42D CONGRESS, } SENATE. { Ex. Doc.
2d Session. } { No. 6.

REPORTS

OF

EXPLORATIONS AND SURVEYS,

TO ASCERTAIN

THE PRACTICABILITY OF A SHIP-CANAL

BETWEEN

THE ATLANTIC AND PACIFIC OCEANS,

BY THE WAY OF

THE ISTHMUS OF TEHUANTEPEC.

BY

ROBERT W. SHUFELDT,
CAPTAIN UNITED STATES NAVY.

MADE UNDER THE DIRECTION OF THE SECRETARY OF THE NAVY.

WASHINGTON:
GOVERNMENT PRINTING OFFICE.
1872.

FORTY-SECOND CONGRESS, SECOND SESSION.

IN THE SENATE OF THE UNITED STATES, *December* 11, 1871.
Referred to the Committee on Naval Affairs and ordered to be printed.

CONTENTS.

	Page.
Letter of the Secretary of the Navy transmitting reports	
Letter of Lieutenant Commander J. R. Bartlett	
Report of R. W. Shufeldt, captain United States Navy, commanding Tehuantepec Surveying Expedition	
Report of E. A. Fuertes, chief civil engineer	25
Embracing—	
The supply of water for summit-level from river Corte, its height, &c	26
Amount of water required for canal-feeder route; its length	28
Dimensions of the canal, its feeders and locks	29
Study of location, &c.; harbor of the Atlantic terminus of the canal	32
Coatzacoalcos Bar	34
Harbors in the Pacific terminus of the canal	37
Permanency of the works and safety of transit	40
Arrangement of parties, &c	43
Explorations of the Coatzacoalcos River	44
from La Puerta to Chivela	47
from Chivela to the Ostuta River	48
Monetza River and caves	50
Chicapa River	51
Explorations of the Ostuta River	54
Impracticability of joining the Chicapa and Ostuta Rivers	55
Exploration of San Miguel Pass	56
Survey of the river Corte and feeder-route	57
Table of river deliveries	61
Table of distances and elevations of prominent points	62
Geographical positions of the prominent places of the Isthmus	64
Table of sea-distances through several Isthmian routes	65
Table of tonnage	66
Building-materials, &c	67
Useful trees, plants, &c	70
Report of Lieutenant Commander N. H. Farquhar on hydrographic work performed on Atlantic coast	83
Lieutenant Commander Alfred Hopkins on hydrographic work performed on Pacific coast	95
Surgeon John C. Spear	101
Embracing—	
Geology and mineralogy of the Isthmus	101
Rocks for constructing-material	105
Thermal springs	106
Earthquakes	106
Climate	107
Health, diseases, &c	108
Insects, reptiles, serpents, &c	111
Agriculture	115
Fruits	119
Medicinal plants, dyes, gums, &c	120
Timber for construction	121
Roads, transportation, and canoe navigation	122
Inhabitants	123
Languages of the aboriginal tribes	128
Towns, villages, haciendas, &c	132
Laborers	135
Natural history	136
Report of Passed Assistant Surgeon H. N. Beaumont, on climatic influences of river Coatzacoalcos	143
Official correspondence	147

MAP INDEX.

		Scale.
No. 1. General map of the Isthmus of Tehuantepec		$\frac{1}{250000}$
No. 2. Map of the Feeder route		$\frac{1}{60000}$
No. 3. Profile No. 1; from Tarifa to the Corte, by way of Cofradia and Santa Maria	Horizontal	$\frac{1}{60000}$
	Vertical	$\frac{1}{2400}$
No. 4. Profile No. 2; from Tarifa to the Corte, by way of the Feeder route	Horizontal	$\frac{1}{60000}$
	Vertical	$\frac{1}{2400}$
No. 5. Profile No. 3; from Chivela to Salina Cruz, by way of Chivela Pass	Horizontal	$\frac{1}{60000}$
	Vertical	$\frac{1}{2400}$
No. 6. Profile No. 4; from Tarifa to the Upper Lagoon, by way of Tarifa Pass	Horizontal	$\frac{1}{60000}$
	Vertical	$\frac{1}{2400}$
No. 7. Profile No. 5; from the Almoloya River to Tarifa Pass, by way of Chivela Plains	Horizontal	$\frac{1}{60000}$
	Vertical	$\frac{1}{2400}$
No. 8. Profile No. 6; from Tarifa to the Atravesado, by way of Tierra Blanca and the Chivela Plains	Horizontal	$\frac{1}{60000}$
	Vertical	$\frac{1}{2400}$
No. 9. Chart of the shore-line		$\frac{1}{60000}$
No. 10. Mouth of the Coatzacoalcos River		$\frac{1}{5000}$
No. 11. Map of the Lower Coatzacoalcos		$\frac{1}{20000}$
No. 12. Comparative charts of the Coatzacoalcos Bar	Horizontal	$\frac{1}{10000}$
	Vertical	$\frac{1}{500}$
No. 13. Map of the Island of Tacamichapa		$\frac{1}{40000}$
No. 14. Reconnaissance of the Uspanapan River		$\frac{1}{60000}$
No. 15. Reconnaissance of the Coachapa River		$\frac{1}{60000}$
No. 16. Chart of the roadstead of Salina Cruz		$\frac{1}{10000}$
No. 17. Chart of the Upper Lagoon		$\frac{1}{60000}$

No. 18. Geological map of the Isthmus of Tehuantepec.
No. 19. Meteorological chart of Chivela.
No. 20. Meteorological chart of Minatitlan.

ILLUSTRATIONS.

Consulate at Minatitlan, with officers of the Expedition.
Minatitlan from rear of consulate.
Coatzacoalcos River at Minatitlan.
Headquarters at Chivela.
Monument Hill, Chivela.
Lieutenant Commander Bartlett's party taking cross-section of Almoloya River
River Verde at old transit crossing.
Tarifa Plain.
Ranchos at Tarifa.
Party under Lieutenant Commander Bartlett in camp at Tarifa.
Rancho at Tarifa, with camp-hunter.

LETTER

FROM

THE SECRETARY OF THE NAVY,

TRANSMITTING

REPORTS OF TEHUANTEPEC CANAL SURVEY.

NAVY DEPARTMENT,
Washington, December 7, 1871.

SIR: I have the honor to acknowledge the receipt of a copy of the resolution passed by the Senate of the United States on the 5th instant, directing that the Secretary of the Navy "furnish the Senate with the report and accompanying maps of the United States ship-canal expedition to the Isthmus of Tehuantepec, Mexico, commanded by Captain R. W. Shufeldt, U. S. N."

The reports of the Expedition, with the accompanying maps, are herewith transmitted.

I am, sir, very respectfully, your obedient servant,

GEO. M. ROBESON,
Secretary of the Navy.

Hon. SCHUYLER COLFAX,
Vice-President of the United States and President of the Senate.

LETTER

TRANSMITTING

REPORTS AND MAPS TO THE SECRETARY OF THE NAVY.

STAMFORD, CONNECTICUT,
November 1, 1871.

SIR: I have the honor to report that, in obedience to orders of the Department, dated August 14, I relieved Captain Shufeldt of the unfinished duty connected with the Tehuantepec Survey.

I now forward the report of that officer, together with others of the Expedition, and maps illustrating the work executed.

Very respectfully, your obedient servant,

JOHN R. BARTLETT, JR.,
Lieutenant Commander.

Hon. GEO. M. ROBESON,
    Secretary of the Navy, Washington, D. C.

REPORT

OF

CAPTAIN R. W. SHUFELDT, U. S. N.

ERRATA.

Page 13, sixth line, "It is conceded" should read, "If it is conceded."
Page 16, fourth paragraph, "obstacles" should be "obstacle."
Page 18, half-way down page, "were" should be "was."
In geological map, light blue at Jaltipan and Uspanapa River should show Asphaltum.
Dark brown at Tarifa, and near by, should show Calcareous Tufa.

J. R. B.

REPORT

OF

CAPTAIN R. W. SHUFELDT, U. S. N.

STAMFORD, CONNECTICUT, *August* 11, 1871.

SIR: On the 9th of September, 1870, I had the honor to receive from the Navy Department an order to command " an expedition for the survey of the Isthmus of Tehuantepec and Nicaragua, in order to ascertain the practicability of a ship-canal at those places between the Atlantic and Pacific Oceans." On the 26th of the same month I submitted to the Department the following memorandum, which was approved of as the basis of the work:

"It is conceded that an interoceanic canal through any of the isthmus passes of the western hemisphere is a necessity for the present or prospective commerce of the world; then it becomes a matter of interest to the American Government to select that route which, while satisfying interoceanic demands, will at the same time conduce the most to the development of our own foreign and domestic trade. In this point of view the Isthmus of Tehuantepec assumes a primary importance, and is the first which claims our attention.

"The canal route will start from some point in the Gulf of Mexico, (probably the mouth of the Coatzacoalcos River.) A glance at the map will show that this Gulf can be held against any naval power; the channels between Cuba and Florida on the north, and between Cuba and Yucatan on the south, being in the aggregate not more than two hundred miles wide, could always be effectually closed by our Navy, holding Key West and Tortugas as a base of operation. No other isthmus presents this military advantage; indeed, over no other is it probable that the United States could maintain any control in time of war. Again, it is the shortest route between our eastern and western possessions, the gain of distance over that of Panama, between New Orleans and San Francisco, being 1,350 nautical miles, and over the other routes proportionately. A steam canal-boat could load at any point on the Mississippi, and deliver her cargo at San Francisco in 10 to 12 days from New Orleans. Thus, a canal at this point becomes a part of our own internal water communication, as well as affording a channel for the external commerce of ourselves and of the world. Both, therefore, in a military and commercial point of view, this route may be deemed of the first importance, and it is respectfully suggested that the expedition may be directed to go first to Tehuantepec, and ascertain the practicability of a ship-canal at that point. This Isthmus has been already thoroughly surveyed by distinguished officers of our Army and Navy, with a view to railway communication, and their maps are in our possession.

"With the advantages of modern science, a canal can be built anywhere, involving only the question of expense, provided water can be found to fill it. This is the problem which the expedition must solve, and for this purpose a thorough exploration must be made at the summit-level. Tarifa, said to be 680 feet above the sea, so far has been considered the lowest elevation, and Señor Moro, in 1843, devised a system of feeders from the adjacent rivers by which water could be brought to that point sufficient for the purpose. It will be the object of the present party to verify his report, and also to ascertain if any additional source of supply can be obtained.

"If water cannot be obtained, either by natural or artificial means, at that point, or some lower level found, then any further work will be useless, so far as this expedition is concerned. But, getting a satisfactory solution to this problem, then I suggest a survey of the lagoons on the Pacific side, and an examination of the outlet of the lagoons into the ocean, with a view of determining their character as a harbor.

"On the Gulf I propose a survey of the bar of the Coatzacoalcos, to estimate the possibility of deepening it. That being found unadvisable, then to examine the adjacent point, 'La Barilla,' with a view to forming an artificial harbor for the entrance of the canal. This work being accomplished, I propose to follow the probable line of the canal between these ports, to form some estimate of the character of the soil, the natural obstacles, and the liability to inundation during the rainy season. We do not propose to define the character of the work to be constructed or to estimate its cost. An undertaking of such magnitude should not be commenced until every foot of the way has been thoroughly examined, and every possible contingency calculated.

"This small party does not desire to be considered anything more than pioneers and explorers for those who, if the project is to succeed, will follow them in broader paths, with more minute investigation and more scientific knowledge."

On the 6th October I received my final orders, in which were placed under my command the United States steamers Kansas and Mayflower, and in which I was informed that a vessel from the Pacific squadron would be detailed for the hydrographic work on that side of the Isthmus.

The expedition, as organized for the land party, consisted of the following personnel:

R. W. Shufeldt, captain commanding; Geo. C. Remey, lieutenant commander; John R. Bartlett, jr., lieutenant commander; P. H. Cooper, lieutenant commander; J. C. Spear, surgeon and geologist; H. A. Bartlett, captain of marines, and photographer; R. T. Jasper, master; C. W. Rae, second assistant engineer.

In addition to the naval officers, Mr. E. A. Fuertes, civil engineer, was appointed chief civil engineer; Mr. R. H. Buel, assistant civil engineer; Mr. T. B. Street, assistant geologist and naturalist; and Mr. E. J. Somers, draughtsman.

I take occasion here to express my appreciation of the untiring zeal and intelligence displayed by Mr. Fuertes throughout our arduous work. His scrupulous adherence to facts, coupled with a knowledge of his profession, entitle his report (herewith appended, and marked A) to the entire confidence of the Government.

These civilians were employed to place the results of the work beyond the reach of that criticism which might allege that naval officers were not competent to perform the duties of civil engineers or draughtsmen. Mr. Fuertes himself, however, bears willing testimony to the fact that the officers who acted as his assistants became in a short time expert in their new profession, and that the whole party at work in the mountains bore exposure and privation without a murmur. Special praise is due Lieutenant Commander Bartlett and his assistants, Messrs. Jasper and Rae, upon whom fell much of the labor and many of the hardships of the field-work, the results of which would be creditable to men of higher pretensions.

On the 11th of November the expedition entered the Coatzacoalcos River. Through the intervention of the Hon. Secretary of State the Mexican government had already been informed of the object of our coming, and had given cordial assent to the proposed survey, as will be seen in a communication received by me from the Hon. Thos. H. Nelson, United States minister in Mexico. (Copy appended, and marked F.) About this time I was informed that a commission of Mexican engineers would join our party in the interior. The following-named gentlemen comprised this commission, viz: Messrs. Manuel Fernandez, Augustin Barroso, and Guillermo Segura, and joined at "La Chivela" on the 10th of January, 1871, working in perfect accord with our own force, and, I presume, making a final favorable report of our joint work to the Mexican government.

It may be as well to state here that President Juarez detailed a battalion of the line, consisting of six hundred men, commanded by Colonel Montesino, for the protection of the surveying party in the disturbed districts, and that this duty was performed by that officer always with alacrity and evident desire to assist us in our work.

In the interval between the 11th and 28th November the Engineer Corps were engaged at Minatitlan in adjusting instruments and making all necessary preparations for the journey into the interior.

The hydrographic party, under the command of Lieutenant Commander N. H. Farquhar, commanding the Kansas, received the necessary instructions for the survey of the waters on the Atlantic side, and commenced work. Lieutenant Commander Farquhar's report is herewith appended, (marked B.)

That officer has displayed so much ability and judgment that I submit his report without any other comment of my own than to draw your attention to the gratifying fact that the Coatzacoalcos Bar is not only deepening from natural causes, as may be seen by comparison with reliable charts of older date, but that, from the nature of the bottom, it may be easily dredged to any requisite depth. The deduction of Mr. Fuertes, after careful investigation into the cause of the currents and their effect at the mouth of this river, will be found of interest. I am satisfied that, at a cost not at all commensurate with the magnitude of the proposed work, the entrance of the Coatzacoalcos can be made easy of access, and the mouth of the river one of the best harbors in the Gulf of Mexico.

It will also be observed by Captain Farquhar's report, that this river can be deepened to 22 feet up to the island of Tacamichapa, at comparatively small expense.

On the 11th of December the surveying party reached the plains of Chivela, and established headquarters in the house of Don Julian Macheo. This gentleman is the proprietor of a hacienda, within the limits of which are to be found all the passes through the Cordilleras on the Isthmus, and to him we are indebted for constant hospitality and assistance.

In pursuance of our preconceived arrangements, first to examine and test the correctness of previous surveys, Messrs. Fuertes and Buel started to look into the plan proposed by Señor Moro, 1843, for feeding the summit-level of a ship-canal by means of the junction of the rivers Chicapa and Ostuta, the route of the canal being through the portillo of Tarifa, with the following results, as reported by Mr. Fuertes, viz: "That the joint delivery of both rivers is not sufficient to feed a canal; that the junction cannot be effected, because the Ostuta is 180 feet below the summit, and if it were at the proper height to insure the supply, in order to bring the water down it would require to cut a prism, whose base would be about twenty miles long; its western depth at the Palmer Rancho 25 feet, gradually increasing to over 1,400 feet at the pass, diminishing from this point to the hypothetical height of the Ostuta. The inevitable conclusion is that, practically speaking, Mr. Moro's project is impossible."

Mr. Moro was a civil engineer of note, and the air of candor and truthfulness which pervades his report inspired confidence which, together with the hope of finding this easy solution of the problem, caused me to accept the disappointment with reluctance; but I am convinced, from the extreme care used in taking the observations and the caution exercised by the above gentlemen, that this project must be abandoned, and it is the only one which has hitherto been made, as the result of personal and practical observation.

The streams in the vicinity of Tarifa and Chivela were examined during the month of December, a period of the year most favorable to measure the mean contents of their probable supply. These streams are the Almoloya, Guichilona, Citune, Verde, Masahua, Tarifa, Chichihua, Monetza, Milagrito, Pericon, and Mentidero. Of these, the Almoloya is the most important; it was gauged the 22d of December, and its delivery was found to be 7.28 cubic feet per second; subsequently, in March, it was nearly dry. Some of the rivers drawn on different maps are simply hill groins, through which water only flows during showers; the Masahua is one of these. The results of the measurement of these waters excluded the possibility of feeding the summit-level from this source, for, in addition to the insignificance of their aggregate delivery, most of them, at available points, do not possess the necessary elevation.

While Mr. Fuertes and his party were making these explorations, Lieutenant Commander Bartlett, with Captain Bartlett, United States Marine Corps, Master Jasper, and Assistant Engineer Rae, were engaged in running a transit and level line from Chivela to the Almoloya River, another from Chivela to Tarifa, and finally, with the hope of finding a more available pass and nearer the possible source of supply, a transit and level line was run by this party from Tarifa to the junction of the Chichihua and Cofradia roads; thence up the Pericon Valley to the San Miguel pass, and down to San Miguel Chimalapa. This duty was performed with zeal and under many difficulties, but it only resulted in disappointment, as the pass was found to be 318 feet higher than Tarifa, and the nature of the cutting difficult. Thus the passage for the canal through the Cordilleras became limited to the portillo of Tarifa.

The problem for finding a natural supply of water and the best pass at the summit, having become simplified by the elimination of the minor rivers and the other portillos, our attention was next turned toward the Rio Corte, or Upper Coatzacoalcos, as the only one large enough to furnish the requisite quantity at the requisite altitude. During the month of February a party was organized, consisting of Messrs. Fuertes and Buel, Lieutenant Commander Remey, and Messrs. Fernandez, Barrosa, and Segura, of the Mexican commission, for the purpose of ascending and measuring that river at the proper point.

It would be tedious to detail all the difficulties and hazards of that duty; the results, however, have manifested the gratifying fact that the Corte contains sufficient water, at a proper elevation, for the supply of a canal of the following dimensions, viz: Breadth at top 162 feet, bottom 60 feet, depth 22 feet. These dimensions were assumed as a basis, because a canal of that width and depth would be amply sufficient to accommodate at least nine-tenths of the commerce of the world, and certainly wide and deep enough for our own domestic trade, and I question if a surface canal, with as many locks as will be required for this one, will not present so many difficulties in the transit of very large ships as to fail to fulfill its object.

Although the strength of our party and the season of the year prevented our running a transit and level line from the Atlantic to the dividing ridge at Tarifa, yet from the thorough surveys and explorations of that portion of the Isthmus by previous parties, for railway purposes, and our own frequent journeys, during which careful observations were made, it is fair to assume that the canal will start at the headwaters of ship navigation, in the river Coatzacoalcos, at the island of Tacamichapa; thence through the valley of that river, utilizing it whenever it may be deemed advisable, to the dividing ridge at Tarifa; descending then through the Tarifa Pass, possibly by the valley of Chicapa to the harbor of Salina Cruz, its Pacific terminus.

The total length of the canal by this route will be 144 miles, the total number of locks required about 140. Throughout this route I am warranted in the opinion, concurred in by the joint commission, that there is no natural obstacles to the construction of the canal which engineering, science, and liberal capital cannot overcome.

To feed this canal with a constant supply of water, it will be necessary to construct an aqueduct or feeder, about 27 miles in length, starting from the Upper Coatzacoalcos, near its junction with the Blanco River, (see map No. 2.) At this point the Corte delivers 1,618 cubic feet of water per second, and the surface of the water, at the dryest season, is 660 feet above the ocean, or 72 feet below the summit-level of the canal. Three miles above this point the river rises to the summit-level. The river Blanco yields 120 cubic feet per second, and is four feet above the summit at a point where its water will be absorbed into the feeder.

It is proposed to construct a dam on the Corte, of suitable strength and sufficient height, and thence, conducting the water-supply to the Blanco, unite the two. The feeder will then traverse the country by a route surveyed for that purpose by the party under Mr. Fuertes, and exemplified on the maps accompanying his report. By reference to these maps and this report, it will be seen that an aggregate amount of tunneling of, say, three miles, and some heavy cutting, will be required. This is beyond all dispute the only feasible route for a feeder, and the only feasible point from which the water can be obtained.

In addition to the expense of this collateral work, it must be observed that the feeder passes through a portion of the country subject at all times to serious terrestrial convulsions. These, however, are incidental to any of the isthmus routes, and while we were among the mountains of Tehuantepec I am justified in saying that no earthquake occurred which could permanently affect the durability of a canal or its feeder.

Taking into consideration these circumstances, a canal supplied with water by such a length of aqueduct, through a mountainous and tropical country, can only be deemed practicable to the extent of its political and commercial necessity, measured by the progress of the age.

By reference to the able report of Surgeon J. C. Spear, (appended and marked D,) it will be observed that the winds pervading the central portion of the Isthmus are of a marked character, blowing at one portion of the year almost directly from the north, with very great force, and during the other portion blowing from the opposite direction, with almost equal violence. I refer to this fact because I consider it as a serious obstacle in the transit of ships through this canal, not insurmountable, but one likely to cause delay, and sometimes to create damage in the passage of the locks.

Dr. Spear has given the subject of material for the construction of a canal great attention, and his report will be found to confirm previous statements, that abundance of wood and stone can be obtained all along the proposed route, of the best quality for the purpose.

While Mr. Fuertes and Lieutenant Commander Remey were thus engaged in defining the feeder-route, Lieutenant Commander Bartlett completed the level and transit line from the Cofradia to the initial point on the Rio Corte, and later in the season, between April 4 and 13, by the joint operation of both parties, a line was run from Salina Cruz to Tarifa, for the purpose of establishing the elevation of the latter point above the Pacific, which during previous calculations had been assumed, and thus completing the line from the level of the ocean at Salina Cruz to the Corte, at the junction of the Blanco.

On the 23d of February, Commander Hopkins reported the arrival of the Cyane, under his command, at Salina Cruz. As soon thereafter as possible I had an interview with him at that port, and gave him the necessary instructions for the survey of the upper lagoon on the Pacific, with a view to ascertain its adaptability as a harbor, and for the construction of an entrance into this lagoon from the sea, at its most available point; the bottom of the lagoon to be examined, with a view to dredging when necessary, and the coast-line of the ocean to be defined between Ventosa and a point as far east as it might be practicable to go. In addition, Commander Hopkins was directed to make a survey of the harbor of Salina Cruz, as the probable terminus of the canal, and to report upon the character of such a breakwater as would make this a secure port. Although this ship, as reported to me by her commanding officer, was short both of men and boats, it gives me pleasure to state that this duty was performed with great accuracy under the many obstacles incidental to the climate and the country. The survey of the upper lagoon was conducted by Master C. B. Gill, assisted by Master T. H. Stevens, Ensigns F. P. Gilmore, and U. Sebree. These are all young officers, and I think that their work manifests in a marked degree the benefits of the high order of training bestowed upon the rising generation of naval officers by the Government. Lieutenant Commander P. H. Cooper also made a reconnaissance of this lagoon. His report and that of Master Gill are annexed to the report of Commander Hopkins, and herewith appended, (marked C.)

It is apparent, from this survey, that the upper lagoon cannot be utilized for the purposes of a canal, for the reasons that it would require an immense amount of dredging, that the bottom is of a changeable character, and that no proper exit for the canal can be made from it upon the adjacent coast.

Commander Hopkins is of the opinion that the harbor of Salina Cruz is better adapted than any other point for the canal terminus. A breakwater of some kind, the materials for the construction of which are immediately at hand, will be necessary to render it a perfectly secure port. I respectfully refer you to the report of Commander Hopkins, and to the observations and deductions of Mr. Fuertes upon this subject. These are confirmed by my own experience. I think it needs but a brief visit to convince even the casual observer that a magnificent port may be made here, with comparatively small outlay of time or money.

The report of Past Assistant Surgeon H. N. Beaumont, concerning the sanitary condition of the crews of the vessels employed surveying the Coatzacoalcos and adjoining rivers, (appended, and marked E) will be found interesting. Dr. Spear has also made observations upon the same subject. There is no doubt that there was much sickness among our officers and men in these waters; and whatever may have been the primary cause, it, in my opinion, was much increased by the want of room and ventilation, particularly on board of the Kansas, for her crew; and to this may be added the fact that both the Kansas and Mayflower left the Washington navy-yard at a time when disease of a similar type was prevalent there. Every care, however, was exercised by the commanding officers of those vessels, and it is undoubtedly due to the unremitting attention of Dr. Beaumont that so few cases proved fatal.

Captain H. A. Bartlett, of the Marine Corps, who acted as photographer, made the best use of the materials he had, and overcame, with praiseworthy perseverance, many provoking obstacles in the way of transportation, &c. A copy of photographic views are herewith transmitted. I am indebted to Lieutenant Commander George C. Remey, who acted as commissary for the Expedition, in a very great degree for the final success of our work. By his prudence, foresight, and economy, our parties were enabled to keep the field, and immense amount of work was performed at comparatively trifling cost.

The liberal provision, by the Navy Department, of officers and men, permitted me to husband the small appropriation made by Congress for the purposes of this survey, and thus I trust to accomplish the objects of the Expedition.

It has rarely been my lot to be associated with men who entered more fully into the spirit of their work, and who labored together more harmoniously. It was a new experience for naval officers to live in the saddle and sleep on the ground, and yet in a few days they were old campaigners, bearing privation without a murmur, and animated only by a determination to succeed.

The question of labor for the construction of a work of such an extent is very interesting, not only in an economical, but in a political point of view.

I am decidedly of the opinion that the main body of laborers cannot be drawn from the native population. A liberal estimate of the inhabitants of the Isthmus will not place them above the number of 60,000. Out of this a force of adult males of, say 5,000, might be found willing to do the work of an advance guard, as canoemen upon the rivers, or muleteers in the interior. The Indians of Tehuantepec are industrious in their own way, handy with the "machete" or clearing-ax, honest, and, while at work, abstemious, but they have absolutely no idea of the value of time or money; you can neither stimulate them by ambition nor excite them by the hope of reward.

This work will have to be accomplished by imported labor. Fortunately the country itself offers a home to any number of emigrants, each one of whom might bring his family, with the assurance of finding a comfortable support in a healthy climate. In this connection I have personal knowledge of the fact that, in the early days of our civil war, President Lincoln contemplated settling the river-bottoms of this Isthmus with negroes from our Southern States, thus endeavoring to solve the problem of the black man's status by means of forced emigration. I am also cognizant of the fact that the Mexican government favored such a project, but the march of events at that time were too rapid to reduce such a scheme to practice. Now, however, the country is still there, offering to the colored men of the South a home contiguous to their native land, easy of access, and probably, by consent of the Mexican government, with all of their rights as American citizens guaranteed and their acquisitions secured. I have a letter upon this subject from an American negro, Mr. Wright, who has lived for twenty years upon the Uspanapa River, and in that time amassed quite a respectable fortune. He has recently made a tour through the Southern States of the United States, and is emphatically of the opinion that there are many discontented men of his own race in that portion of our country who would willingly emigrate to Mexico if any such public work should be undertaken, and if they might live there for a term of years, at least, under treaty protection.

I do not offer this idea as a complete solution of the labor question, but as by no means an unimportant element, and as a nucleus around which might rally the political and religious ideas which in the course of time must pervade that Isthmus, through which an American canal is to pass.

The main body of laborers, however, would probably have to come from China. Fortunately the Isthmus presents every inducement to the Chinaman—streams overflowing with fish, and plains abounding with cattle; but particularly a scanty population, leaving thousands of acres of fertile land to be cultivated, in a congenial climate, and with no obstacles or prejudices in the way of his religious, social, or industrial ideas.

It is easy to imagine this land, now so desolate and deserted, peopled by Chinese on the southern slope and by negroes on the northern; teeming with the products of every climate, and enlivened by human industry from the Atlantic to the Pacific.

The political condition of this part of Mexico must have such an important bearing upon any public work undertaken there, that I consider it pertinent to this report to call your attention to it.

The greater part of a canal, as well as its most costly portion, must pass through the State of Oaxaca. This State has been for years in a condition of revolution and internecine strife, resulting at present in irreconcilable geographic divisions, in political " partidos," whose governing motives are revenge, in insecurity for life and property, and lastly, as most significant for ourselves, in distrust and dislike for every foreign element, however apparent it may be that the introduction of that element can alone bring peace and develop the resources of the country. In the suppression of these revolutions by the State authorities, civil law seems to be held in abeyance, and the life and property of every individual is subject to the caprice of the military commandant. Thus a local and irresponsible despotism exists, dangerous alike to the native and the foreigner. It can scarcely be conceived that in a country professing to be a republic, contiguous to our own borders, and in the nineteenth century, such a state of things can be, and yet this is apparent to the most casual observer. He who reads as he rides over this Isthmus, learns, with profound regret, that through this system of terrorism, a land rich in natural resources furnishes but a scanty living for a sparse population, and that the inhabitants are daily becoming more debased, ignorant, and imbecile. The causes for this state of things are manifold; first, perhaps, is the fact that the large majority of the population are Indians, preserving the language and the customs of their ancestors with wonderful pertinacity, and inheriting their feuds intensified by time. No efforts are being made by the government to educate them out of their primitive barbarism, and while they have nominally conferred upon them the privileges of citizenship, they remain the veriest slaves to authority, whether legal or usurped. They are impressed as soldiers by any armed force, compelled to fight, and, if caught, shot without mercy. Thus, with life and property liable at any moment to forfeiture, added to apathy, natural to the race, they have no motive for the acquisition of wealth, no ambition for the cultivation of the higher qualities of humanity. From year to year their degradation is becoming more and more complete.

Out of a population of, say fifty thousand, the number of people in the vicinity of whose towns a canal or railroad would pass, some four or five hundred are white men, "gente de razon," as they conceitedly style themselves. These are the "rancheros" in the country and the shop-keepers in the villages; they form the ready instruments of designing leaders, to collect the Indians and steal the horses, and make "pronunciamientos." Ignorant, immoral, hating innovations, revengeful, these form the real impediments to progress—the willing tools in the initiation of civil war and anarchy.

The foreigners, or "strangers," as they are called, whatever the length of residence or amount of pecuniary interest in the country may be, have exercised a considerable influence upon the commercial status of the Isthmus, but their lives never seem to be safe from assault or their property from confiscation. The "so-called" Americans have added to the opprobrium of the American name by presenting claims against the republic to the "mixed commission" in Washington, outragous in amount, and many of them false in point of fact. This course, on their part, has been seized upon by the local authorities to add fuel to the flame of popular dislike to foreigners of whatever nationality.

Again, the geographical divisions of the State stand in the way of political harmony. The capital, Oaxaca, is situated in the heart of a mountainous and inland district, while the city of Tehuantepec and the contiguous towns lie upon the Pacific plains, adjacent to the ocean, Tehuantepec being the only port of entry for the State. The consequence is, that in a country where intercommunication is so difficult, the interests are not only antagonistic, but the antagonism is very much exaggerated. The people of the plains complain that all the employés of the government come from the Oaxaca district, while all the revenue collected goes to the same point.

Lastly, the right of the State government to make war upon its own citizens, to raise troops and to levy taxes for war purposes, irrespective of the federal authorities, is a constant source of revolution and disorder, as well as of abuse of power by irresponsible rulers. In a late revolution in Juchitan, while we were upon the Isthmus, that town, one of the most flourishing in the country, was destroyed, (a thousand houses being burned,) and its people either shot or driven into exile, and this while the federal troops and civil authorities remained inactive and inert. Such an exemplification of "State-rights" operates in a way to nullify the wise and liberal policy which the federal government seems desirous to inaugurate.

Owing to these and other causes, the southern and central portion of the Isthmus presents nothing but stagnation in business, distrust and animosity between neighboring towns, insecurity for life and property, disaffection against the government, and indeed an entire absence of all the elements which constitute the public and private happiness of a people. Judging from the past, also, there is no hope for the future. I traveled over this country fifteen years ago, buoyed with the hope of its regeneration; to-day, the evidence is convincing that there has been no improvement and no progress.

That portion of the Isthmus which lies in the State of Vera-Cruz is not so much subject to these influences. The Indians are inoffensive and docile, and the foreign population at Minatitlan predominate. In consequence of this, insurrections are rare and progress apparent.

This is written with no spirit of hostility to the Mexican people, but it is essential to know that the central government, inspired as I believe it to be by the spirit of the age, yet exercises no visible control over this distant portion of its jurisdiction, and I am convinced that, before any public work is undertaken here, it will be necessary for its security that treaties are made, affording national guarantees that the federal power asserts its authority over all local powers; and if ever deemed by the United States the point for the construction of an interoceanic canal, the first stipulation should be the right in some way of protecting American interests and the lives of American citizens.

The world has been accustomed to regard the separation of this hemisphere by means of a canal as a work of great *international* necessity; and so perhaps it was, until forestalled by the completion of the canal at Suez but I think the result will show that even Suez has not as yet radically affected commerce or changed the main channels of trade, yet that canal is essentially more of an international route, from its geographical position, than one through any American isthmus ever can be. It is the short connecting-link between the capital, political influences, and the trade of all Europe, and the teeming population of the East. I have, therefore, regarded canal communication through this hemisphere as *American*, and local in its main object, incidental only as to the rest of the world. Viewed from this stand-point, a single glance at the map demonstrates not only the necessity of a canal, but its location. Each isthmus rises into importance as it lies nearer to the center of American political and commercial influence, and the intrinsic value of this eminently national work ought to be based upon the inverse ratio of the distance from that center.

A canal through the Isthmus of Tehuantepec is an extension of the Mississippi River to the Pacific Ocean. It converts the Gulf of Mexico into an American lake. In time of war it closes that Gulf to all enemies. It is the only route which our Government can control. So to speak, it renders our own territory circumnavigable. It brings New Orleans 1,400 nautical miles nearer to San Francisco than a canal via Darien, and such is the character of the intervening waters, that it permits a canal-boat to load in Saint Louis and discharge her freight in California with but little more than the risk of inland navigation. As a matter of political economy, therefore, as well as of commercial necessity, a canal here assumes the gravest proportions. It may be that the future of our country lies hidden in this problem—whether, in the demonstration of which, our principles of government, and our commerce under the flag which represents them, are to go hand in hand to further development, until are reached and taught the remotest corners of the East and the rudest barbarians of the Pacific Isles, or whether, resisting the struggles and checking the aspirations of the American heart for space and freedom, we are to live in disregard of natural law, and leave to another nation a glorious mission unfulfilled.

Finally, although we are fully justified in reporting this canal practicable as an engineering work, yet, from the length of the main canal and the number of locks, as well as from the expense of construction of its feeder, the question becomes a serious one—so serious that it will probably require *national* resources to build it.

For twenty years the Isthmus of Tehuantepec has been the butt of speculation, the sport of railway financiers. People, both native and foreign, have lived and died there, in the vain hope of the coming of the "company" which was to build railroads and develop the river navigation. They have lost confidence in American enterprise, and have left but little faith in American projects. This work, of so much importance to ourselves and to the world, ought to be placed beyond the pale of speculation—out of the region of doubt. It needs national resources and national guarantees. It should be based upon a treaty between the two governments. A simple canal concession, subject to revocation by the same power which granted it, is valueless. It neither interests our Government nor inspires confidence among capitalists.

Upon this question of cost, I would reduce the dimensions of the canal until the original outlay would form the basis of a permanent and remunerative investment, because I believe that the financial success of the project will depend upon our domestic trade, and not upon the general commerce of the world. In other words, I would make the Tehuantepec Canal bear the same relation to the trade of the United States that the Erie Canal does to the State of New York. In a few years it will have tended as much to the aggrandizement of the whole country as that canal has to the " Empire State."

On the 27th April, 1871, the Expedition left Mexico, and 25th May arrived in Washington with the results of our labor, which are herewith respectfully submitted by

Your most obedient servant,

R. W. SHUFELDT,
Captain Commanding Tehuantepec and Nicaragua Surveying Expedition.

Hon. GEORGE M. ROBESON,
Secretary of the Navy, Washington, D. C.

A.

REPORT

OF

SURVEYS FOR A SHIP-CANAL

ACROSS

THE ISTHMUS OF TEHUANTEPEC, MEXICO,

BY

E. A. FUERTES, CIVIL ENGINEER.

REPORT

OF

E. A. FUERTES, CIVIL ENGINEER.

HEADQUARTERS TEHUANTEPEC AND NICARAGUA SURVEYING EXPEDITION,
Stamford, Connecticut, August 27, 1871.

SIR: I have the honor to submit the following report of the work executed on the Isthmus of Tehuantepec:

This report is divided into two parts and an appendix.

The first part contains a summary of the results obtained with reference to the ship-canal, its feeders, and harbors.

The second part contains an abstract of the operations performed in the field, and a discussion showing the impracticability of joining the Chicapa and Ostuta Rivers, as proposed by Sig. C. Moro. This part also furnishes the data which proves that the summit western streams are unavailable for canal-feeders.

In the appendix many tables and data will be found, to be used as references in the study of this project.

PART I.

Object of the Expedition.
At 11 a. m., of the 10th of October, 1870, the Tehauntepec and Nicaragua Surveying Expedition sailed from the city of Washington, bound for Mexico, its object being to determine, in the most absolute manner, if it was practicable to construct a ship-canal across the Isthmus of Tehauntepec.

Instructions.
My instructions from you were to the effect that I was to leave aside all questions appertaining to the politico-economical bearings of the problem; and my mission was technically circumscribed to the scientific and engineering conditions of the project. Further, after consultation, the following plan was adopted and made a part of your instructions to me: I was to declare the project impracticable if I should find deficiency of water; tunneling in the ship's transit; excessive cutting; and either unsafe or extraordinarily difficult harbors at either terminus of the route.

What would make the project impracticable.
Any scheme contemplating to feed the canal from other than natural sources of supply, should be considered impracticable; though in the case of failing to obtain a natural supply, studies and calculations might be made, in order to expose the degree of difficulties to be encountered in obtaining an artificial supply by means of collecting reservoirs and pumping.

Conditions for its practicability.
On the other hand, if the solution of this problem should present no extraordinary difficulties, or obstacles that could not be overcome with the ordinary appliances of engineering skill in its present state of development, I should declare the project practicable, unless the expense to be incurred in its construction should appear palpably incommensurable with the importance of the undertaking.

Why the project is declared practicable.
The data obtained from our explorations and surveys prove that a ship-canal is practicable on the Isthmus of Tehauntepec, because the difficulties to be encountered in its construction are of the ordinary type, or such as are inherent to works of a similar nature, with the difference that they will be met on a larger scale. This fact is due to the assumed dimensions of the canal, and is inherent to the conception of the project, in whatever part of the world it might be located.

A "through-cut" canal impracticable.
The nature of the Isthmus of Tehauntepec makes it impossible to construct across it a "through-cut" canal. The use of locks becomes indispensable in order to reach the summit-height at Tarifa. This point is the lowest and most available pass in the mountains traversing the Isthmus from east to west.

Lowest summit pass.

Elevation of the summit.
Its true mean elevation above the Pacific Ocean is 754.4 feet, as given by the spirit-level. This height can be easily diminished to 732 feet by a cut 22 feet in depth on the Tarifa Pass. In this manner, the summit-reach of the canal will have the same elevation as the Tarifa River, upon the point at which the summit-level will be fed with water.

Point of emplacement of the waters.
The only point from which the canal can be fed is from the Upper Coatzacoalcos or Corte River, near its junction with the Blanco, at the point marked "A" in map No. 2. At this place the Corte delivers 1,618 cubic feet of water per second, and the surface of the water in the dryest season is 660 feet above the ocean, or 72 feet below the summit-level of the canal.

Delivery of the Corte River.

Height of the Corte.
Three miles up stream from this point the Corte's waters ascend to the summit-level height.

Delivery of the Blanco River.
The river Blanco yields 120 cubic feet per second, and is 4 feet above the summit at the point marked "B." The banks and bed of the Corte at "A," (map No. 2,) are of clay, rocks, feldspar, and granite. The direction of the stream, width of its bed, which is free from gravel, and the topographical features of the locality, are admirably constituted for the erection of a dam. The materials are at hand and of the most durable nature.

Banks of the Corte and Blanco.

TEHUANTEPEC CANAL SURVEY.

It is proposed to construct a dam on the Corte of suitable strength, 122 feet in length at the lip, and 86 in height, immediately below the point marked "A" in map No. 2. *Dam at the Corte.*

At this place there is a strong depression or pass in the ridge separating the Corte and Blanco Rivers, between "A" and "B." Taking into account the fall or head to be given to the feeder, the horizontal distance between the Corte and Blanco is 1,750 feet, and the height of the pass above the feeder will be 257 feet. In order to turn the water of the Corte into the feeder, on the Blanco Valley, it will be necessary to excavate less than 400,000 cubic yards upon the ridge which separates the Corte and Blanco Valleys. This excavation will just supply the material for the Corte dam, the dam at the Blanco, and the inlet chambers, and the revetment wall of the feeder at the Blanco dam. *Blanco Pass. Distance between the Corte and Blanco. Excavation of Blanco Pass.*

Two thousand feet below "B," a dam 16 feet high must be erected on the Blanco. The river-bed is here 130 feet wide, though the river itself is hardly 20 feet across. The dam, however, will have to be built 140 feet long. Eighty feet of this length will be reserved for the Blanco, and whatever surplus waters may fail to pass through the gates and weirs of the Corte in time of floods. *Dam at the Blanco.*

The balance of the length of Blanco dam will be used for the feeder.

This dam will be pierced by the feeder-chamber, provided with regulating flow-gates, and the waters of the feeder will thus run across the left end of the dam, and between the left bank of the Blanco and a wall buttressing the dam and dividing the waters of the feeder and the Blanco River. *Feeder chamber at the Blanco dam.*

This buttressing and dividing wall will not be more than 300 feet in length, and from this point forward the feeder will run through a side cutting, and entirely above the reach of the heaviest floods. A few hundred feet below the dam a series of falls occur, which make it impossible for extraordinary floods to reach the feeder. *Protection of feeder from floods.*

In map No. 2, all the black dotted lines show the lines and country explored. All the continuous black lines show the lines levelled and surveyed with the transit. A heavy double line shows the approximate location of the feeder. *Conventional signs.*

The waters of the Blanco, Maxiponac, Capepac, Coyolapa, Escolapa, Pita, Chichihua, Pericon, Otate (and, if necessary, the Coquipac) Rivers can be utilized to feed the Pacific side levels, furnishing jointly about 495 cubic feet of water per second. The Corte River will supply any deficit that may occur at the summit for the Pacific side and the upper reaches of the Atlantic side. Water can never be wanting for the summit, because only the Pacific plains will draw heavily from it; while on the Atlantic side not less than 30,000 cubic feet flow into the Coatzacoalcos, between the Almoloya and Uspanapa Rivers. This amount is delivered by the Almoloya, Malatengo, Sarabia, Jumuapa, Jaltepec, Chalchijalpa, Naranjo, Coachapa, and Uspanapa Rivers, and many other small streams. All the rivers are distributed along the shores of the Coatzacoalcos, at very suitable distances from each other. *Available waters for the summit-supply, in addition to the Corte. Permanency of the summit supply — waters of the Atlantic side.*

The general estimates for water-supply made in the sequel, call for 1,618 cubic feet per second, as the amount required to work the whole canal, under the exacting supposition that it is to be fed exclusively from the summit. *Amount of water required for the whole canal.*

The available summit streams were gauged at the height of a remarkably dry season, and found to yield jointly 2,113 cubic feet; so that, strictly speaking, 495 cubic feet per second will have to be disposed of by means of waste-weirs from the very summit, in the dryest season, and supposing an extravagant expenditure of water. *Delivery of the summit streams; surplus water.*

Since a large portion of the water brought to the summit is to be used on the Pacific side-slope, this fact might lead to the supposition that the Coatzacoalcos would lose thereby its present importance as a large river. This objection is met thus: Abreast of Minatitlan the cross-section of the river has an area of 31,900 square feet, and though the velocity of its current is always more than 1.6 feet per second, even taking it at one foot per second, this would give nearly 32,000 cubic feet of water per second, as the delivery of the river. One-twentieth of this amount is taken for canal purposes, *Status of the Coatzacoalcos. Approximate delivery of the Coatzacoalcos at Minatitlan.*

and is obtained near its source, and before any of its large tributaries swell the mighty volume of the river. While the diminution occasioned by subtracting so small a volume from the river will be less perceptible than the fluctuations produced by small freshets, this small amount will be sufficient to supply one-half of the canal necessities, and to irrigate the sterile lands of the Pacific plains, where the indigo culture languishes for want of water. Besides, when the canal shall have been built, the valley of the Coatzacoalcos will assume its commercial and political importance. At present it is valueless, and the river can hardly be ascended as far as Súchil in Indian canoes.

Feeder-route. Having demonstrated that there is an abundant supply of water to feed the summit-level and the whole canal, I will now proceed to describe the feeder-route, and the practicability of bringing the water to the summit. The feeder-route is divided into five sections.

First division; description. *First division.*—After leaving the point marked "B," in map No. 2, the feeder will follow the left bank of the Blanco and Corte Rivers, until it reaches station 395, on the Capepac River. The whole of this division will be in side-cuttings, with very little filling, and only three inconsiderable full cuts. (See profiles Nos. 1 and 2.) The ground was explored at the points marked with dotted lines. The topography is accurately sketched.

Streams crossed. Nature of the ground. Length of first division. The most important stream crossed is the Maxiponac, (Sardine Brook,) insignificant as to volume, and remarkable for the number of its beautiful falls. Sand-stones and clay are abundant, feldspars crop out in many spurs, and the excavations will be difficult and expensive. The approximate length of this division, including the Blanco Cut, is four and one eighth (4⅛) miles.

Second division; description. Aqueduct. Streams crossed. Feeder-tunnel. *Second Division.*—From the Capepac, (Reed Brook,) the feeder will commence at Lemon Ridge, at the proper grade; and following the Capepac Valley on the left bank of its western branch, it will extend nearly to its head-waters; 227 feet above the bed of the Capepac, it will be necessary to construct an aqueduct about 1,200 feet long, connecting the Lemon and Devil's Ridges. The western portion of this division ends at the gap which forms the water-shed divide of the Milagro and Capepac Rivers. Midway between their sources, and at right-angles with their direction, flows the Sona-pac, (Lemon Brook,) traversing the divide, and having its source at Cliff Ridge. The bed of the Sona-pac is 118 feet above the summit; and the width of the gap is 4,150 feet at the grade; therefore a tunnel of that length becomes here indispensable.

Nature of soil. The nature of the soil is sandstones at the Lemon ridge, clay and slates in the upper branch of the Capepac, and marbles at the tunnel. The length of this division is one and a third miles, including the tunnel and the aqueduct. This will be the most expensive portion of the whole route.

Third division; description. *Third division.*—This division extends from the tunnel, near the source of the Milagro, to the second ford of the river Pita, (Hemp River.) It follows the left bank of the Milagro on the lap of the main range, which extends from Cliff Ridge to Tarifa.

When abreast of the town of Santa Maria, the feeder, whose general direction has been from east to west, turns now to the southwest, to escape the lowlands of the Chimalapa Potrero, (or flat lands,) searching for the lowest pass between the Chocolate Hill and the Sierra Madre. Since this pass is 160 feet above the summit-level, another tunnel will become necessary at this point. (See profile No. 2.) Its length will be *Feeder tunnel. Streams crossed.* 3,550 feet. The streams crossed by this division are a few very insignificant brooklets in the eastern end. The Coqui-pac, (Black River,) I believe, can be turned into the feeder without difficulty, by simply connecting a small dam and a waste-weir. Its floods are said to be inconsiderable, even when other rivers are much swollen; and this looks plausible on account of the small area it drains. After passing the Chocolate Hill, the feeder will encounter a sort of corrugated soil, forming the bed of many little streams, tributaries of the Coyolapa, (Second River,) and Escolapa, (First River;) but they do not complicate the difficulties of the feeder-route. The Cuchara (Spoon-

TEHUANTEPEC CANAL SURVEY.

brook) is passed near its source. This division ends at the Pita, whose waters have the same height as the summit-level. The excavations of the eastern part of this division are in compact limestones and clays. Drift and shales are found in the Chimalapa Potrero, plastic clay on the Chocolate tunnel, and drift and clay in the western terminus of this division. The length of this division will be eleven and three-eighths miles. {Nature of soil.}

Fourth division.—North of the town of San Miguel the main chain of mountains sends northward a heavy spur, which, ending at Santa Maria, turned the Corte from its western descent and sent it northward. We have named this spur the Cofradia Range. It is solid, and uninterruptedly high throughout its length, with but two exceptions, at the mouth of the Escolapa and at the Pita Brook. Even beyond the Corte, this range lifts again the last of its many heads, as a huge cone, which Indian wit has named the "Runt." I will now explain how this range is traversed by the feeder. {Fourth division; description.}

The Corte at Santa Maria is 373 feet below the summit. The Pita, which crosses the Cofradia Range, is at the summit-height, and is, besides, a tributary to the Corte fifteen miles below Santa Maria; therefore, by following the Pita Valley, we can cross the Cofradia Range below the summit-grade, since the Pita runs below this grade. The Chichihua, west of Cofradia Range, was found 71 feet below the summit, at the point marked Q, and the Pericon is 60 feet above, at the point crossed by the transit line; hence, the feeder must be located about half-way between these last points. The whole route of this division is easily excavated, and consists of clay at the Pita Brook, sandstones in the valley formed across the Cofradia Range, and humus and loose earth in the potreros of Chichihua. The length of this division is eight and three-eighths miles. {Nature of soil.}

Fifth division.—This division comprehends the tunnel from the Otate River to Tarifa Plains. {Fifth division.}

The only important features of this division is the length of the tunnel, but the excavations can be easily and cheaply made, the ground being very soft. The excavations need not exceed 205,000 cubic yards. {Fourth tunnel. Nature of soil.}

The following table contains a condensed statement of the important features of the feeder:

Number of divisions.	Limits of divisions.	Length of divisions.	Remarks.
Division No. 1	From Corte to Capepac	4½ miles	1 tunnel 1,750 feet long.
Division No. 2	From Capepac to Cliff	1⅜ miles	1 tunnel 4,150 feet long. 1 aqueduct 1,200 feet long.
Division No. 3	From Cliff to Pita	11⅜ miles	1 tunnel 3,550 feet long.
Division No. 4	From Pita to Sierra Blanca	8⅜ miles	Only 3 miles heavy cutting.
Division No. 5	Sierra Blanca Tunnel	2 miles	1 tunnel 9,650 feet long.
Total length of feeder		27¼ miles	Joint length of all the tunnels = 3.61 miles.

DIMENSIONS OF THE CANAL—ITS FEEDERS AND LOCKS.

Calculations for the water-supply, and best form of cross-sections to be given to the artificial water-courses.

The length of the canal proper will be about one hundred and forty-four miles from the harbor at Salina Cruz to the island of Tacamichapa on the Coatzacoalcos River. Fifty-two miles of this length will form the descending branch from Tarifa to the Pacific. With the exception of Tarifa Pass, there will be no necessity for using lock-flights, and even here, every reach may hold two full lock-lengths, and enough development can be found on the hill-side to avoid the grouping of more than two locks at a flight. {Length of the canal. Length of the Pacific branch of the canal. Lock-flights.}

The dimensions proposed for the canal are:

<small>Transverse dimensions.</small>

	Feet.
Top-breadth	162
Bottom-breadth	60
Depth of water	22

And for the locks:

<small>Lock dimensions.</small>

Length between miter-sills	320
Breadth	42
Depth of water	21
Depth of prism of lift	10.14

I should recommend double locks; but the estimates that follow suppose each lock subdivided by gates affording respectively 130, 218, and 320 feet of lockage length.

It is extremely difficult, nay, impossible, to determine the amount of water required to feed a canal unless the condition and nature of its trade are known. This is especially the case when the transit has to be effected through an undeveloped country, under very anomalous political, social, industrial, and economical conditions. I do not feel justified in using the custom commercial statistics before me of the probable commerce that may seek this channel, because for my purpose I have no confidence in them, and no good reason to suppose that this manner of guessing is more rational than any other one, so long as any guessing element enters into the problem. I believe that, through this canal, an immense impetus will be given to the commerce of our Pacific States; that the politico-economical laws of our development demand its immediate construction; that the length of many trading channels will be shortened, and that the capital now eliminated through losses of money, time, and deterioration of merchandise, will be redeemed, and made useful in its application to cheapen produce and increase trade; but I also believe that the data required to estimate upon the nature of the Tehuantepec Canal trade for water-supply purposes can only be approximated after long study and diligent research of uncollected trade statistics at home and abroad, requiring a length of time made impracticable by the nature of our Expedition.

The following table will explain the necessity of knowing the amount of trade to estimate the water-supply:

On level stretches if—	And finds the locks—	The vessel will draw from the summit—	And consequently will leave the locks—
The vessel is descending from the summit.	Full	No water	Empty.
	Empty	One lock full	Empty.
The vessel is ascending to the summit.	Full	One lock full	Full.
	Empty	One lock full	Full.

On a flight of locks if—	And finds the locks—	The vessel will draw from the summit—	And will leave all the locks—
The vessel is descending from the summit.	Full	No water	Empty.
	Empty	One lock full	Empty.
The vessel is ascending to the summit.	Full	One lock full	Full.
	Empty	As many locks full as there are contiguous chambers.	Full.

<small>Basis of calculation for water supply.</small>

Although the estimates made are based upon a trade of about twenty thousand tons crossing the summit daily, they have been made under conditions so exaggerated, that I believe under ordinary circumstances this canal can accommodate thirty thousand (30,000) tons daily.

<small>Lockage distribution.</small>

I have also distributed the canal trade among small vessels, which will consume a large lockage in proportion to their tonnage, thus: 120 lockages, of 170 feet length, for vessels of 200 tons and under; 20 lockages, of 218 feet length, for vessels of 500 tons; 5 lockages, of 320 feet length, for vessels of 1,000 tons. These conditions will require special machinery to attend to the rapid demands upon the gates.

The lockage-water for the whole canal will then be expressed by *Water required for lockage.*

$$\frac{42' \times 10'.14 \, [170 \times 120 + 218 \times 20 + 320 \times 5]}{24^{hs} \times 60^{m} \times 60^{s}} = 146.94$$

cubic feet per second.

Referring to the meterological chart, it will be seen that the mean daily evaporation on the summit-plains does not exceed the 0.19 of an inch.

It is customary among French engineers to allow in temperate latitudes from three-fourths of a millimeter to two millimeters, while American and English engineers use one-fourth of an inch, as the depth lost by evaporation in twenty-four hours. But we were on the Isthmus at the only season of the year in which it does not rain frequently, and the evaporation is never so high as when the observations were taken; therefore I have adopted 0.016 foot per twenty-four hours as the basis for calculation, this being the mean amount observed.

Length of canal, 144 miles	760,320 feet.
Breadth	162 feet.
Area of surface	123,171,840 square feet.
Depth of daily evaporation	0.016 of a foot.
Total evaporation in twenty-four hours	1,970,749 cubic feet.
Amount of evaporation per second	23 cubic feet.

Water required to supply evaporation.

The losses by filtration depend upon the nature of the soil, workmanship, and accidents that cannot be foreseen. Experiments made in the canals of Du Midi, Givors, Briare, and Bourgogne, and from experiments extending over one month at Weyneport, and in the Palmyra and Clyde levels, I feel safe in adopting 8,090 cubic feet per second per mile as the losses from filtrations. Taking into account the increase wet perimeter of this canal, calculations give 897 cubic feet per second as the total amount of filtration throughout the length of the canal.

The water lost through any gate is replaced by the loss from the upper gate, and this same source of waste can be traced to the summit-level. M. Minard makes them equivalent to 0.13 feet per second. *Losses by filtration.*

I will admit for gate-leakage 0.30 cubic feet per second. The losses through waste-weirs are equally uncertain, though they are unnecessary. If cast-iron gates are used throughout, and properly cared for, lock and weir wastes can be reduced to a minimum. I have allowed for weirs two cubic feet per second. *Gate leakage.*

The feeder will experience losses by filtration, evaporation, and at the weirs. The Saint Privé feeder (26,000 feet long) loses three-fourths of its water; while the feeder of Boulét, which is 56,000 feet in length, leaks four-fifths of the volume it receives. These feeders are under comparatively unfavorable circumstances, while the nature of the soil of our feeder is well calculated to prevent filtration. I have supposed that the losses under this head will amount to 550 cubic feet per second, or more than three times the lockage-water necessary for the whole canal. *Weir losses.* *Feeder losses.*

Total amount of water required to supply the ship-canal.

For lockages	146.94 cubic feet per second.
For evaporation	23.00 cubic feet per second.
For filtration	896.00 cubic feet per second.
For leakage at gates	0.31 cubic feet per second.
For leakage at weirs	2.00 cubic feet per second.
For feeder losses	550.00 cubic feet per second.
For the whole canal	1,618.25 cubic feet per second.

Total water required to supply the canal.

32   TEHUANTEPEC CANAL SURVEY.

Transverse section for the artificial water-courses.

Best form of transverse section for the feeder, in order to deliver at the summit, say 1,618 cubic feet per second, with a velocity of 2.7 feet per second—

$$\frac{1618}{2.7} = 599.26 \text{ square feet} = \text{area of transverse section.}$$

The angle of slope can be safely assumed at 40°; hence the sought depth of water in the feeder will be—

$$\sqrt{\frac{599.26 \sin 40°}{2 - \cos 40}} = 17.668 \text{ feet depth of water};$$

also,

$$599.26 - 17.668 \cos 40° = 12.862 \text{ feet, breadth of bottom.}$$

The absolute slope .... 21—053 feet.
And upper breadth .... 54—98 feet.

To find the fall or head necessary to be given to the feeder to deliver the required amount of water, with the given velocity at Tarifa, the formula is—

$$h = \zeta \frac{l\,p}{F} \times \frac{c^2}{2g} \quad \text{Weisbach, volume I, page 446.}$$

Where h = fall required

Length of feeder, 27¼ miles.

Where l = length of feeder = 144,000 feet.

Where p = the wet perimeter $= 12.862 + 2\sqrt{17.668^2 + \left(\frac{54.982 - 12.862}{2}\right)^2} = 68.67$ feet.

Where F = transverse section = 599.26 square feet.
Where c = the given velocity = 2.70 feet.
Where g = the acceleration of gravity = 32.20 feet.
Substituting above, we find—

$$h = 13.97 = \text{fall of the feeder that will fulfill the conditions.}$$

Feeder-head.
Comparative data.

The following table establishes a comparison between the water dimensions and water-supply estimates of the Caledonian Canal; the ship-canal proposed through the Isthmus of Panama by the engineer-in-chief of the Royal Corps of Miners, Paris, 1841; the Albany and New Baltimore Ship-Canal, proposed by William I. McAlpine, A. M. S. of C. E., Albany, 1853, and the estimates made for the Tehuantepec Ship-Canal:

Designation.	Panama.	Caledonian.	Albany.	Tehuantepec.
Length of canal	47¼ miles	25 miles	12½ miles	122 miles.
Breadth of canal at water level	148 feet	122 feet	120 feet	162 feet.
Breadth of canal at trench bottom	66 feet	50 feet	50 feet	60 feet.
Depth of water in canal	23 feet	20 feet	2 feet	22 feet.
Lock-length between miter-sills	210 feet	172 feet	115 to 300 feet	170 to 320 feet.
Lock-breadth	47 feet	40 feet	31 feet	42 feet.
Lock-depth			20 (?) feet	21 feet.
Estimated trade per day	5,000 tons		10,000 tons	20,000 tons.
Estimated supply for lockage, in cubic feet, per second.	25,148		98.11	146.94
Estimated evaporation, gate, and leakage losses, cubic feet, per second.	0.462		42.33	22.31
Estimated filtration, cubic feet, per second.	62,224		84.78	1,446.00
Total supply, estimated in cubic feet	87,834		225.22	1,618.00

Study of the location of the Atlantic branch of the canal.

It will be well to say, before proceeding to the description of the canal-route, that the main efforts of the Expedition were dedicated to its immediate object, viz, to determine the practicability of the canal. Considerable time was spent in summit explorations and in testing the feasibility of projects previously proposed. Disappointment met us everywhere; and when at last the feeder-route and its water-supply were discovered, the season was so far advanced that it was impossible to extend our level lines to the Atlantic side, and locate the north branch of the canal. However, the ground has been thoroughly explored, the work previously performed for railroad and other purposes, and the profile and plans obtained from the studies of Barnard, Sidell, Orbegozo, and others, coupled with our own observations, enable me to assert with confidence, that below the confluence of the Malatengo there is no obstacle whatever in the way of the canal. The broad Coatzacoalcos Valley has room enough, and is flat for a long distance on either side of its Thalweg.

The soil at Tarifa is impermeable, and the feeder will deliver its waters directly upon the plains. *Delivery end of feeder.*

A crescent-shaped lake will be formed, which, owing to the nature of the ground, will retain its waters at all points, except at the Tarifa River. At this point, where the soil drains naturally to the Atlantic, the north summit-gate will be excavated. *Tarifa Lake.*

The Pacific summit-gate will be twenty-two feet lower than the lowest point of the Tarifa Pass. The houses now at Tarifa will form a peninsula, where store-houses, repair-shops, &c., will be built. *Pacific end of the Summit Reach.*

From Tarifa the first level will start northward. *Atlantic end of the Summit Reach.*

From barometric observations behind the Campanario Hill, as well as on account of the grade of the Tarifa River, it appears that there will be required nine locks between the summit and the point of confluence of Chichihua and Tarifa Rivers, or one lock per mile. *A lock per mile between Chichihua and Tarifa Rivers.*

From this point to Mal-paso, below Rio Chico, the bed of the Chichihua has a small slope, which necessarily widens the distance between the locks. Then the canal will run along the valley of the Coatzacoalcos, as shown in map No. 1. *Approximate location of the north branch of canal.*

Twenty-one miles above Rio Chico, the Coatzacoalcos falls only three hundred and sixty-three feet in more than one hundred and forty miles of river-course. This fact, together with the already large size of the Corte at Rio Chico, guarantees a convenient distribution of the locks.

On the Pacific side it is necessary to descend with sixty-three locks from the summit to La Venta de Chicapa, and this must be done in eight miles; the length of development required for one flight will be 20,160 feet, while the amount furnished by the ground is 42,240 feet, or, as I have said before, no more than two locks need be grouped in flights. Beyond this point, eight locks will be used in a horizontal distance of forty-seven miles. *Pacific side flight.*

It will be seen, by comparing jointly the several profiles of the Pacific plains, that in some places embankments will be required to elevate the surface of the canal to its proper grade. *Canal embankments.*

Profile No. 5 shows the low range of hills at the Salina Cruz point, but the prominent elevation seen near the ocean can be overcome by an insignificant cut, because the level line was run upon a ridge, which is at least fifty feet higher than the small valley upon whose western ridge the road has been built. *Southernmost range of hills.*

I have been unable to obtain a copy of the profile made by Orbegozo, between the Tarifa Pass to the Upper Lagoon, by way of La Venta de Chicapa; but from recollection, and notes entered in my journal when I examined these profiles, I have no manner of doubt in stating that the ground descends very uniformly from La Venta to the Lagoons, and also that the ascent, though rapid, is quite uniform from La Venta to Tarifa Pass. I have visited this pass three times from opposite directions. The last time I inspected it was from La Venta upward, in company with the chief of the Mexican commission, for the sole purpose of studying the development of the hill-curves and the location of the locks. We found no place where the locks could not be easily placed to advantage, with regard to economy of time and water, even if double locks were built, with a water-pit between them. *Configuration of Tarifa Pass.*

Lieutenant Commander Bartlett ran a transit and level line down the Tarifa Pass, to the point where all difficulties disappear; but pressure from other quarters compelled me to suspend this work, for the more important one of determining the height of Cofradia Pass. This line was to be continued to the ocean, after a return from the Corte region; but finding then that the Mexican commissioners were engaged in this *Determination of the height of Tarifa Pass.*

work, in order to obtain the greatest possible number of profiles across the Isthmus, the height of the summit was determined by way of La Chivela, San Geronimo, Tehuantepec, and Salina Cruz.

I expect to receive a copy of the La Venta line from the Mexican commissioners, and if it should arrive in time, it will be appended to this report and credited to them.

Abruptness of mountain range. An inspection of the general map would seem to indicate that high ground might exist on the plains, between the Chicapa and Verde Rivers, on the line traversed by the canal; but this is not the case. The south slope of Masahua Range starts *The Verde an insignificant river.* abruptly from a dead level; the Lagartero Hill looks like a huge boat stranded on the beach. The Verde, which looks formidable in the maps, was crossed twice near Cofradia without knowing it, though looking sharply for its bed.

Crossing the Juchitan River. The Juchitan River is the only one that deserves special mention, because it will require to be spanned over by the canal; but its floods are powerless when they reach Juchitan. Small culverts along the canal-line in the area covered by the river-floods will overcome this obstacle. These same circumstances obtain in the Tehuantepec River, but in a lesser degree, since this river now runs through a permanent channel, which it was said the river excavated for itself; but while studying the *Regimen of the Tehuantepec River.* regimen of this river, I ascertained that the witchcraft attributed to this peaceful stream arose from ignorant tinkering with its waters, for irrigation purposes. A trench had been dug unprotected below the flood-line, and the river found an outlet over soft ground to the old sunk turnpike, which was washed away, and ever since kept by the river for its bed.

Floods of the Tehuantepec River. The highest floods of the Tehuantepec River never reach fifteen feet above its bed. An inspection of profile No. 5 will show that there is no difficulty in crossing over the stream.

HARBOR OF THE ATLANTIC TERMINUS OF THE CANAL.

Coatzacoalcos Harbor. On the Atlantic side of the Isthmus there is a natural, well-protected harbor, made by the banks of the Coatzacoalcos. The harbor varies its depth, but from its entrance to the island of Tacamichapa it can easily be deepened to twenty-two feet.

Shallow points. Between the harbor bar and Minatitlan the river is very deep, with but five exceptions, viz: at the harbor entrance; near the southern ends of the islands of Guerrero and Diablo; and at the points of confluence of the streams Tierra-Nueva and Camarones. This last point is deep enough, but quite narrow. All these bars *Uspanapa Bar.* but two can be removed without much expense, owing to the nature and extent of the deposits, which are sand and gravel, under twenty feet of water. The narrow Uspanapa Bar is covered by eighteen feet of water at low tide. It is made by deposits from the latter river. The Coatzacoalcos is very deep above and below the point of confluence.

Elimination of the Uspanapa Bar. Piles driven on the Uspanapa, or a partial damming of the river, will cause the sands to deposit farther up stream, on its own bed.

Average depth of the Coatzacoalcos from the bar to Minatitlan. With the exception mentioned above, the river varies from twenty-two to eighteen feet in depth in the old as well as in the Kansas channel. The latter channel was discovered in 1871, by the hydrographic party.

The length of the whole trunk is twenty-one miles, counted from the center of the harbor bar to the Minatitlan custom-house.

THE COATZACOALCOS BAR.

This bar has been often surveyed, and its depth, condition, and geographical position have been variously stated by different observers.

The following table will give an idea of the discrepancies of results, which place the bar anywhere between four and eleven miles from where the extreme observations indicate:

TEHUANTEPEC CANAL SURVEY.

Position of light-house of Coatzacoalcos Bar.

Latitude.	Longitude west of Greenwich.	Authorities.
° ′ ″	° ′ ″	
18 03 27	94 21 25.5	Memoirs of the Spanish Navy.
18 04 50	94 25 00.0	Murphy.
18 08 30	94 17 00.0	Robles.
18 11 00	94 24 00.0	Commodore Perry, United States Navy.
18 08 15	94 21 00.0	Miller, United States Navy, United States Expedition, 1871.

Mr. Miller's results are nearly the mean of the results which have the most weight. The same disagreement is found with regard to the depth of water over the bar.

Depth of water over the bar.

Authorities.	Date of survey.	Depth of water over the bar.
Dampier	17—	14 English feet.
Cramer	1774	17 English feet.
Robinson	1820	22 English feet.
Orbegozo	1824	14 English feet.
Robles	1842	20¼ English feet.
Perry	1848	12¼ English feet.
Tehuantepec Expedition	1871	14 English feet.

Not knowing what to make with these results, which cannot all be correct, and being absolutely sure that the tides are insignificant, and the bar permanent for all practical purposes, I have compiled the surveys of our Expedition and of Commander Perry's, and carefully interpolated soundings deduced from those given by the actual surveys. The contour curves were then constructed, and are appended, with longitudinal and transverse profiles. (See map No. 11.) *Comparison of surveys.*

A period of twenty-three years has elapsed between these surveys, and in that time the following changes have taken place: *Interval of 23 years between the two surveys.*

1. The channel at the mouth of the river retains its depth of forty feet, but it is now twice as long as it was in 1848.

2. The horizontal distance between the 40 and 18 foot curves has been elongated one and a half times; but now the channel is narrower.

3. The first contour curve, returning upon itself, and limiting the southern edge of the bar, has receded toward the sea one-tenth of its original distance, as counted from the deepest part of the river abreast of the old fort; but vertically over the place of this curve there are now four feet more of water.

4. The width of the bar has not altered sensibly, and is now generally four or five feet deeper.

5. The 24-foot curve of depth has neither shifted nor sensibly altered its shape. It is inside of the bar, convex toward the sea, and its apex is nearly tangent to the coast-line.

6. Between the apex of this curve and the southern edge of the bar, great changes have taken place. The channel has become narrower, and though much deeper, it is quite crooked in the line of maximum depth. *Material changes.*

7. No results have reached my hands of the nature of the drift upon the bar before 1840. Now it is made up of coarse and fine, gray and black sands, shells, and clay, with red and black specks. *Drift upon the bar.*

8. The black sands belong to the Uspanapa, and, as has been remarked, can be prevented from reaching the harbor by inducing the formation of a bar at the mouth of the Uspanapa, in front of which the sands will naturally settle, practically, for an indefinite period. *Uspanapa sands.*

9. The Coatzacoalcos Bar is an external bar, and is often disturbed by northers. Since the drift, held in suspension by the agitated sea, cannot run up against the Coatzacoalcos current, it is deposited outside of and parallel to the coast, especially toward the eastern side of the entrance. This conclusion seems plausible from the shape of the 6-foot curve.

10. The 18-foot curve shows the limiting height of greatest deposits, and it has advanced toward the channel with an irregular serrated outline, confining the effective cross-section of the river; consequently the increased depth of water over the bar is accounted for, because the increased velocity, due to the stricture in the channel, has blown away the fine sands.

11. The bar is permanent, with a clay sub-soil. This can be shown by the 18-foot curve, thus: The nature of the deposits should be considered with regard to their cohesion and density; as is shown by the slopes of the profiles, the particles deposited over the lower portion of the river slide easily upon each other, and are of light weight. If the bar and river deposits were of uniform density, the current would cut a channel with sensibly parallel outlines; but if the bar is made up of a substance harder than the drift upon it, it will act as a dam, against which the current will impinge, and, becoming divided and thrown sideways, it will excavate irregular channels through the material that collects in front of the bar. Also, since the edge of the bar acts as the lips of a dam, the current will wash away the light particles, no drift will be found upon it, and eddies will be found in close proximity to the obstructions, which will produce both shallow and deep holes, not far removed from each other.

If we look at the chart of 1871, it will be seen that these effects, which are the irrevocable sequence of dynamical laws, obtain in the Coatzacoalcos Bar in a very remarkable manner; hence they must be attributed to the hardness and permanence of the bar. It will also be observed that those points of the bar which should expose the subsoil to the action of the currents, are the only places where the sound gives "hard clay."

12. The profiles and sections accompanying the chart of 1871 will give an accurate idea of the present state of the bar. The parts ruled in black lines represent the required amount of dredging, under the supposition that the entrance channel will be 1,200 feet wide at the bottom throughout its length, and 25 feet deep from the entrance until after crossing the present bar. Beyond this point the channel is very deep, and only small excavations will be required on the sides to increase the width of its bottom to the large dimensions proposed.

The nature of all the surveys made of this bar, though sufficiently accurate for navigation purposes, do not offer the minuteness of detail necessary to determine the amount of excavations necessary for the improvement of this harbor.

But I feel no hesitation in asserting, with unusual confidence, that the Coatzacoalcos River can be made a very safe and snug harbor for any class of ships with but comparatively small expense.

The excavations between Tacamichapa and Minatitlan can be reduced to a minimum by a proper arrangement of the locks, which will slack the water up stream.

The hydrographic party, in charge of Lieutenant Commander Farquhar, surveyed accurately the Coatzacoalcos Bar, triangulating from a measured base-line on its western shore, and checking by auxiliary measurements.

Soundings were taken by finding the angles at each sounding with the sextant, from known stations, at given intervals of time, and locating the average line of soundings by the sextant and bearings.

Nearly the same system was employed in the Coatzacoalcos River. The coast-line was plotted from magnetic bearings and measured distances, with check-sights to all available stations.

I have every reason to believe that this work is accurate and reliable. The balance of the hydrographic work on the Atlantic side must be considered as reconnaissances and sketches.

TEHUANTEPEC CANAL SURVEY.

HARBORS IN THE PACIFIC TERMINUS OF THE CANAL.

The roadsteads of Ventosa and Salina Cruz have been proposed as the available Pacific harbors.

Ventosa and Salina Cruz.

In their present state they are both unsuitable for our object, and while Salina Cruz can be converted into a safe artificial harbor, the Bay of Ventosa never will be used, on account of its exposure, the nature of its shores, the limit of the surf-line, shape of the coast, and holding character of the ground.

The astronomical position of Salina Cruz, as given by Trastour, is nearly correct, though by some great error creeping into our calculations we made it nearly seven miles south of its true place. The Mexican commissioners kindly volunteered to solve the doubt entertained at the time with regard to our accuracy, and their results agree remarkably well with the true position of Salina Cruz, as given by our transit-line.

During my stay in Salina Cruz, I cross-examined nine of the coast pilots, by requesting them to remain in a room without telling them my object, until I called them out one by one, asked them the same questions, and sent them out without giving them a chance to converse with their companions. These pilots, or "patrones," had been employed on this coast from three to eighteen years, with a license from the government to take command of crafts. The points on which their answers were identical are given below.

Its present condition, as stated by pilots.

1. The south wind is the most dangerous, on account of the surf.
2. A breakwater at Point Salina Cruz will destroy the surf.
3. They think so because the "stones" now at that point protect the landing considerably.
4. The norther impedes now only the entrance of sail, but a steamer can enter the roadstead without danger, with any norther short of a hurricane.
5. The stiffest norther does not interfere with the landing of merchandise.
6. Point Ventosa, or Morro Point, defends this roadstead from the north, east, and northeast winds.
7. The east wind is always tame, and only blows from May to September. During this period it does not blow from the east more than thirty days—never consecutively nor regularly—and the wind never lasts a quarter of the day. It generally begins at 12 o'clock in the night, and ceases when the sun is hot, say by 10 a. m. A launch, with six men, can carry on the landing with any east wind.
8. One of the pilots, Lorenzo Pablo, says that there is plenty of water in the Upper Lagoon, near the islands; that toward this place the water deepens rapidly, but turns gradually shallow as you approach any shore-line. The last time he worked in the lagoon, he found that the soundings had changed from the islands toward Punta de Agua. This happened in December, January, and February last. He entered the Boca Barra in May, and will never do it again, because "the feat is dangerous."
9. All the pilots agree that the inward current at Santa Teresa is small, but the outward current is very strong, and cannot be crossed.
10. There are breakers from Boca Barra to Ventosa Point, and the surf extends from half to three-quarters of a mile toward the sea. They are formed by a hard sand bank parallel to the coast.
11. Inside the Ventosa Bay the Tehuantepec River spreads out a current for a mile toward the sea, and destroys, during its floods, the sand-bars made by the sea during the dry season.
12. The present captain of the port at Salina Cruz is D. Benito Perez, a very intelligent sea-faring man, quite expert in the use of the sextant for navigation purposes, and well acquainted with the coast. He says that he has often surveyed the Salina Cruz port, and that—
13. The swell begins at 8 a. m., and ends at 5 p. m., and is strongest from 12 to 2, or at low tide.

14. In June the highest tides occur, also occasional squalls. From April to the middle of June, one man can pull a pair of sculls in any part of the bay.

15. From his soundings in the direction of the buoy and custom-house, Perez has found 3 fathoms of water near the shore, and the depth increasing gradually to over 11 fathoms at the buoy.

16. No point of the roadstead has less than 3 fathoms of water over it, except close to the shore.

17. At two-thirds of the distance measured from the custom-house toward Point Ventosa, there is a sand-bank, formed and destroyed alternately by the north and south winds; but there are always 11 fathoms of water over it.

18. The surface currents in the bay are periodical, and coincide in direction with the prevailing winds.

19. The normal tides are four feet, but are increased to six feet by the south wind.

20. Salina Cruz Point protects the roadstead very much. The current from that quarter is generally from the sea toward the beach, in a northeast direction.

21. The holding-ground at Salina Cruz is excellent.

22. The holding-ground at Ventosa is very poor, and the bay is gradually getting filled with sand and mud.

23. There are no rocks on the coast for a long distance east and west, except so close to the shore that no vessel will venture to go near.

Beyond these questions all their answers were discordant; but the unanimity in the above particulars, obtained from different sources, gives them considerable weight.

Deductions from data obtained. Coupling the above statements with the results of the surveys of this coast, made at different times, with my own observations, I feel warranted in making the following deductions:

Position of Salina Cruz. The position of Salina Cruz is in latitude 16° 10′ 11″ north, and longitude 95° 20′ 00″ west of Greenwich.

Lagoons believed to be unavailable. The lagoons offer no natural facilities that would recommend their use as a part of the canal, except in the case that the Pacific branch of the canal should be located in a northerly and southerly direction. But under this condition, the necessity of crossing the Chicapa may by itself offset the problematic advantage of a diminished length of excavation.

I believe that it is impracticable to reach the Upper Lagoon by an artificial channel from the sea.

The volumes of water of the many rivers traversing the plains bring large deposits from these sandy districts, which are shifted by the tides and currents.

It will be very expensive to excavate, under water, fifteen miles of channel, which may fill up immediately, and having no suitable outlet for a harbor entrance, they are no better than an inland lake for the purposes of this canal.

The surveys made by Master C. B. Gill, United States Navy, the remarks of Lieutenant Commander A. Hopkins, and Lieutenant Commander P. H. Cooper, and the statements of the pilots and of the captain of the port, prove that Salina Cruz is preferable to La Ventosa, for the purposes of a port of entry.

Direction and length of breakwater. A breakwater 1,500 or 2,000 feet long, and S. 67° E., will protect this Salina Cruz port, and convert it into a snug harbor.

I apprehend no difficulty in constructing this breakwater with the suitable material at hand. The artificial port at Algiers is not unlike Salina Cruz, with regard to the nature of its exposure, but very different as to the violence of the sea, which is milder at Salina Cruz.

Transmitted swell at Salina Cruz. I believe that the swell entering the roadstead is due to lateral transmission, and absolutely there is no swell by reflexion. I went on board the Cyane during a heavy swell, and observed its motion along the coast, and immediately after landing I ascended to Salina Cruz Point, to watch the swell from a height. The wind was south, but the swell came from the west, and after being considerably broken by a clump of rocks which advance toward the sea at Salinas del Marques, it was *sent* out toward the sea.

The transmitted motion reached the Salina Cruz Point, where the swell was distinctly seen to diminish in height, and to enter the roadstead through the crevices in the rocks at Salina Cruz Point and south of the rocks in a northeast direction. A breakwater in the direction proposed above will make this port as smooth as Marseilles, though with much better entrance.

I do not think it will be necessary to construct a jetty on the eastern end of this port, believing that the breakwater will be sufficient to protect an area large enough to shelter forty vessels riding their anchor at two cables' length. <small>Area sheltered by the breakwater.</small>

Although the well-known "Mexican double-current" runs northward and sensibly parallel to the west coast, its influence does not reach the coast itself; and there must be an inner counter-current in close proximity to the land. This fact was unmistakably observed by me during four days, with north and south winds; and the captain of the port states that though the surface-currents coincide with the wind, they are so light as only to affect the course of small boats; the normal-currents are from the southwest to the northeast. He has had many years of experience on this coast.

The line of surf begins almost opposite the custom-house, and gradually widens as it advances toward the Morro Point. The absence of surf on the west end of the port illustrates the shelter afforded by the few rocks at Point Salina Cruz, and serves as an index to what may be expected from a breakwater. <small>Present position of the line of surf.</small>

A wharf 300 feet long could now be used for the discharge of vessels during a great portion of the year; but, since they have no wharf, a rope-ferry is used instead.

I do not desire to convey the idea that it would be easy or inexpensive to convert the Salina Cruz roadstead into a harbor, for the simplest problem of this nature requires special studies absolutely beyond the purpose and means of the Expedition. <small>Uncertainty as to the character of the improvements of the Pacific harbor.</small>

There is no engineering undertaking more fruitful of mistakes than the formation of artificial harbors, even after protracted study and thorough surveys. The complications arising from littoral alluvium often require to destroy a whole series of plans, and to start upon a new system, with loss of time and heavy expenses.

With regard to Salina Cruz, I know nothing about the difficulties to be encountered in the foundation of the breakwater, and next to nothing about the nature, intensity, and effects of prevailing currents and winds. The data I have been able to compile have been given above, and all I can say, as an expert, is: That taking into account the results of surveys and other information obtained, and having inspected the localities referred to, I am not able to see anything impracticable in the proposed formation of this harbor. <small>The improvement believed practicable.</small>

Judging by comparison, I believe I am safe in stating that the sea-works performed in many places appear to me to have been constructed on a scale greater than their importance warrants, when they are compared with Salina Cruz, as the terminus of this ship-canal. Thus— <small>Comparative condition and importance of Salina Cruz and other artificial harbors.</small>

Antibes.—Has a double mole, one of them 24 feet above the sea, protecting the harbor against the mistral winds. It has been a most expensive work, requiring many additions to the original plan, as well as corrections.

La Ciotat.—Which, like Cherbourg, struggles against reflected swells.

Cannes.—Where the sand-deposits will forever give trouble.

Olonne.—Port of Sands; open to the southwest winds, with protection against lateral transmission.

Islands of Yeu and Ré.—In the latter, the ports of Saint Martin and La Flotte have given a great deal of trouble, with complications that could not be foreseen before the construction of their moles.

I might mention eight or ten other artificial harbors of a limited commercial influence, whose importance is insignificant when compared with that of Salina Cruz.

Should the commerce of the canal assume such dimensions as would crowd the harbor of Salina Cruz, it can be easily conceived that heavy expenditures would be warrantable in the construction of a channel from the canal to the upper lagoon.

Upper lagoon as a harbor to Salina Cruz roadstead.

The hydrographic work on the Pacific side was executed by a party of officers of the United States sloop Cyane, in charge of Master C. B. Gill, United States Navy. The transit line run around the Upper Lagoon, and all the details of the surveys, as inclosed in chart No. 16, bear evidences of thoroughness and intelligence. It has given me pleasure to look over Mr. Gill's work and find it correct.

Character of the hydrographic work.

The work around Salina Cruz was not completed, owing to want of time and scarcity of provisions. The points located in detail agree with the surveys of Trastour and a hasty triangulation made by myself on the coast-line.

In the chart of this roadstead, No. 15, the geographical position of Salina Cruz has been corrected to its true position, and details filled in from other surveys, when known to be correct.

PERMANENCY OF THE WORKS AND SAFETY OF TRANSIT.

Wear and tear of the works.

Taking for granted that the dimensions to be given to the canal and accessory works will be such as will fulfill the laws of their stability, the only forces that will conspire against their permanence are the necessary wear and tear incident to the nature of the works, accidents, and cataclysms. The former cannot be avoided, and the engineer has nothing to do with the latter. But it will be well to say that earthquakes are not unfrequent in the Isthmus, although I would state that they are not as dangerous as is popularly believed. Their damages have been circumscribed to small localities, and their effects upon the canal may be considered under two points of view: 1st. The immediate damage that the canal itself may suffer; 2d. The result of these damages, as they may affect the character of inundations, and destruction of life and property.

Earthquakes.

Inundations.

Since the feeder and the north branch of the canal are to be built upon the valleys of large water-courses, and using the water of the same valleys, no damage to property nor destruction of life can be anticipated, as inherent to the artificial channel. On the Pacific side, the land being flat, no torrents can be formed; and its many and large water-courses will carry the water from the feeder to the sea.

I have studied diligently the subject of earthquakes, and their effect upon the Isthmus, having consulted the following authorities: Baron A. Von Humboldt, Pilla, A. Erman, Perrey, Sarti, Soldani, Dr. Yung, and Dr. A. Rojas.

No cataclysms recorded on the Isthmus.

The cataclysms and earthquakes recorded in South and Central America have never proved destructive on the Isthmus to an extent that would injure seriously a canal.

From observations by Perrey during many years, the following is the yearly average of earthquakes throughout the earth: 23 in winter, 15 in spring, 20 in summer; 22 in autumn; 80 the whole year.

Earthquakes during the survey.

We visited the Isthmus during the two seasons of maximum recurrence, and only experienced three earthquakes, one strong, but which would have been harmless to the canal, and the other two quite insignificant.

Direction of earthquake-waves.

Quito, Venezuela, and Chili are the points of the continent whence earthquake-waves are mostly propagated toward the Isthmus.

General earthquakes.

The earthquakes of 1852 are the most striking general earthquakes recorded, and in Oaxaca and Vera Cruz only a few houses were cracked. At all events, they were not calamitous. These earthquakes began on the 17th of January, by an eruption of the Mauna Loa, nearly destroying the Sandwich Islands. In July, Cuba and Porto Rico suffered terrible losses in life and property; on the 17th of the same month it was felt in Ceuta; on the 18th in Santo Domingo, and in Austria it was so violent that the shock rung the church-bells; on the 25th it was felt in Georgia, United States; on the 16th September, the inhabitants of Manila experienced the heaviest oscillations in their records; St. Iago of Cuba was completely destroyed, and at almost the same instant the Etna entered into one of its most terrible eruptions. It will be seen that there must be some reason holding good for the safety of the Isthmus, when it escaped the commotion of a center of disturbance comparatively close, while distant points were violently shaken.

The general earthquake of 1867, which proved so calamitous in the West Indies, was harmless in the Isthmus.

The above is not presented as a proof, but only as a plausible deduction, tending to show the stability of the Isthmus.

There are strong reasons to confirm the belief that Calabria, Tuscany, Portugal, Cuba, and Japan are subject to heavier commotions than any Isthmian route will ever be; and yet this danger is never taken into account in connection with public works, or commercial and political enterprises. *Development of regions exposed to earthquakes.*

The data obtained from our surveys are not sufficient to make estimates as to the cost of the canal. *No estimates of the cost of this canal can be furnished at present.*

I have thought it advisable to exaggerate the dimensions of all the elements tending to exhaust the summit water-supply, and to tunnel for the feeder in localities in which I had reason to believe that an open cut would be less expensive. *All unfavorable conditions have been exaggerated.*

I believe that the cost of the feeder is not incommensurable with the importance of the canal.

For the purpose of comparison, we have the Croton Aqueduct, which brings water to New York from a distance of 41 miles. In its construction, it has been necessary to prepare an immense drainage area, to make costly improvements, and an expensive dam at the Croton River; to bring the water through an arched aqueduct to the elegant High Bridge over the Harlem. The old reservoir was constructed in Central Park, the distributing reservoir in Forty-second street, and many accessory works, more or less expensive, were finished, at an average expense of $1,000,000 per mile. *Croton Aqueduct, compared with canal feeder.*

Many years of connection with the Croton Aqueduct have made me familiar with the character of its works, and the thorough survey made of the feeder-route enables me to believe that the construction of the ship-canal feeder cannot exceed one-fifth of the entire cost of the Croton Aqueduct.

The expenses to be incurred for the canal proper need no defense; they depend upon the assumed dimensions of the trench and locks, while the class and number of obstacles to be overcome are of the most ordinary nature. *Cost of the canal proper.*

Although the construction of this ship-canal is truly a large project, when compared with many ancient works its magnitude disappears. *Magnitude of the project compared with ancient works.*

One thousand one hundred and seventy-eight years before Christ, the pyramid of Chemnif was commenced. In its construction 360,000 slaves were employed during twenty years, and ten years were spent in the building of the causeway, over which 100,000 men, in gangs of 10,000, brought the materials to the pyramid.

The canal built by Nitocris, Queen of Babylon, and which protected her kingdom against the Medes, was made by turning the Euphrates into an artificial channel, probably provided with gates and sluices, and with so many windings that it was a three days' voyage to pass the town of Ardericca.

To prevent the city from inundations, Nebuchadnezzar, five hundred and sixty-two years before Christ, built an immense lake to receive the flood-water, while facing the banks of the Euphrates with brick and bitumen walls the entire length of its course through the city.

Modern Rome is abundantly supplied from three of the twenty aqueducts that once brought water across the Campagna, in lines from 30 to 60 miles in length. One of these aqueducts passed over 7,000 arches.

The Thermae of Augustus and Diocletian were magnificent conceptions of luxury. In the latter, 40,000 Christians were employed, and it furnished baths for 32,000 people, in sumptuous buildings covering an area nearly a mile in circumference; while the ruins of the baths of Caracalla still attest to their ancient vastness, being the largest ruins inside the city, next to the Coliseum.

One-third of the walls of the Coliseum still remain, inclosing the area where 100,000 spectators once witnessed a naval battle fought upon an artificial sea.

I believe that, taking into account the transcendental importance of the Tehuantepec Ship-Canal, and the power of our present civilization, other reasons than "natural obstacles" and the "expense of the undertaking" must be given for postponing any longer the opening of whatever Isthmian route may prove most beneficial to the national interest and the commerce of the world.

CONSULATE AT MINATITLAN, WITH OFFICERS OF EXPEDITION.

MINATITLAN FROM REAR OF CONSULATE.

PART II.

I reported for duty in Washington immediately after my appointment as chief engineer of the Expedition under your command, and on September 22, 1870, I proceeded to New York to purchase the necessary instruments, and obtain as much information as possible upon the literature of our subject. Our outfit in instruments was very modest owing to our small resources, but every necessary thing was purchased of the best quality for its object; and in no instance has the Expedition suffered for want of appropriate contrivances to carry out its work to the best advantage.

Instrumental outfit of the Expedition.

Our instruments and papers, carefully packed, were placed on board the United States steamer Mayflower. On October 20, 1870, a furious cylone struck our vessels when not far from Jupiter Inlet, and the violent motions of the ships, as well as the large amounts of water in their holds, damaged our instruments very considerably. The stationery, many books, and similar articles were nearly destroyed.

Instruments, &c., damaged by a hurricane, Oct. 20.

The Engineering Corps of the Expedition spent thirteen days at Key West, working incessantly in order to repair, clean, and adjust our instruments.

Repair of damages.

The Expedition left Key West on November 5, and arrived in Minatitlan on the 11th of the same month.

Arrival in Minatitlan.

During our stay in Minatitlan the Expedition was occupied in the following manner:

Preliminary arrangements.

A copy of your General Order of November, 1870, was given to officers in charge of parties in the field, together with my instructions upon the work to be executed by the sections under their command.

The different parties had been previously arranged thus:

Arrangement of parties.

Commissary Department, in charge of Lieutenant Commander G. C. Remey.

Hydrographic Party, in charge of Lieutenant Commander N. H. Farquhar; assistants, officers and men of the United States steamers Kansas and Mayflower.

Astronomical Party, in charge of Lieutenant Commander P. H. Cooper; assistants, Third Assistant Engineer T. Skeel.

First Engineering Party, in charge of Lieutenant Commander J. R. Bartlett; assistants, officers detached from other parties, sailors United States Navy, and natives.

Second Engineering Party, in charge of R. H. Buel, civil engineer; assistants, Second Assistant Engineer C. W. Rae, sailors United States Navy, and natives.

Third Engineering Party, Master Robert T. Jasper, United States Navy; assistants, officers detached from other parties, sailors United States Navy, and natives.

Department of Natural History, Surgeon J. C. Spear, United States Navy; assistant, Thomas H. Streets.

Photographic Department, Captain H. A. Bartlett, United States Marine Corps; assistant, William Bush.

Draughting Department, Ernst J. Somer.

Meteorological Department, Coast-station Mate A. E. Bateman; intermediate Coast-station, captain's clerk A. W. Smith.,

Contractor, Don Benito Suarez.

An inventory was made of the instruments and other effects, giving the makers' numbers, and the quantity or weight of the articles, and charged to party commanders. The balance of supplies not disposed of in this manner were charged to headquarters.

Distribution of instruments, &c.

The coast meteorological observatory was erected at Minatitlan, and continuous

44   TEHUANTEPEC CANAL SURVEY.

Adjustment of instruments and determination of errors, &c. — observations taken in regular rotation, in order to determine the errors of all the instruments with the "standards," establish constants of corrections, &c.

The field instruments were readjusted; chains, tapes, &c., tested with the standard, the nature of constants for our micrometer determined; and observations were taken of latitude, time, longitude, and magnetic variation.

The native contractor was engaged, and preparations were made to insure our instruments against damages from the rude transportation they were to undergo.

Greenwich time. — True Greenwich mean time was adopted for all meteorological observations.

Hydrographic work commenced. Meteorological stations. — The hydrographic party commenced the reconnaissance of the western bank of the Coatzacoalcos, selecting the location for their base-line, and the coast observatory began the series of hourly observations, which were kept up until 11 p. m., Greenwich mean time of April 20, 1871. The coast station contained the following instruments, properly mounted, and protected against accident and inaccuracies:

The station at Chivela contained the same kind of instruments, but those that were apt to break had been doubled in number: 1 chronometer, Negus, No. —; 1 sextant, Gambey, No. —; 1 barometer, James Green, No. 1764; 1 Holosteric P. H. B., No. 32440; 1 psychrometer set, James Green; 1 maximum and minimum set, James Green; 1 anemometer, 1 rain-gauge, 1 evaporation-gauge, 1 dew-gauge, 1 tide and flow gauge, 1 solar thermometer.

Standard chronometer. — The Kansas chronometer, Negus, No. 777, was assumed as the standard.

Barometric calculations. — Uniform field-note forms were distributed to all the parties.

All barometric heights have been calculated by A. Guyot's tables, after eliminating the instrument's proper errors.

EXPLORATIONS OF THE COATZACOALCOS RIVER.

Start for the mountains. — On the 28th of November, at 6.45 a. m., the Kansas steam-launch and four canoes shoved off the Coatzacoalcos bank, opposite the American consulate, having on board our instruments and all the officers and men, bound for the mountains.

Almagres. — With a clear day before us, we moved slowly up stream, meeting many mahogany and cedar rafts. At 8 p. m. we landed at Almagres, a dilapidated town containing 98 voters, and situated thirty-seven miles south of the bar.

Head of ship navigation. — This is the highest point of the river that could be utilized for a ship-canal, on account of its small depth and frequent bars. It will be more economical and expedient to commence the canal at the town opposite the Rancho del Mariscal, cutting through the Island of Tacamichapa, in the direction of Absalotitlan, and by clearing the entrance of the Mistan Fork avoid the sand deposits which come from this river. Although the Jumuapa River has a fine sand bottom, either the configuration of its outlet, its internal bars, or the shape of its shores prevent its sands from drifting into the Coatzacoalcos, because the general character of the bottom of the latter river consists of plastic clay, with a remarkably small amount of gravel and sand.

Jumuapa River.

The Coatzacoalcos below Almagres. — For a description of the Coatzacoalcos below Almagres, see extracts of Captain Farquhar's report.

The river banks below Almagres are very low, frequently flooded, and the country is crossed by many creeks, which complicate the regimen of the river, not only with regard to the tides, but also in connection with the floods.

It will be seen in the meteorological report that the river rises and falls, often without apparent cause, and independently of the tides and wind.

The most important of these creeks drain the country west of Minatitlan, and are the Menzapa, Apepeche, Ocosapa, and Jacoteno, on the left bank; and the Coatajapa, which drains the country north of the San Antonio River. All river depths referred to in this report relate to the dry season, unless otherwise stated.

Two and a half miles south of Minatitlan, a haven exists, made by the confluence of the Ojosapa and Tacojalpa, where the Spanish government water-cured pine masts that were afterward taken to the Havana and Carraca arsenals.

TEHUANTEPEC CANAL SURVEY.

The breadth of the river from the Coachapa to Almagres varies from 400 to 500 feet, while at the confluence of the Uspanapa in the south extremity of Guerrero Island, near Tierra Nueva, and near its mouth, this majestic river is nearly half a mile wide. Breadth of the Coatzacoalcos.

These and other important facts developed by the accurate surveys of this river by the hydrographic party, shows that a secure harbor can be obtained on the Gulf side of the Isthmus and safe navigation for any sized ships, as far as the Island of Tacamichapa. Security of the Atlantic harbor

The improvements required can be easily and cheaply effected. The description of this river given by Señor Moro is very accurate, from the Milagro River in the Chimalapa region, down to its mouth in the Gulf.

I differ from his opinion that the Coatzacoalcos could be utilized as far as its confluence with the Malatengo. To straighten a large water-couse is extremely expensive, and above Almagres this river is abruptly tortuous, and shallow in very long stretches. Also Señor Moro never went north and east of Santa Maria Chimalapa; and Señor Robles, who surveyed the Upper Coatzacoalcos very hastily, was often deceived by the native Indians. The Coatzacoalcos not navigable above Almagres.

We left Almagres on November 29, and proceeded up the river. Two miles above Almagres we saw the first bluff upon its shores. It consisted of green slate, and was about 60 feet high. A decided change in the heighth of the shores became noticeable, and not unfrequently we saw evidences of strong flood-currents. Change in appearance of the banks.

Five miles above Almagres the river becomes uninterruptedly tortuous, being filled with extensive bars and snags. Its current flows at the rate of 3 and 4.5 feet per second, in long shallow stretches; 7 miles above Almagres one of these bars had dammed the river so high that it broke through another place, or "rompido," in about 1848, running then through the old channel that it had excavated in 1834. This rompido shortened the river course 6 miles, but the bar now below this point is so shallow that the next flood may again alter its course. From the best information I have been able to obtain, these breaks take place every twelve or fifteen years. Our travel through this part of the river was very unpleasant, as it rained in torrents, and the current was so swift that the canoes passed the steam-launch with ease, though the latter carried 70 pounds of steam. The launch became disabled and was sent back, though she could not, in any case, have proceeded much further up stream, on account of the frequent bars, over which our canoes now often found difficult crossings. River tortuous. River's velocity above Almagres. Rompidos. Frequency of the rompidos. Navigation difficult for canoes above Almagres.

At Peña Blanca we saw the first indication of stratified rocks thus far noticed; the banks were 60 feet high, composed of white and green strata of clay, with a shallow synclinal. The average strike was about 12° and dipping south. The natives use this clay in the manufacture of their rude pottery. Stratified rocks. Pottery clay.

The river bottom is here hard, and is made up of sharp sand, small gravel, and clay. River bottom.

From the island of Guapinoloya to Pedernal Island, the river is very deep, with a clean clay bottom, and only occasionally sandy. Guapinoloya to Pedernal Island.

The temperature of this river is about 3 degrees cooler than the air in the morning, and 4 degrees cooler at noon. This was only observed during our journey of eight days up the river. Temperature of the river.

After passing the Chalchijalpa River, the banks are quite high, and the Coatzacoalcos grows wider and shallow opposite the island of Oaxaqueña, where it is about 1,400 feet wide, with 12 feet of water in the channel, which is about 200 feet wide. The river branch on the northwest side of this island was nearly dry. In latitude 17° 27′ north there is a dangerous bend, with a high bluff in the receiving shore, and a large sand deposit on the salient shore. Farther up we passed the Perla and Platanal Islands, covered with camalote, gimba, and crocodiles. The camalote is a tall grass eaten by cattle; the gimba is a species of bamboo. Oaxaqueña. Dangerous bends. Perla and Platanal Islands.

The roots of both plants afford a most effective protection to the banks against the heaviest floods.

Bank protection.

Opposite these islands the bottom is clean, plastic clay, which occasioned great difficulty to the pole-men, whose poles were buried fast.

In latitude 17° 23' north, longitude 94° 25' west of Greenwich, the country becomes wild and wooded; the current is swifter, and the river narrow, although the volume of water appears undiminished, even after passing above the Chalchijalpa.

Country becomes wild.

The Chalchijalpa is a large river, whose different sources come from the direction of the Chimalapa Mountains. Señor Moro says: "The Indians of Santa Maria ascend it on rafts to a point 38 miles distant from their village."

Source of the Chalchijalpa.

Although it may be possible to utilize isolated portions of the river for the canal, even in these high points, it is my opinion that flood-gates and other accessory works will overbalance the economy of excavations. Be it as it may, future surveys must determine these points, with the study of details.

Portions of the river might be used for the canal.

We then passed the Jaltepec, or "Rio de los Mijes," which, although 300 feet wide at its mouth, has an extended bar, with a channel 12 feet wide at its mouth, and less than 6 feet deep. A short distance above this river, on the Coatzacoalcos, we encountered the first dangerous rapids, having a very strong current, which spends its force in lateral deep holes, with extensive whirlpools.

Jaltepec river. Dangerous Rapids.

The river Jaltepec has its source in the Mije Sierra, a district densely wooded, and originally inhabited by the powerful Indian tribes whose few remaining descendants are now passing away. The remnants of these races are only found here at San Juan Guichicovi.

Source of the Jaltepec.

The Coatzacoalcos widens, and again has the appearance of a great river, until after passing Súchil.

Coatzacoalcos above Jaltepec.

At Mal-paso it again contracts; the channel is narrow, tortuous, and filled with large stones.

It contracts at Mal-paso.

"Súchil," which, translated from the Mexican, means "a flower," is the head of canoe navigation in the dry season. This small settlement is on the left high bank of the river, and from this height an extensive view can be obtained over the low banks of the opposite shore. Above Súchil, and until we reach Mal-paso, the river remains wide, and the banks are generally formed by green slate.

Súchil the head of canoe navigation.

The first hills become visible on the right bank, between the Jumuapa and Chalchihalpa Rivers.

First hills visible.

They are low and broken in outline, and from among them flows a brook, latitude 17° 22' north, longitude 94° 35' west of Greenwich, which Don Benito Suarez says is fifteen miles long, and whose waters in times of flood run through the bed of the Chalchijalpa. One mile and a half above this brook we left the Coatzacoalcos, and entered the Jumuapa River. Its appearance is different from that of the Coatzacoalcos, though with identical geological characteristics. It is about 300 feet wide at its mouth, with deep banks, and so shallow that our canoes could hardly get along through its tortuous channel filled with snags. A few days later in the season, travel by water is interrupted, and canoes can ascend as far only as Súchil.

Don Benito's Brook and the Chalchijalpa.

Description of the Jumuapa.

After passing the Jumuapa's mouth, the average width of the river cannot exceed 100 feet, with a current of three and a half miles per hour at this season, and a general depth of from 3 to 5 feet; but the channel is traversed by innumerable sand-bars, with only a few inches of water over them.

Its breadth and depth.

The waters of this river are about 2° colder than those of the Coatzacoalcos, and as we ascend the stream the bottom looks blacker, the texture of the clay is coarser, the rocks on the banks more granular, red clay becomes more abundant than green, and many patches of oil, from vegetable distillation, are seen floating over the water. On our first camping out on the Jumuapa, latitude 17° 18' 30" north, longitude 94° 33', I picked up from the beach several pieces of water-worn lignite.

Temperature of the Jumuapa. Petroleum. Lignite.

In latitude 19° 18' 30", longitude 94° 33' west of Greenwich, we found large deposits of iron-sand, and what, perhaps, may be gold. It is not mica, and although the little bright particles might be copper or iron pyrites, still they could be sensibly flattened by pressure.

Above this point rapids are met at every bend, and the river is constantly breaking through new channels, though these changes are circumscribed to very narrow lateral limits. Four rompidos are found here in less than two miles. *Rompidos abundant.*

During our journey all the officers made independent notes and observations which, being compared at night, were found to agree very fairly while on the Coatzacoalcos; but after entering the Jumuapa, it was found impossible to compare our notes satisfactorily. This river and the Sarabia are said by Señor Moro to descend from the Guienagate Mountains. Finally we passed the Fortuguero Brook, which enters the Jumuapa on its left bank, and all the surveying parties landed at La Puerta on December 6, after eight days' canoe traveling. *The Jumuapa imperfectly surveyed. Its source. Landing at La Puerta.*

EXPLORATIONS FROM LA PUERTA TO CHIVELA.

After leaving La Puerta, we reached the picturesque plains of Sarabia, traveling on mules over very bad roads.

The whole district up to San Juan Guichicovi is made up of red clay in its plastic state, and slates of several colors, and of all degrees of hardness and denudations. Compact limestone here makes its first appearance in our journey, and its constant association with silicates indicates the presence of hydraulic limestone. *Geology of the route.*

The extensive district of San Juan Guichicovi contains jasper and argillaceous limestones. From the latter a good cement is made, as can be attested by the huge pile of this material opposite the old unfinished church commenced by Cortes. *Cement.*

While passing through this wild and romantic region, we crossed the Mogañe and Pachiñe, both torrent streams, tributaries of the Malatengo, and of no value to our purposes, being low as to elevation and insigificant as to volume. *Mogañe and Pachiñe insignificant brooks.*

The geological features of the country do not again change much until after crossing the Malatengo near its junction with the Cituñe River. The clay then becomes more sandy, compact limestone forms the base of the mountains, and gray slate and quartz bowlders are seen in abundance. *Change in geological features.*

In the neighborhood of Petapa a greenish slate was often met with, and on the road I picked up a piece of blue and green malachite. *Petapa.*

Gaining very little information here, we left for El Barrio, after taking note of the traditional rumor about some large lakes in the Petapa Mountains. *El Barrio.*

Leaving El Barrio, we crossed several small dry streams, and, lastly, came to the Almoloya, which was spoken of as the great dependence of the summit-level. We found it about 20 feet wide, with a sluggish current, and hardly 6 inches deep. Its bed of sand and gravel was often dry, the water percolating through the gravel. What we had seen convinced me of the impossibility of using the streams that could be found high enough for supplying the summit-level of a ship-canal. *The Almoloya nearly dry.*

Still, to place these facts beyond doubt, transit and level lines were run, with the results given in the sequel. From the Malatengo near the Cituñe River, the ground rises constantly toward the north, and after we crossed the Almoloya it descends steadily toward Chivela.

This hacienda is situated on the southwest course of the remarkably level table-land of the summit of the sunk Cordilleras, which join the Andes by the east and the Rocky Mountains by the west. *Chivela.*

ORGANIZING THE ENGINEERING PARTIES, AND PRELIMINARY EXPLORATIONS.

As soon as the officers arrived at Chivela, the following work was planned and carried out:

The meteorological station was established at headquarters, and its monotonous work placed in charge of A. W. Smith, captain's clerk. *Meteorological station at the summit.*

It gives me unusual pleasure to attest that Mr. Smith's devotion to his duty enables us to present a good set of meteorological data.

Temporary datum-plane. The height of Chivela was temporarily assumed at 680 feet. All intermediate stations were referred to the Chivela barometers; and all level and transit lines to the permanent monument opposite headquarters.

The true height of the summit was to be determined by the spirit-level, in case that water-supply for the summit could be found.

Base-line. A base-line was established on the Chivela plains. Its direction is that of the stem of the cross opposite the Chivela House, and the cross on Monument Hill. Both of these monuments are permanent.

A mean of several astronomical observations gives the true bearing of this base-line from headquarters, south 49° 18′ 12″ west.

Testing Moro's triangulations. From Monument Hill, fourteen angles of prominent points were measured from this base-line, and found to agree perfectly with Moro's triangulations.

Similar results obtained from Tarifa, Rosetta Hill, near Ultimo Rancho, and also from the Atravesado Mountains. The use of the base-line for triangulation purposes was deferred for the time being, and it was only used as the starting reference-line of **Moro's triangulation adopted.** transit surveys. Moro's triangulation was accepted for reasons of economy. The only errors detected in his work were in a few triangles of a low order, which he established very obliquely from his base, evidently because they were deemed to be of small importance.

First engineering party organized. A party was organized in charge of Lieutenant Commander Bartlett, assisted by Second Assistant Engineer Rae, and Master Jasper, with sailors and natives.

Their instructions. Their instructions were to explore, locate, level, and gauge all the western rivers proposed by Williams as summit-feeders.

The same party was to explore, as above, the passes of Chivela, Tarifa, Masahua, Piedra, Parada, and any other passes they might discover.

The Guichilona and Almoloya Rivers alone were found available as to height. The former was entirely dry, and is formed during the rainy season by the water that flows along the hill-groins of mountains almost denuded of woods.

If this torrent, which sheds on the Pacific side, were to be used for the summit-supply of a storage-reservoir, it would require very heavy cuttings to get over the ridges lying between itself and the Arroyo Marques.

The volume discovered by these rivers will be found in the appendix.

Astronomical party. Instructions were given to Lieutenant Commander P. H. Cooper, in charge of the astronomical party, to locate Chivela, Tarifa, San Miguel, Santa Maria Chimalapa, El Barrio, Petapa, &c.

I regret to say that very little astronomical work has been accomplished, since from the beginning of our survey, this party seemed to be destined a failure. Severe rheumatism attacked Mr. Cooper, disabling him completely for a long time, and his party, already crippled, became practically extinct after the resignation of Mr. Skeel.

Points determined by triangulation and transit lines. Accordingly, with very few exceptions, I have depended altogether upon the engineer's transit for the location of points.

I also regret to say that when we arrived at Chivela it was deemed inexpedient to **Photographic party.** employ the photographic department in charge of Captain Bartlett, U. S. Marine Corps, since our limited resources did not seem to warrant the expense of transporting and subsisting his party.

Photographic views. A set of views were taken of some places that could be photographed without much expense, and will be found intercalated in these reports.

EXPLORATIONS FROM CHIVELA TO THE OSTUTA RIVER.

While Lieutenant Commander Bartlett's work was under way, I went to Tarifa, accompanied by Mr. Buel, principal assistant civil engineer, to explore the environs of

HEADQUARTERS AT CHIVELA.

MONUMENT HILL, CHIVELA.

LT. COMDR. BARTLETT'S PARTY TAKING CROSS SECTION OF ALMOLOYA RIVER.

RIVER VERDE AT OLD TRANSIT CROSSING.

the summit-plains, and the rivers Tarifa, Chichihua, Monetza, Chicapa, Ostuta, and the Corte or Upper Coatzacoalcos.

The locations explored are marked on the maps by a fine dotted black line.

The Tarifa and Chivela plains are one and the same table-land of the summit, but the valley seems divided into two parts, the hills approaching each other a little to the southwest of Tarifa. <small>Summit table-lands.</small>

The remarkable Chivela plains can be said to be the flat, broad valley of the Otate Brook, and having an area of ten and one-half square miles. <small>Area of Chivela plains.</small>

The soil is sandy to the depth of about twenty feet, as is shown by the wells of the locality, and the easily excavated and deep banks of the many brooks that traverse its surface in the rainy season. <small>Its soil.</small>

North of the Chivela House, the eastern slope of all the gently rolling hillocks are covered with stones of different sizes, hinting by their direction and position that they may have been deposited there contemporaneously with the drift of the Pacific plains, or by the action of floods of a more recent period. <small>Drift on the plains of Chivela.</small>

There are eight dry-brook crossings before entering the contracted part of these plains, and they show that the sand deposit becomes thinner as we approach Tarifa, where many pools of stagnant water prove that the soil is impermeable. <small>Impermeable soil of the plains.</small>

The houses at Tarifa are on a slight elevation, and all the surrounding country becomes flooded during the heaviest rains; but soon after the waters find their way to the Atlantic by the Almoloya and Chichihua Rivers. These plains are covered with grass, and, in the places not cleared, a thick underbrush shelters abundant game, and a few beasts of prey. <small>Tarifa.</small>

Royal palms, the silk-tree, and three species of sensitive plant are very numerous. We remained in Tarifa a week, waiting by appointment for Don Julian Macheo, the owner of extensive lands of the Isthmus. We made many explorations with a leveling transit and two barometers, measuring distances with the micrometer on the speaking-rod. <small>Preliminary explorations.</small>

Simultaneous barometric observations were taken hourly on the coast, at Chivela, and at whatever point explorations were under way.

We found the details of the country very imperfectly given in maps, and became convinced that we should be obliged to do the topographic work over again, especially in the neighborhood north of Tarifa. Señor Macheo informed me that the lake supposed to exist by some, near the headwaters of the Chicapa, was simply an invention; because his father visited the source of the Chicapa, and never found the lake. Later in our explorations, I saw the principal source of the Chicapa as it poured from among the crevices of the large rocks in the neighborhood of Mr. Scarce's rancho. <small>Source of the Chicapa.</small>

The Tarifa River has its source in the Pasapartida hills. <small>Tarifa River.</small>

On December 18 its breadth was 20 feet, its mean depth 0.08 foot, and its mean velocity 0.03 foot per second; consequently its delivery was at the time less than one-half cubic foot per second.

FROM TARIFA TO CHICHIHUA RIVER.

On December 19 we left early in the morning, to explore the Chichihua River. (See map No. 2.) We crossed the Tarifa River three times, the first part of our journey being toward the north, and upon its valley, a beautiful and grassy plain. At the end of the first three miles we left the Albricias Mountains and the Convento Cerro to the southeast, and began to ascend rapidly to the north, by the complicated system of hills which divide the Tarifa and Otate water-sheds. <small>Chichihua River, and Potrero and Sierra Blanca Pass.</small>

I will be very particular in describing this, the last northwest spur of the Albricias chain, because here lies the heaviest part of the cutting for the canal-feeder.

The Albricias Mountain is made up of marbles and magnesian limestones, from the Convento Cerro, till it reaches a point east of Santa Maria; it follows parallel to the <small>Albricias range.</small>

Corte River for a short distance, and then turns east; in other words, compact limestone and dolomites skirt the base of the highest Isthmian Mountains, at a height of six or seven hundred feet above the ocean.

Due north of Tarifa are found soft limestones, very different from the dolomites above referred to, partaking more of the character of travertine.

They were deposited in strata, whose dip is now vertical, with a north and south strike, and this character is common to the whole of this spur; but the quality of its material varies a great deal, since sometimes it is calcareous tufa; then it passes into argillaceous marl, and again the clay disappears, and sand predominates.

This material is so soft that the foot-travel over it grinds it into impalpable dust.

The furrows made by each rainy season compel the Indians to leave last year's tracks for new ones, until they have made so many paths over these hills that it is confusing to select the best road.

Plains or potreros of Chichihua. North of this ridge the country descends to the Chichihua Valley, and is formed by soft sandstone, until the junction of the Chichihua and the Pericon, where jasper and argillaceous rocks are again seen ascending toward the north, forming the hilly district inclosed by the Chichihua, Malatengo, Corte, and Coyolapa Rivers.

Occasionally plastic red and green clay are met with, as well as granular quartz bowlders.

Bed of the Chichihua. South of the Pericon the streams have cut their way through the rocks in situ, and neither drift nor indications of heavy floods are visible; but the bed of the Chichihua has clear, sharp sand brought down from the potreros east of Cofradia range.

Sierra Blanca Pass.
Sierra Blanca tunnel.
The summit of Sierra Blanca Pass is 1,232 feet above the ocean, and in order to get the waters of the Corte into Tarifa, it will be necessary to cut the thin web at this pass to a depth of 483 feet, or to tunnel through it, if it is found cheaper than either an open cut or a detour up the Tarifa River Valley. In the present state of my knowledge of the locality, I would propose a tunnel, that may be of small dimensions, through rocks that I know are very soft. This tunnel will be 9,650 feet long, and its area need not exceed that of a rectangle, 19 feet by 12 feet, surmounted by a semicircular arch of 12-feet span. Under these conditions, its cost will be less than $600,000.

Its probable cost.

Brooks of the Chichihua plain. From the pass we descended by the northeast to the Otate Brook; crossed a gently rolling plain, with rich pastures, and ascended the Chichihua Mirador, a high hill, from whence the surrounding country could be easily inspected. We took several observations with the barometer, and measured several angles to test Moro's triangulation. We descended to a small valley, crossed the brooks Mentidero and Milagro, and, after one and a half miles' travel to the north, we ascended the hills which form the left bank of the Chichihua. Their general direction is to the east; and these hills are highest at the Pericon junction, where there is a cañon about 100 feet wide, with nearly vertical walls, about 150 feet high. A gradual descent to the east brought us to the Chichihua below the Corazo Brook, and where we cross-sectioned the Chichihua at a point 71 feet below Chivela; a short distance below, the Chichihua flows into the Corte River. It was here that I conceived it possible to use the Corte as a summit-feeder, because its tortuous course and probable rapids naturally led me to think that it would be easy to overcome the small difference of level without going very far up stream.

Cros-section of the Chichihua.

MONETZA RIVER AND CAVES.

Tabla Bolsa.
Source of the Monetza.
We left Tarifa December 21, 1870, very early in the morning, under a leaden sky, from which poured a blinding rain. Our route was by the northeast until we reached Tabla Bolsa, which is a very small valley, lower than Tarifa, since it sheds toward the east. The Panecillo, which we crossed and followed after the last Tarifa Ford, led us to the source of the Monetza. This river flows from under a natural Gothic arch, cut by its waters in the southwest extremity of the Convento Hill. This hill consists of pure black marble, and the walls of the arch or tunnel which traverses it are perforated

TARIFA PLAIN

RANCHOS AT TARIFA.

PARTY UNDER LIEUT COLOMB. BARTLETT IN CAMP AT TARIFA.

and jagged, pouring in all directions fine transparent streams of crystalline and delicious water. This natural arch or bridge is 25 feet high, 23 feet broad, and about 120 feet long. A thousand yards below this point, the stream, which flows over a black bed of rocks fantastically water-worn, plunges into a beautiful cave about one-half a mile long, and called the Large Convento.

The Monetza was found 112 feet below the summit at its source, and delivering 2.8 cubic feet per second. After this river emerges from the mountain, it is joined by the brook Leña del Monte, and, with a uniform grade, runs along a fertile valley which terminates in the Chicapa River, at the town of San Miguel, 300 feet below the summit. The material of the Convento Mountain is admirably suited for construction purposes; and a marble and lime quarry can be easily opened at a very convenient distance from the summit works. I will not describe the exact route from Tarifa to San Miguel, being of little importance to our subject. The topography is accurately given in map No. 2. *Height of the Monetza. Its volume. Building material.*

The Chicapa was first cross-sectioned at San Miguel, near the Niltepec Ford, though with a result higher than its minimum value, since copious rains had been falling for the past six days. *The Chicapa at San Miguel.*

Six experiments were made for velocity, at the end areas of the portion of the river chosen, using the surface velocity reduced to mean velocity by Weisbach's formula, (Vol. 1, p. 363.) This same method was employed in all important rivers. *Gauging of rivers.*

The village of San Miguel is on the right bank of the Chicapa, and at the point of confluence of this river with the Monetza and Xoxocuta Rivers, being shut in by high mountains on all sides. *San Miguel.*

The Xoxocuta comes from the mountains north of San Miguel, and flows to the Pacific, while a small stream on the north slope of these same mountains flows to the Atlantic. The sources of this stream, which are quite near, were explored; and since San Miguel is so low, and the streams are so short, I conceived the hope of finding here a low pass to bring the Corte waters to the east end of Cerro Albricias, using the Lower Chicapa Valley for the canal-bed. The San Miguel Pass was subsequently leveled, and found impracticable. (See profile No. 7.) *The Xoxocuta. San Miguel Pass.*

We spent two days in San Miguel, weather-bound, but making short excursions in the surrounding country. Afterward, we here obtained, in fair weather, five long series of barometric observations, and found the altitude to be 403 feet above the ocean. The same, as given by the level, is 404 feet. On December 24, Chimalapa Indians were engaged to accompany us into the woods, and early on the morning of the 25th we started up the Chicapa Valley, with the intention of testing the practicability of joining the Chicapa and Ostuta Rivers, as suggested by Señor Moro. *Explorations around San Miguel. Its elevation. Explorations of the Chicapa Valley.*

During our journey we took profuse notes on the topography of the country, and they will be found incorporated in map No. 2.

It will be well to say that, from San Miguel to Mr. Scarce's rancho, bearings were taken with the compass, and the distances were estimated by the watch, keeping a uniform gate in our walk. All I can claim for this exploration is, that it is a very conscientious reconnaissance of the ground, giving an accurate idea of its topography. It has been plotted with the bearings taken all along, and the latitude of three points, after calculating our rate of travel. It is also abundantly checked by the bearings of prominent points, taken from Tarifa, Convento Summit, San Miguel, Xoxocuta, Palmar, near an indigo-plantation, before descending to Ultimo rancho, at Rosetta Hill, on the Espiritu Santo Hill, and on the Atravesado, at three different points. This route can be said to have been surveyed by intersecting bearings from known points. *Claims as to accuracy in this exploration.*

The whole Chicapa River can be ascended to its source without great difficulty, through a wild and uninhabited region. *The Chicapa easily explored.*

The only remarkable feature of this stream is its extraordinary rise, which takes place at the rate of one foot in a hundred, since it falls 1,000 feet in less than 18 miles. *Remarkable rise of the bed of the Chicapa.*

This river was cross-sectioned four times, and the following table shows the difference of the delivery between the points gauged. *Gauging the Chicapa.*

Table showing the delivery of the Chicapa River at different points along its course.

Chicapa River gauged at—	Sum of ordinates of depth, in feet.	Distance between ordinates, in feet.	Mean area of cross-section, in feet.	Mean velocity, in feet, per second.	Mean delivery, in cubic feet.	Height above or below the summit, in feet.	Date of cross-section.
San Miguel	46.16	4.000	184.64	1.14	143	341 below	December 24, 1870.
Ultimo rancho	45.34	4.125	187.03	0.82	103	272 above	December 26, 1870.
Scarce's rancho	25.34	4.000	101.36	0.72	49	616 above	December 29, 1870.
At its mouth					2	754 below	March, 1871.

Scarce's rancho. — The last cross-section was made by the officers of the Cyane. On the 26th of December we arrived at the rancho of Mr. Louis Scarce, who told me he had traveled from the Blanco River, at its junction with the Corte, in a straight line, to his rancho, or hut, and was sure that the Corte was at least 1,000 feet above Chivela.

Statement of Mr. Scarce.

Believing that he knew the country well, I engaged him as a guide, and sent him immediately to cut a path to the source of the Chicapa River, while we took series of barometric heights, time, latitude, and magnetic observations. (See appendix.)

Elevation of Scarce's rancho. — Mr. Scarce's rancho was found to be 616 feet above the Chivela Station; and the Chicapa at this point passes less than 50 cubic feet of water per second.

Survey of the Upper Chicapa. — At the end of four days, we again started up the stream, following the bed of the Chicapa with the compass, and leveling by angles of elevation and depression, and reducing to the horizon the distances as given by the micrometer. About 1,700 feet from Scarce's rancho we came to the main source of the Chicapa. The water pours from among the crevices of very large bowlders, which have fallen over the bed of the river, from a cliff about 800 feet high. From this point forward the river, which delivered about 50 cubic feet at Scarce's rancho, hardly carries two or three cubic feet of water.

Source of the Chicapa.

Left the bed of the Chicapa. — Beyond this point, and about $1\frac{1}{8}$ miles from Scarce's, the little water that flows, and the reduced size of its bed, made me abandon this thalweg for that of a dry brook with a very wide bed, whose direction seemed to lead toward the Atravesado Mountain. This brook was named Arroyo Providencia.

Providencia Brook.

Geological features of the valleys. — The small tributary of the Chicapa, just abandoned, turned toward the north behind a high chain of near hills, and is evidently a very small and short stream. Up to Ultimo rancho, the rocks are argillaceous; but near the source of the Chicapa, compact and blue limestones abound, which grow coarser as we ascend to the Arroyo Providencia.

This stream runs through a deep cañon, two or three hundred feet high, and its precipitous sides are covered with overhanging stalactites.

We also found quite a large deposit of nitrate of potassa about two miles east of Scarce's rancho. After four days' travel we ascended to a high spot, where the underbrush ceases to grow.

Traveling in the lowest valley. — We then ascertained that we had followed the lowest valley, which leads directly to the gap between the highest point of the Sierra and the Atravesado Peak; in other words, we had followed the valley supposed by Moro to be the bed of the Chicapa River. A reconnaissance from a high point advised us to leave Providencia Brook, which had become impossible to ascend, for another more southerly and marked valley, which was named Aguas Nuevas, in commemoration of the day, January 1, 1871. When we struck it, at 7 a. m., our height was 1,375 feet above Chivela, and at 4 p. m. our elevation was 3,245 feet. Feeling convinced beyond any possible doubt that this was the lowest thalweg within five miles from north to south, I determined to leave its bed, and see how the country looked east of us, or toward the Ostuta. Ten minutes up-hill travel brought us to a cleared eminence, from which I saw, with a feeling of disappointment I cannot describe, that the chances of bringing a feeder through this route were very few, because our height was so great, and the Ostuta, running from north to

Aguas Nuevas Brook.

Rise of the largest valley.

Disappointment.

south, had to descend an astonishing distance, in order to make a junction of these rivers possible, since the Pacific plains reached to our latitude, and from this point northward the mountains rise abruptly from the plains. I hoped that our labor might still bear some fruit, because, turning to page 11 of Señor Moro's original report, in my possession, entitled " Reconocimiento del Ystmo de Tehuantepec, London, June 1, 1844," I read the following words, which I translate. Señor Moro, standing on the Atravesado Mountain, says: " Toward the north I saw the deep ravine through which the Chicapa runs; and on the east the high lands of the Ostuta's bed, which I had just visited and recognized perfectly, were less than three miles off. The difference of level between the two points is so inconsiderable, that there is no doubt as to the possibility of effecting the junction of these rivers. And it is no less evident that there is not the least obstacle to prevent it, in the short distance intervening between them." Filled with hope at this precise statement, although very short of provisions, and with the Indians who accompanied us very discontented and rebellious, I turned to the southeast, in order to ascend the Atravesado. Failing to see from the Atravesado anything in the direction of the Ostuta, on account of an intervening mountain, we moved south and then east, in order to descend by a detour to the most southeasterly spur of the Atravesado.

With the exception of the high point just abandoned on the south, everything else east or north of us appeared under our feet; and had it been possible to see the high land of the Ostuta from any point of this mountain, this was the place from which to view it. This point is marked M, in map No. 2. The highest part of the Sierra bears north 2°, east from us, and a spur from it hides the place through which Moro thought he saw the Ostuta. Since his assertion, quoted above, is so positive, I must conclude that he lost his bearings, and mistook, for the Ostuta, the small valley running behind Trespicos Hill, and the peculiarly sharp and craggy limestone hills near them, called the Cucumates; but these points are evidently low, too far south, and proved to be at least fifteen miles away from where Moro proposed to begin his feeder. The deep valley we saw at our feet with terrible distinctness proved to be the Ostuta's; but we could not believe it, because it appeared to be 4,000 or 5,000 feet below us. After all our notes were plotted, the Fortuna Brook was found to run up so near the gap that it may be possible that Moro mistook it for the Chicapa. This opinion is strengthened by the fact that Moro ascended the Atravesado from Niltepec, and not by the bed of the Chicapa. I declare distinctly that there is no point on the Atravesado, nor near it, from which the Chicapa and Ostuta Valleys, nor the land through which they run, can be seen at the same time.

All lands in direction of the Ostuta seen at our feet.

Valley of the Ostuta not recognized from the Atravesado, it being impossible to conceive that Moro had reference to the extremely low valley we saw.

Did Moro mistake the Fortuna for the Chicapa?

I was accompanied on this expedition by Mr. Buel and Señor Macheo—two of the most courageous and daring men I have ever known. We considered this solution of Moro's project as the only hope for a canal; since the Corte project, besides being as yet problematic, the weight of evidence was against it; therefore, we studied these mountains with anxious interest, sparing no personal discomfort, till the country was explored as far as it was possible for a human being to go.

The mountains were thoroughly explored.

Moro's assertion was not verified, and, since our steps were barred by the precipices which bind the eastern edge of the Atravesado, we determined not to give up hoping until we had seen the ground from below, upward. Accordingly, we decided to descend to the town of Niltepec, explore the Ostuta as far as possible, and endeavor to reconnoiter the gap referred to by Señor Moro.

As we left Aguas Nuevas Brook, the climate, as well as the fauna, flora, and geology of the country, changed visibly. Nothing but the pine grew over the nearly bare rock of finely laminated shale, which, as we ascended, became transformed into a breccia, very much decomposed on the surface, but bearing no vegetation. The summit of Cerro Atravesado consists of porphyry and argillaceous rocks. This hill is ingrafted into the main sierra from north to south, and in a very conspicuous manner blocks the valley of the Chicapa at right angles to its thalweg. Its top surface is flat, about 5,000

Change of climate, fauna and flora in the Atravesado.

Remarkable drift.

feet above the sea, and covered with rich pasture. All along its extensive top, and in a southwest direction, we found immense blocks of granite which do not belong to the place, and can only be accounted for by supposing either that they had fallen down from the highest part of the Sierra Madre, previous to the formation of the gap through which Moro proposed to pass the canal-feeder, or that they were there through glacial action.

In Niltepec we parted company with Don Julian Macheo, who was called away to one of his plantations, after the burning of the town of Juchitan by the Juchiteco Indians, then in a state of revolt. I feel that many thanks are due from us to Señor Macheo. Two of his best houses in Chivela were given up by him for the use of the Expedition; we also shared his hospitality in Tarifa and La Venta. He was of the greatest service to us in many ways; and, besides volunteering to perform the difficult task of catering for our party in the mountains, his presence and influence among the Indians prevented a great deal of trouble.

EXPLORATIONS OF THE OSTUTA RIVER.

Drift on the Pacific plains.

On the 6th of January we left Niltepec for the Ostuta. The whole river to Piedra Grande is level and covered with drift, remarkable for its size and the direction of its dispersion. The whole Pacific plain forms a basin of about 1,400 square miles, and its shape can be likened to that of a half cone, of small height, hollow and inverted, having its apex at Boca Barra. Toward this point flow all the rivers on the Pacific side in a radial direction; but the dispersion of the drift takes place in a southwesterly

Erratic blocks. direction, whatever the shape or inclination of the ground on these plains. Erratic blocks are found in this direction from the Ostuta, which flows southwesterly to the Tehuantepec River. This latter stream runs from west to east, and even in the mountains, as on the Atravesado, there are blocks of granite at an elevation of five thousand feet above the ocean, and arranged in *lines*, sensibly parallel to those of the coarse drift on the plains thirty miles off. Some of the blocks have a volume of over 120,000 cubic feet. These blocks are also found arranged in the same direction north of the dividing ridge of the Isthmus, in the town of St. Maria.

Most of the Pacific rivers have considerable beds; but with the exception of the Ostuta, they all pass very little water at this season.

Pacific rivers nearly dry. Jicara tree.

The Niltepec was nearly dry, and the brooks Chocolate, Huacamaya, Agua Zarea, Petaca, Roble, and Juamol were entirely dry. The plains are arid, hot, and sandy. Besides a parched under-brush hardly any other vegetation is seen, except a poor quality of grass and the Jicara tree, (*Crescentia cujete.*) This tree is variously called in

Delivery of the Ostuta at Piedra Grande,

different places Jicara, Totuma, Higuera, Dita, and China; it is small, not unlike the apple tree in appearance, and bearing a green sesile fruit or gourd, used by the natives extensively as cups, vessels, &c. When ripe it possesses in a most extraordinary degree the properties of ergotine; but fortunately the Indians are not aware of it, and use it for no medicinal purposes. The Ostuta River was gauged at Piedra Grande, (see Appendix,) and found to deliver only 203 cubic feet per second.

On the 9th of January we left Piedra Grande by the northeast, and camped by the Ostuta, nine and a quarter miles north of our starting-point.

Northern limit of the Ostuta explorations.

In all, we made four camps, and ascended the river for seventeen miles from Piedra Grande, or where the highest peak of the sierra bore south 89° west from us. Two and a third miles after leaving Piedra Grande, we turn north to ascend the Cristalinas Hills, in order to see the valley of the Ostuta and Moro's Gap on the Atravesado. We soon reached the top of a steep hill, at the point marked on the map No. 2, El Portillo.

View of the Ostuta and Moro's Gap from El Portillo.

This point is 122 feet below Chivela; and looking to our left, we had a discouraging bird's-eye view of the Ostuta. Its tortuous course could easily be traced in the deep valley at our feet, until it turned sharply to the west, behind a mountain lower than the one we stood upon. Moro's Gap was square in front of this turn, and considerably higher than El Portillo.

We descended then to the river, and after fording it without difficulty, ascended up stream by the right bank, cutting our way through the dense foliage. Occasionally we ascended near hills, or climbed trees to study the topography. Our barometric observations were taken very carefully, though in our two first tents the atmospheric state was unpropitious.

Fording the Ostuta. Unpropitious weather for barometric observations.

Still, I feel confident that, in these cases, the errors are within 40 feet of the truth; although an error even of one thousand feet (which is impossible) would not affect the result, since Moro's Gap is more than 3,000 feet above the summit at Tarifa. Moreover, the important observations on the Ostuta are those taken at its highest point; in these four observations were taken—at, before, and after the hour of the day in which the barometric column has the same height as the daily mean height, and all the indications of the barometers, coupled with the precaution taken to insure accuracy, warrant the confidence I place in the fact that the height of the Ostuta at the point V, in map No. 2, is between 170 and 190 feet below the lowest point of the Tarifa Pass. The Ostuta was explored more than four miles up stream from the point from which Moro intended to start his feeder. I did not mistake Moro's Gap for any other gap. This water divisory has a northeast direction; is about four miles long; its southern extremity joins the characteristic northern prominence of Cerro Atravesado, and it is limited on the north by the highest peak of the Siérra. In fact, it is formed by two spurs from these mountains, which, from opposite directions, meet at the lowest point of the gap. This gap, besides being the same one that we ascended from the Chicapa side, is the lowest one of the range, and was inspected and always recognized from the points marked El Portillo, R, S, T, and V, map No. 2. Also, the eastern thalweg of this pass is made up of steps, forming small valleys, and descending toward the Ostuta and Fortuna.

Height of the Ostuta at the highest point explored.

Identification of Moro's Gap.

IMPRACTICABILITY OF JOINING THE CHICAPA AND OSTUTA RIVERS.

Señor Moro makes Ultimo rancho and Chivela at the same height. A glance at the barometric data on the appendix shows it to be 275 feet above Chivela; but although the heights for each set of observations agree within six feet, since only three observations were taken, I will pass to the rancho Scarce, where five sets of good observations were taken, giving a mean of 624 feet. The distance between these two points is less than eight miles; following the river turns, and applying the rise per mile of the river between San Miguel and Scarce's rancho, which are points well determined, we should find that the Chicapa, at eight miles from the rancho Scarce, must fall about 422 feet. Hence—

Elevation of Ultimo rancho.

Elevation of Scarce's rancho.

624 = elevation of Scarce's rancho.
422 = fall of river in eight miles.
———
202 = height of Ultimo rancho, by calculation.
275 = height of Ultimo rancho, by the barometer.
———
73 = difference, which probably would be less if the true length of the river were known.

It needs no demonstration to prove that the Chicapa Valley is the only route for Moro's feeder.

At San Miguel this river is over 369 feet below the summit, and at El Palmar it is 24 feet above; hence, the cutting below the Chicapa bed must commence 2,400 feet before reaching the Palmar Brook. This cutting, gradually increasing in depth, will be eleven miles long and 3,245 feet deep by the time it reaches that point of Aguas Nuevas Brook, from which we turned away to descend the Atravesado. (See P, map No. 2.) But this is not all. There are fully one and a third miles of ascent from Aguas Nuevas Brook to the lowest point of Moro's Pass, and beyond this point the tunnel must extend through the base of the mountain, before reaching the Ostuta's bed.

Amount of cutting required to carry out Moro's plan.

56 TEHUANTEPEC CANAL SURVEY.

Exploration of the Ostuta abandoned. The above supposes the Ostuta to be at a convenient height; but since it is 180 feet below the summit, besides the above cutting, 180 feet of depth of cutting must be added throughout the whole length of the feeder and summit. We became convinced of how useless was the attempt to explore any further the source of the Ostuta, and, taking additional barometrical observations, and cross-sectioning the river at the highest point visited, (V, map No. 2,) we turned back extremely disappointed.

Delivery of the Ostuta at the highest point explored. The Ostuta delivers at the highest point 84 feet less than at Piedra Grande, or 119 cubic feet per second.

Geological features of the Ostuta Valley. On the mountains north of Niltepec, the southern slopes are of clay; as we ascend we meet sandstone, compact limestone, and, lastly, gray and green slate, breccia, and porphyry.

Our next step, after leaving the Ostuta, was to try the San Miguel Pass, by way of the streams Chichihua and Pericon.

EXPLORATION OF SAN MIGUEL PASS.

Preliminary studies of the San Miguel Pass. We explored the San Miguel Pass, and the hasty study of its valleys convinced me that it was of importance to settle its practicability instrumentally.

Transit and level lines from Chivela to the town of San Miguel, by way of the Chichihua Plains. Accordingly, while we were on our way to the Corte, orders were given to continue the transit and level lines from Tarifa to San Migual via Sierra Blanca and San Miguel Passes. Lieutenant Commander Bartlett was detailed for this work. The detour given to this line had for its object to study the range of hills dividing the Tarifa plains and the Chichihua potreros, in order to bring the feeder by this latter place in case the San Miguel Pass should prove impracticable. The work was performed by Mr. Bartlett with the care and accuracy characteristic of this efficient officer. The San Miguel feeder-pass was found to be 1,071 feet above the ocean, and the Sierra Blanca Pass is 1,238 feet above the same plane. Although San Miguel Pass offers less height, the facts developed by the topographical and geological survey make Sierra Blanca the most feasible route for the feeder, for the following reasons: The Pita Brook is a forced point of pass of the feeder. (See map No. 2.) In order to reach the San Miguel Pass, the feeder must turn south, up the valley of the Arroyo Corozo, and its grade will soon intersect the northern base of the Albricias Cerro, in a cutting of hard limestone and marble; it must then turn a right angle to the west, and skirt the southern lap of the Albricias Cerro, until it reached the Tarifa Plains.

Elevation of San Miguel Pass.
Elevation of Sierra Blanca Pass.
Sierra Blanca Pass preferable.

The Sierra Blanca Pass is right at Tarifa, and its material is made up of soft calcareous tufa.

Topography of the Chichihua at Corozo Brook. The Chichihua, at the point marked Q, is 71 feet below the summit, and the Pericon, at the point marked C, is on the grade of the feeder, so that the length of cutting to Tarifa will be less than 10,000 feet, through easy ground, across the thin web-like spurs that divide the Tarifa and Chichihua potreros. The rise of the ground is gradual from Chichihua toward Sierra Blanca, and abrupt from north to east, as can be seen by the Pericon, which runs quite parallel to the Albricias Hill, up to Sierra Blanca. At this point it is sent northward, while the Naquipa runs north and south from the pass to the Chichihua. The Corozo route will require six miles of hard tunneling, and seven miles of equally hard deep cutting. The direct route has five miles, requiring no extra cutting, and only three miles of heavy cutting, through soft soil, and in which a short tunnel will be found economical.

Topography of end of feeder-route by Sierra Blanca Pass.
Typography of end of feeder route by San Miguel Pass.
Additional advantages of Sierra Blanca Pass.

Since Tarifa River is lower than the Tarifa Plantation, and the Arroyo Pita is also lower than Tarifa River, it will be seen that there can be no doubt as to the possibility of supplying the summit with water, if it can be brought down to the Pita.

First failure to explore the Upper Coatzacoalcos. From San Miguel Pass and Cofradia we went to Santa Maria Chimalapa, where, after suffering many hardships, we were obliged to return to Chivela, and make such arrangements as would insure our passing through the Chimalapa region in order to reach the river Corte.

TEHUANTEPEC CANAL SURVEY.

We arrived at headquarters on January 25, and found there the scientific commission appointed by Mexico, and composed of Señors D. Manuel Fernandez, Don Agustin Barroso, and Don Guillermo Segura. These gentlemen very kindly offered to co-operate with us in our work.

Mexican commissioners.

Lieutenant Commander Bartlett had by this time completed the survey and levels between the Almoloya River and Tarifa, and was instructed to continue the line to San Miguel. Lieutenant Commander Farquhar had also completed the survey of the Coatzacoalcos Bar; Surgeon Spear had made a preliminary report upon the geology of the country explored to date; Mr. Skeel had resigned and left for the United States; Lieutenant Commander Cooper had been sick and unable to perform any duties; still, he had gone to Petapa, to obtain information about the lakes spoken of by Mr. Hermandorff and Señor Gives, but was unable to procure guides, on account of the disturbed state of the country from the Juchitecan revolution.

State of affairs upon arrival at headquarters.

Dr. Spear and the Mexican commissioners explored these lakes subsequently, and found them to be only insignificant pools, of very small extent, and unsuitable for any purpose.

The Petapa lakes found to be insignificant pools.

SURVEY OF THE RIVER CORTE AND FEEDER-ROUTE.

On the 30th of January we again left Chivela for Chimalapa, accompanied by the Mexican commissioners; but after nineteen days of ineffectual endeavor to induce the Chimalapa Indians to carry our provisions into the woods, I was again compelled to return to headquarters, because neither our efforts nor the presence of the federal troops could overcome the superstitious fears of the Indians with regard to the dangers to be encountered in the wild country we intended to explore. Having determined to become independent of Chimalapa help, I organized a small heterogenous force of unmarried men from different Indian tribes, and returned again to the Corte region. Three engineering parties were placed in the field, working toward each other with the transit and level.

Second failure to reach the Corte.
Success of a party selected from different tribes.
Three parties on the field.

On the 31st of March these lines met upon a joint bench-mark, near the Sona-pac Brook. The results obtained (see profile No. 1) settled definitely the practicability of supplying with water the summit-level at Tarifa.

Joint bench-mark.
The water-supply question settled.

Although we spent many days in useless negotiations with the Indians, no time was lost, because daily excursions were made to the Corte, the Milagro, and the adjoining country. In this manner accurate sketches were made of the ground explored, so that, when our arrangements were completed to go through with the transit and level, no random or trial lines were run, because the instruments passed so closely over the route of the feeder, that its center line could be staked out from our present note-books with but small trouble. In these explorations, beset with many hardships and dangers, Mr. Buel took a very active and prominent part, and also Lieutenant Commander Remey, who volunteered to take a share in this work. The Mexican commissioners accompanied us on the preliminary reconnaissance, and lent us valuable assistance. They shifted their headquarters to La Venta before we started on our instrumental survey to the Corte; and, when returning from this survey, I heard that they were working near La Venta.

Co-operation of the Mexican commissioners.

I wrote you officially, giving you an account of the satisfactory result of our survey to the Corte, and sent the same information to the Mexican commissioners, notifying them besides of the near end of our work on the Isthmus. I subsequently met the commission by appointment in La Venta; but finding that they had nearly finished the line of levels from Tarifa to the ocean, and since I already had the important part of this line, I deemed it an act of deference to the commissioners not to continue the level-line over their own stakes. Accordingly, I placed four parties in the field to determine the height of the summit by way of Chivela, San Geronimo, and Salina Cruz, and reconnoitered the ground of the plains over which the canal will pass, as well as

Captain Shufeldt and the Mexican commissioners officially notified of the success of our undertaking.
Why the Tarifa transit-line did not extend to the ocean.
Elevation of the summit determined by the spirit-level.

S. Ex. 6——8

58   TEHUANTEPEC CANAL SURVEY.

Exploration of the plains and homew'rd bound. many other points of the coast. I then returned to headquarters, by way of Tarifa Pass, inspecting the Masahua Pass, and many points of this range of hills. Soon after all the officers returned to Minatitlan, which place we left, homeward bound, on April 27, 1871.

I cannot close this report of our operations on the Isthmus without expressing my thanks to all the gentlemen with whom I was associated in the field, not only on account of personal considerations, which they must feel that I appreciate, but mainly for the valuable services that they have rendered to the Expedition. Captain Bartlett, when not busy with the duties of his party, lent his aid whenever his services were required. Master Jasper proved himself to be a genial, ready, and always hard worker. Second Assistant Engineer Rae, United States Navy, and civil engineer, had charge of the levels in the field, and of very hard work in the office. His work, often checked, is extremely accurate. Lieutenant Commander Bartlett had charge of the transit-lines, and has earned the highest commendation on account of his zeal, accuracy, and unassuming high worth. In the civil list, Mr. Buel, principal assistant engineer, joined to a rare executive ability a clear mental power, trained by exercise, and based upon scientific knowledge. Mr. Somer, principal draughtsman, lent valuable assistance to the hydrographic work on the Atlantic side of the Isthmus, and has made all the chart projections, and some trigonometrical calculations. Dr. Streets volunteered to act as rodman in the perilous ground of the Upper Coatzacoalcos, and all the gentlemen connected with this work have undergone many dangers and trials, always cheerfully and without a murmur.

I feel under obligations to the Tehuantepec Railway Company, and to several gentlemen mentioned in this report, for their contribution of maps and topographical information.

Respectfully submitted.

E. A. FUERTES,
Chief Engineer United States Expedition to Tehuantepec.

Captain R. W. SHUFELDT,
United States Navy, commanding U. S. Tehuantepec Surveying Expedition.

APPENDIX.

APPENDIX.

TABLE OF RIVER DELIVERIES.

Names.	Date.		Breadth of rivers.	Mean velocity per second.	Mean area of cross-section.	Mean delivery.	Remarks.
1870.			*Feet.*	*Feet.*	*Sq. feet.*	*Cubic feet.*	
Almoloya	Dec.	22	20.50	0.86	12.445	7.28	At the ford from Chivela to El Barrio. By Lieutenant Commander Bartlett, United States Navy.
1871.							
Blanco	March	18	46.00	2.24	53.600	120.00	At the site for the Blanco Dam.
Corte	Feb.	21	122.00	2.11	767.015	1,680.00	At Camp No. 2.
Corte	Feb.	25	188.00	2.79	551.230	1,538.00	At Camp No. 4.
1870.							
Chicapa	Dec.	24	99.00	1.14	184.640	143.00	At the Niltepec Ford, excluding the Monetza River.
Chicapa	Dec.	26	66.00	0.82	187.030	103.00	At Ultimo rancho.
Chicapa	Dec.	29	....	0.72	101.36	49.00	At Scarce's rancho.
1871.							
Chicapa		x	x	x	x	2.00	At its mouth, by officers United States Steamer Cyane.
1870.							
Chichihua	Dec.	19	31.05	2.63	21.22	37.94	Near Corozo Brook.
1871.							
Coyolapa	April	3	20.00	2.52	19.46	33.32	At the Santa Maria Ford.
1870.							
Guichilona	Dec.	2	12.?	0.00	0.00	0.00	Entirely dry.
Masahua	Dec.	—	x	x	x	0.51	Joins the Verde and is dry at the ford.
Mentidero	Dec.	19	x	x	x	0.54	At the ford.
1871.							
Milagro	March	30	62.00	1.78	153.56	186.00	At Santa Maria Ford. Gauged by Lieutenant Commander Bartlett, United States Navy.
1870.							
Milagrito	Dec.	19	x	x	x	0.24	On the road to Chichihua.
Monetza	Dec.	21	10.00	0.90	4.540	2.78	Below the Little Convento.
1871.							
Ostuta	Jan.	8	81.00	1.81	164.910	202.64	Behind Piedra Grande.
Ostuta	Jan.	12	46.96	2.50	70.160	119.00	Highest point explored.
1870.							
Otate	Dec.	19	10.50	0.30	2.415	0.72	On the road to Chichihua.
Pericon	Dec.	19	x	x	x	2.17	On the road to Chichihua.
Rio Verde	Dec.	—	x	x	x	0.26	Dry at the second ford from Chivelo to San Geronimo.
Tarifa	Dec.	18	20.00	0.30	1.60	0.32	On the road to Chichihua.

TABLE OF DISTANCES AND ELEVATIONS OF PROMINENT POINTS OF THE ISTHMUS OF TEHUANTEPEC.

Measured from Tarifa Cross to—	Distances.			Elevation above the ocean.			Authorities.
	By way of—	Miles.	Feet.	By the spirit-level.	Barometrically.	Trigonometrically.	
				Feet.	*Feet.*	*Feet.*	
Almoloya River	Chivela	16	2905	755.40			Bartlett U. S. Ex., 1871.
Do					738.0		Moro.
Almoloya River, (highest crossing)	Sidell's line			557.00			Compiled.
Almoloya River, (lowest crossing)	do			312.00			Do.
Almoloya River, (crossing)	Barnard			780.00			T. R. R. Co.
Almagres							
Atravesado Mountain, (camp 3)	Chicapa Valley				3,962.8		Fuertes.
Atravesado Mountaain, (Point P. of transit-line.)	do				3,189.30		Do.
Atravesado Mountain, (peak)	do				4,778.30		Do.
Do						5,016.60	Moro.
Atravesado Mountain, (highest p'k of range)						7,687.40	Do.
Atravesado Mountain, (Camp 5)	Chicapa Valley				1,642.20		Fuertes.
Blanco River, (camp)	Transit-line	37	600	736.20	738.20		Fuertes and Bartlett.
Do	Feeder-route	27	144	736.20	738.20		Do.
Blanco Pass to Corte River	do	27	1694				Fuertes.
Do	Transit-line	37	1550	1,012.00			Buel.
Blanco Ridge, (summit)	do	36	859	1,889.30	1,851.90		Buel and Fuertes.
Capepac River	Transit-line	32	2401	508.40			Bartlett.
Chalchijalpa River							T. R. R. Co.
Cerro Prieto Peak						1,509.30	Moro.
Chivela Cross	Transit-line	10	875	717.80			Buel and Bartlett.
Do					689.00		Moro.
Chivela Pass	Transit-line	11	†145	778.60			Bartlett and Buel.
Do					796.00		Sidell's profile, 1859.
Do					779.00		Williams.
Chichihua River	Transit-line	15	3725	1,114.40			Bartlett.
Do					620.10		Moro.
Chichihua, (near Corozo Brook)				646.80	643.63		Bartlett and Fuertes.
Chicapa River at San Miguel	Transit-line	14	5000	385.40			Bartlett.
Chicapa, (Puerta Vieja rancho)				272.30			Moro.
Chicapa, (Palmar rancho)	Chicapa Valley			724.60			Fuertes.
Chicapa, River, (at Ultimo rancho)	do				993.10		Do.
Do	do				682.20		Moro.
Rosetta Hill	do				2,013.90		Fuertes.
Chicapa, (at Scarce's rancho)	do				1,378.60		Do.
Chicapa, (Providence Brook, Camp 1)	do				1,457.30		Fuertes and Buel.
Chicapa, (Aguas Nuevas, Camp 2)	do				2,093.60		Do.
Chocolate Brook	Transit-line	21	845	1,152.00			Bartlett.
Chocolate Hill, (Jacal on summit)	do	21	3130	1,252.30			Do.
Do	do				1,069.60		Moro.
Cofradia Huts	do	12	695	1,269.00	1,250.40		Bartlett and Fuertes.
Do	do				1,233.70		Moro.
Cofradia, (summit of range)	do	12	5180	1,769.20			Bartlett.
Coachapa River							
Comitancillo	Chivela Pass	32	3415	221.80			Bartlett.
Convento Pass	San Miguel route					750	Williams.
Convento Hill						1,463.30	Moro.
Corte River, (Milagros mouth)					350.00		Fuertes's estimate.
Corte River, (at Capepac)	Transit-line			479.00	419.80		{ Fuertes and Buel. Stormy weather.
Corte, (N. of Santa Maria)	do			636.40	636.60		Bartlett and Fuertes.
Corte, (at the Chimalapilla)	By Corte grade				490.00		Fuertes's estimate.
Do					390.40		Moro.
Corte, (Camp 1)	Transit-line	37	3300	662.40	660.60		Fuertes and Buel.
Corte, (Camp 2)	do	39	520	689.30	692.80		Do.
Corte, (Camp 3)	do	39	4600	705.00	729.36		Do.

TEHUANTEPEC CANAL SURVEY.

Table of distances and elevations of prominent points of the Isthmus of Tehuantepec—Continued.

Measured from Tarifa Cross to—	Distances.			Elevation above the ocean.			Authorities.
	By way of—	Miles.	Feet.	By the spirit-level.	Barometrically.	Trigonometrically.	
				Feet.	*Feet.*	*Feet.*	
Corte, (Camp 4)	Transit-line	42	2395	723.30	725.40		Fuertes and Buel.
Corte, (highest point explored)				756.00			Do.
Coyolapa River	Transit-line	18	3820	612.10			Bartlett.
Cochara Brook	do	18	60	654.90			Do.
Daniguiati Summit						900.60	Moro.
Daniguibixo						977.70	Do.
Devil's Ridge	Transit-line			1,800.00			Bartlett and Buel.
De los Perros River	do	24	3510	150.00			Bartlett.
Do				63.00			Sidell.
Do				111.00			Barnard.
Encuntordar Mountain	Railroad lines, 1851			256.00			Barnard and Sidell.
Escolapa River	Transit-line	19	970	595.70			Bartlett.
Do					164.00		Moro.
Guiévixi Mountain						1,364.90	Do.
Guiévixia						1,962.00	Do.
Guiexila						3,779.70	Do.
Huacamaya, (east summit)						2,542.80	Do.
Huilotepec	Sidell's profile			97.00			Sidell.
Jaltepec River	Barnard's profile			75.00			Barnard.
Do	Sidell's profile			149.00			Sidell.
Juchitan	do			67.00			Do.
Do						59.10	Moro.
Joint B. Mark, near Sonapac Bk	Transit-line	31	1535	1,059.60			Bartlett and Buel.
Jumuapa River	Barnard's line			136.00			Profile, 1857.
La Puerta							
Laollaga Hill						4,678.30	Moro.
Malatengo River	Sidell's crossing			217.00			Sidell.
Malatengo River, (highest crossing)	Barnard's railroad			494.00			Barnard.
Malatengo River, (lowest crossing)	do			256.00			Do.
Masahua, (east summit)						2,283.60	Moro.
Masahaua, (middle summit)						2,254.00	Do.
Masahua Pass				843.00			Barnard.
Masahuita						2,017.80	Moro.
Mata, rancho of	Railroad line			260.00			Sidell.
Do	do			255.00			Barnard.
Maxiponac River	Transit-line	34	3388	1,149.00			Buel.
Mentidero Brook	do	5	900	827.80			Bartlett.
Milagros River, Santa Maria Ford	do	25	2830	432.80			Do.
Do					275.00		Moro.
Monaportiac						364.20	Do.
Monetza River, (source)	Tabla Bolsa				600.80		Fuertes.
Monetza River	do				643.10		Moro.
Minatitlan							
Niltepec, (house of Señor Sesma)					312.00		Fuertes.
Nisiconejo Pass	Railroad line			930.00			Barnard.
Ocotal Hill	Transit-line	35	2080	1,662.20			Buel.
Ostuta River, (behind Piedra Grande)					290.00		Fuertes.
Ostuta, (Camp 6)					514.80		Do.
Ostuta, (Camp 7)					517.80		Do.
Ostuta, (highest point explored)					541.70		Do.
Otates River	Transit-line	3	4840	837.80			Bartlett.
Do	Feeder-route			725.00			Estimated.
Palo Blanco Hill						1,217.30	Moro.
Paso Partida Hill						1,528.90	Do.
Pericon River, (first crossing)	Transit-line	6	457	795.80			Bartlett.
Pichincha	do	14	3910	1,018.00			Do.
Do						902.30	Moro.
Piedra Parada, (east pass)						825.00	Williams.
Piedra Parada, (west pass)						800.00	Do.
Piedra Parada, (summit)						1,346.90	Moro.
Pita Brook	Transit-line	17	2095	716.80			Bartlett.
Potrero Brook	do	24	930	479.20			Do.
Salina Cruz	do	57	4715				Buel and Bartlett.
Sarabia River	Railroad line			299.00			Williams.
Do	do			275.00			Sidell.

*Table of distances and elevations of prominent points of the Isthmus of Tehuantepec—*Continued.

Measured from Tarifa Cross to—	Distances.			Elevation above the sea.			Authorities.
	By way of—	Miles.	Feet.	By the spirit level.	Barometrically.	Trigonometrically.	
				Feet.	*Feet.*	*Feet.*	
Sangre Brook	Transit-line	28	240	689.40			Bartlett.
San Gabriel Boca del Monte					164.00		Moro.
San Juan Guichicovi					817.00		Do.
San Geronimo	Transit-line	24	3755	193.40			Bartlett.
Santa Maria Brook	do	26	1370	808.80			Do.
Santa Maria church	do	26	5059	972.60	947.80		{ Fuertes and Bartlett. Stormy weather.
Do					859.00		Moro.
San Miguel Pass	Transit-line	11	2000	1,071.30			Bartlett.
San Miguel church	do	14	3100	400.40	399.20		Fuertes and Bartlett.
Do	do	14	3100		390.40		Moro.
Sonapac Brook	do	32	2401	868.90			Bartlett and Buel.
Súchil settlement							
Tarifa Cross	Transit-line			735.70	732.90		Fuertes and Bartlett.
Do	do				684.10		Moro.
Tarifa Pass	do	4		754.40			Bartlett.
Do	do			753.79			Mexican com'rs, 1871.
Tehuantepec	do	45	1930	124.09			Buel.
Do					137.80		Moro.
Do	Railroad-line			146.00			Barnard.
Tierra Blanca Pass	Transit-line	2	5000	1,237.60	1,232.00		Bartlett and Fuertes.
Tierra Blanca, (delivery end of tunnel)		2	940	807.00			Bartlett.
Tesistepec	Railroad-lines			208.00			Barnard and Sidell.
Transit station 272	Transit-line	3	4840	837.80			Bartlett.
Umalalang					721.80	715.30	Moro.
Uspanapa River							
Vontosa	Transit-line	53					
Zanatepec					164.00		Moro.

GEOGRAPHICAL POSITIONS OF THE PROMINENT PLACES OF THE ISTHMUS.

Places determined astronomically.	North latitude.	West longitude.
	° ′ ″	° ′ ″
Harbor of Salina Cruz, (custom-house)	16 10 11.4	95 20 00
San Mateo Huazontlan del Mar	16 12 47	95 07 06.5
Boca Barra	16 13 00	94 53 22
San Dionisio Tepehuazontlan	16 16 30	
Juchitan, (church of)	16 26 10	95 09 37.5
Chivela	16 42 48	95 08 14
San Miguel Chimalapa	16 43 00	94 53 05
Tarifa	16 43 30	95 01 00
El Barrio	16 48 40	95 14 55.5
Santa Maria Chimalapa	16 55 06	94 49 12.4
San Juan Guichicovi	16 57 38	
Paso de la Puerta	17 12 35	
Coatzacoalcos, near the Jumuapa River	17 21 05	
Don Benito's Brook	17 22 00	94 35 00
South end of Pedernal Island	17 27 45	
Island of Tacamichapa, at Horqueta	17 43 00	
Almagres	17 46 36	
Minatitlan	17 58 54	94 29 36
Mouth of the Coatzacoalcos	18 08 15	94 21 42
Places determined by other than astronomical measurements.		
Cerro del Morro	16 10 24	95 17 34.5
Xunivahui Peak	16 12 40	95 22 47.5
Huachilaif	16 13 32	94 44 48.5
Santa Maria del Mar	16 13 33	94 59 41
Daniguibixo	16 14 36	95 16 54

TEHUANTEPEC CANAL SURVEY.

Geographical positions of the prominent places of the Isthmus—Continued.

Places determined by other than astronomical measurements.	North latitude.	West longitude.
	° ′ ″	° ′ ″
Buxmumbáh	16 14 42	94 47 10.5
Town of Huilotepec	16 14 54	95 17 19.5
Malumbiamlaif	16 14 59	94 45 06.5
Tilema Island	16 15 30	95 02 04.5
Umalang	16 16 39	94 58 24
Mitiachuaxtoco, (Santa Theresa Hill)	16 17 10	94 56 15.5
Danilieza, (Cave Hill)	16 20 07	95 22 53.5
Daniguibedchi, (Tiger's Hill)	16 20 10	95 21 32.5
Tehuantepec church, (cathedral)	16 20 16	95 22 01
Monaportiac Island	16 20 34	95 02 24.5
Danigú or Camotepec, (Sweet Potato Hill)	16 22 06	95 13 21.5
Mitiacix or Iguana Island	16 23 09	95 00 09.5
Tiactinayix	16 26 12	94 55 57.5
Zopilote Hill	16 26 31	94 38 01.5
Espinal church	16 29 26	95 10 55.5
Iztaltepec church	16 30 27	95 11 34.5
Daniguiati	16 31 59.5	95 13 21.5
Laollaga Hill	16 32 32	95 22 29
Venta de Chicapa	16 34 00	94 57 23
Lagartero Hill	16 34 15.5	95 03 12
San Geronimo church	16 34 20	95 14 06.5
Pie de Banco Hill	16 34 41	94 49 08
Chihuitan church	16 35 44.5	95 17 53.5
Rinconchapa Peak	16 37 13	94 58 23
Guievichi Peak	16 37 26	95 15 07.5
Palo Blanco Hill	16 38 17.5	94 55 46
Zapata Hill	16 39 05	94 54 34
Piedra Parada Hill	16 39 08	95 00 03
Prieto Hill, (east peak)	16 39 41	95 07 34
Xoxocuta Hill, not on Xoxocuta River, but south-southeast of San Miguel	16 42 11	94 53 23
Paso Paxtida Summit	16 42 17	94 58 09
Huacamaya, (east peak)	16 42 28	95 10 53
San Miguel church	16 43 02	94 52 58
Guie Vixia	16 43 08	95 14 52.5
Convento Hill	16 43 11	94 57 22
Atravesado Peak	16 43 12	94 39 20
Tarifa	16 43 31	95 00 40
Almoloya Peak	16 44 08	95 13 25.5
Peak west of San Miguel Pass, (Albricias)	16 44 21	94 53 48
Summit of Chichihua, (west peak of Albricias Range)	16 44 34	94 56 40
Ostuta River, at the highest point explored	16 48 00	
Petapa church	16 49 36	95 15 25.5
Santo Domingo church	16 49 45	95 16 42.5

Table of sea distances through several Isthmian routes, compiled from H. Stuckle's Essay on Interoceanic Canals.

Ports.		Cape Horn.	By way of—			Advantages of—	
			The Isthmus of—			Tehuantepec over Cape Horn.	Tehuantepec over Darien.
Vessels sailing from—	In order to reach—		Tehuantepec.	Darien.	Suez.		
		Miles.	Miles.	Miles.	Miles.	Miles.	Miles.
New York	Hong-Kong	19,000	10,750	11,500	11,658	8,245	745
	Shanghai	18,300	10,355	11,100	12,458	7,945	745
	Melbourne	12,720	9,600	9,890	13,357	3,120	290
	Yokohama	17,340	9,435	10,210	13,493	7,905	775
	Honolulu	14,100	5,955	6,730		8,145	775
	San Francisco	14,200	4,400	5,300		9,800	900
	Mazatlan	13,000	3,135	4,060		9,865	925
New Orleans	Hong-Kong	19,300	9,400	10,830		9,900	1,430
	Shanghai	22,300	9,020	10,430		13,280	1,410
	Melbourne	13,000	8,260	9,250		4,740	990
	Honolulu	14,400	4,620	6,030		9,780	1,410
	Yokohama	17,600	8,100	9,510		9,500	1,410
	San Francisco	14,500	3,070	4,650		11,430	1,580
	Mazatlan	13,300	1,800	3,390		11,500	1,590

SEA DISTANCES.

COMPILED FROM DON JOSÉ DE GARAY.

TABLE OF DISTANCES *to the principal ports in the Pacific and Indian Oceans, compared with the voyages to the same places via the Isthmus of Tehuantepec, compiled from "An account of the reports of the scientific commission appointed by Don José de Garay, London, 1846."*

No.	Voyage. From—	Voyage. To—	Description of the route.	Distance in—	Distance, via Tehuantepec.	Difference saved.
				Nau. miles.	*Nau. miles.*	*Nau. miles.*
1	New York	Salina Cruz	Round Cape Horn, crossing the line in longitude 26° west, touching Rio Janeiro, Valparaiso, Callao, and Salina Cruz.	12,417	3,330	9,087
2	New York	Canton	By the Atlantic and Indian Oceans, crossing the line as above, with the course of No. 12.	15,540	11,950	3,590
3	New Orleans	Boca Barra	Round Cape Horn, touching St. Thomas, Rio, Valparaiso, and Callao.	12,510	900	11,600
4	New Orleans	Columbia River	Round Cape Horn	14,830	3,220	11,610
5	The Lizard	Boca Barra	Round the Horn, touching Madeira, Rio, Valparaiso, and Callao.	11,820	5,360	6,460
6	The Lizard	Tahiti	Round the Horn, touching Madeira, Rio Janeiro, and Valparaiso.	12,830	9,170	3,660
7	The Lizard	Wellington, New Zealand.	Round the Horn, touching Valparaiso and Tahiti.	15,160	11,500	3,660
8	The Lizard	Wellington, New Zealand.	Round the Horn, direct from Valparaiso.	13,990	11,500	2,490
9	The Lizard	Wellington, New Zealand.	By the Atlantic and Indian Oceans, touching Madeira, Rio Janeiro, to latitude 41° south; thence eastward.	15,820	11,500	4,320
10	The Lizard	Wellington, New Zealand.	Touching at Madeira, and crossing equinoctial line in long. 26° west.	14,740	11,500	3,240
11	The Lizard	Sandwich Islands.	By the Horn, touching at Valparaiso	14,300	8,860	5,440
12	The Lizard	Canton	Touching at Madeira, crossing in longitude 26° west, going to latitude 41° south and eastward to longitude of St. Paul's, and thence by the Straits of Sunda.	14,750	13,980	770
13	The Lizard	Canton	Touching Madeira and Rio	15,830	13,980	1,850
14	The Lizard	Manila	Same route as No. 12	14,210	13,630	580
15	The Lizard	Manila	Touching at Rio Janeiro	15,290	13,630	1,660

TABLE OF TONNAGE, COMPILED FROM H. STUCKLE.

It may be stated approximately that whatever Isthmian route should be opened to the commerce of the world, it will at once command the trade between Europe and California, our own trade with the western ports of Mexico, our Pacific States, and the west coast of South America. The tonnage from this trade amounts to more than 1,500,000

In addition to the above, the European commerce that will seek the American Isthmus in preference to Suez for the trade with Chili, Bolivia, Peru, Ecuador, New Granada, Central American states, and the western coast of Mexico, amounts at present to more than 700,000

Making a total of 2,200,000

BUILDING MATERIALS, ETC.

A.—MINERALS, ROCKS, ETC.

The absence of hydraulic limestones on the Atlantic plains makes it necessary to look for a substitute.

The remains of many ancient walls, built by the Indians at a very remote period, are still extant; and the cement used by them was so strong that, at the present time, the stones cannot be separated but with a crowbar. This cement, so far as I have been able to study its composition, is made with sand and asphaltum.

Asphaltum is found in abundance in the following places:

At Paso Nueva	Right bank of Coatzacolcos, three miles north of bar.
Tshuatlan	Near the town.
Rio San Antonio	At its ford, on the road to Ocuapa.
Rancho del Tigre	Three miles east of above, on same road.
Uspanapa River	Left bank, at rancho Longinos.
Uspanapa River	Right bank, six miles up stream from above.
Uspanapa River	One-fourth mile northeast of above, toward San Antonio River.
Chichigapa River	At a lake near San Cristóbal.
Almagres Town	One mile southeast of the village.
Coachapa River	Near Cerro de Cal, south of Almagres.
Coatzacoalcos River	Right bank, near Guapinoloya Island.
Coatzacoalcos River	Right bank, half a mile below Narango River.
Tatugapa River	At Encantada Mountain.
Sayulá	One-third of the way on road from Acayucan to Almagres "Plantation," south of Acayucan.
Jaltipan	Near to and northeast of the town.
Mecayapan	Near the town.

CHIVELA.

Milk quartz	In detached bowlders.
Sandstones	In the hills west of plantation.
Sand	In the plains.
Coarse chalk	In the pass.
Specular iron ores	In the pass.
White marble	Chivela and Masahua Passes.
Compact limestones, calcspar	Rancho del Zapotal.
Quartzose and argillaceous sandstones	Southeast of Chivela houses.
Variegated and siliceous marls	Chivela Pass.
Clay, plastic	Below the plain sands.

TARIFA.

Shale	Above the gneiss at the pass.
Quartz rocks	At the pass and at Agua Escondida.
Granites; gneiss, clay slates	Upper part of pass.
Plastic clay; argillaceous rocks	Lower part of pass.
Pearl stones	Espinosa and Paso Partida hills.
Compact sandstones	Piedra Parada.
Sandstone schist; decomposed granites	Around Tarifa hills.
Calcareous tufa	At Sierra Blanca.

Compact limestones	Convento Hill, Albricias chain.
Marbles, dolomites	Convento Hill, Albricias chain.
Diorites, calcareous spar	Convento Hill, Albricias chain.
Gray and purple slates	On the road from Tarifa to San Miguel, at the Cienaguilla Hill.
Clay and loam	On the Tarifa plains.
Specular iron-ore	At Campanario Hill.
Red hematite	At Tarifa Brook.

SAN MIGUEL.

Compact limestones	Albricias Range.
Green-stones, clays	Upper Chicapa.
Schists, gold sands	Upper Chicapa.
Orthoclase and albite	Upper Chicapa.
Rocks	Upper Chicapa.

ATRAVESADO.

Sandstones, decomposed breccia, finely laminated shale, clay-stone, and porphyry	Providence Brook and upper part of the Aguas Nuevas Valley.
Quartz breccia	On the porphyry of the summit.
Talc slates	Above the limestones of Buenos Ayres.
Argillaceous sandstones	Southern spurs of Atravesado.
Immense granite bowlders	Deposited by glacial action on the flat top of Atravesado in a southwest direction.

NILTEPEC AND ZANATEPEC.

Syenite	Below the limestones of Zanatepec.
Magnetic iron-ore	North of Niltepec.
Quartz, broken and disintegrated	Ostuta River ford.
Talc slates	Above the limestones of Niltepec.
Clay, talcose slates and schists	Ostuta banks east of Atravesado.
Argillaceous sandstones	South lap of Atravesado.
Pearl stone breccia	Foot of Tres Picos Hill.
Most interesting moraine terraces and drift	Near Tres Picos Hill.
Marbles and compact limestone	Cucumates hills.

VENTA DE CHICAPA.

Clay and limestones	Masahua Range.
Calcareous tufa	Masahua Range, near Agua Caliente.
Compact and laminated limestone	Foot of Tarifa Pass.
Travertine	Foot of Tarifa Pass.
Calcareous breccia	North of Zapata Hill.
Hypersthene rock, quartz, nodules, and green-stone schist	At Palo Blanco.
Clays and sands	Near La Venta.

FEEDER-ROUTE.

Trachytic porphyry, granites, syenites, albite, and other decomposed feldspars, granite bowlders, limestone bowlders, plastic clays, argillaceous and siliceous rocks	Upper Coatzacoalcos, near the Blanco.

Sandstones over ferruginous red and blue clays	Fisherman's Ridge, near the Blanco.
Clay rocks, slates, and clays	Upper branch of Capepac Brook, Chocolate Hill, and Pita Brook.
Sandstones	Lemon Ridge and Cofradia Range.
Marbles and compact limestones	Cliff Ridge, upper part of the Milagro Valley.
Clay rocks, jasper, trachytic porphyry, kaoline, sandstones, calcareous tufa	Near the town of Santa Maria.
Sandstone, limestone drift	Southeast of Santa Maria.
Limestones	Below and north of Santa Maria.
Calcareous tufa	On road, after crossing the Milagro.
Calcareous tufa	Tierra Blanca tunnel.

SAN JUAN GUICHICOVI.

Hydraulic limestones, clays, slates, antique porphyry.

EL BARRIO.

Graywacke, sands, clays.

XOCHIAPA PLAINS.

Graywacke schist	On surrounding hills.
Sandstones, plastic clays	On the plains and hillocks.
Compact limestones	Near the source of the Malatengo.

GUIECHILONA; GUIE-VIXIA; GUIE-VICHI.

Dioritic porphyry, gray and green slates, compact limestones, sandstones, greenstone schist, hornblende and translucent hornstone rocks, graywacke schist, magnetic iron-ores, and dolomites like the magnesian limestones of Convento	In the Lao-Llaga hills.
Argillaceous sandstones	At Guie-Vichi.
Very hard sandstones	At foot of Guie-Vixia.

ZOPILUAPA RIVER.

Trap-rocks, as hypersthene and pyroxenic porphyry, also modern limestones.

SALINA CRUZ.

Veined porphyry	At Cerro Morro.
Petro siliceous porphyry	At Point Salina Cruz.
Amygdaloidal porphyry, with crystals of phonolite	At Point Salina Cruz.
Graphic and fine-grained granites	At Point Salina Cruz.

Phonolite is very abundant at Xunirahui and at the Guie-Agola Rivers. The Xunirahui named after a noted Zapoteco woman, is a large chunk of phonolite in the shape of a headless female bust. Viewed from the sea, it appears conspicuously like a house-chimney. (See chart of Salina Cruz.)

Dioritic porphyry and syenite	At Daniguibedchi.
Splendid granite, syenite, quartz, and albite conglomerates	At Huilotepec.
Graphic granite	At Hazontlan.

Many varieties of dioritic porphyry granites and syenites	Around Salina Cruz.
Tertiary soft limestones, compact blue limestones	At Dani-Lieza.
Compact blue limestones	At Tehuantepec, across the river, and behind Santa Maria Dani-Lieza.
Clays	In the plains.
Sands	In the plains above the clay.

LAGOONS AND SOUTH COAST.

Trap-rocks, laminated granites	At Monopostiac.
Porphyry	Umalalang.
Graywacke	Iguana Island.
Dioritic porphyry	Manguixtiac.
Syenitic porphyry	Pixixixi, Uxinduic Santa Teresa.
Syenite, syenitic greenstone	Monopostiac.
Stratified greenstone, beautiful granites	Cerro Prieto.
Basaltic rocks,? peperino,? basaltic tufa	Monopostiac.
Granite, tremolite veins	Santa Teresa.

IN THE PACIFIC PLAINS.

Sands, loam, recent and fossil, living shells, clay, below the sands, at a depth varying from a few feet to 40 or 60 feet.

IN THE ATLANTIC PLAINS.

Loam; alluvial drift in the valley of the Coatzacoalcos, often of immense depth; sandstones and clay in the upper part of the valley near Chichihua; clay and talcose slates are often met with between Almagres and La Puerta; lignite in several parts of the coast associated with asphaltum chunks; also on the Coatzacoalcos banks, and at La Puerto, near the Tortuycrero River. Asphaltum is very abundant.

B.—USEFUL TREES, PLANTS, ETC.

No. of varieties.	Name.	Diameter of trunk in feet.	Location and remarks.
1	Almendro	½ to ¾	Pacific plains; brown, coarsed-grained, brittle.
1	Almendrillo	½ to ¾	Pacific plains; red, very strong, and indestructible.
	Baba		Pacific plains; white, porous, light.
	Bia a guibesa		Pacific plains; violet gray, fine, long fiber, tough, very useful.
2	Boj, (box-wood)		Pacific plains; yellow, hard, tough; used for wood-engraving, &c.
	Biza duné		Pacific plains: orange, hard, heavy, brittle, peculiar grain.
	Brasil, (*Cæsalpina crista*)	1 to 1½	All parts; used for red and black dyes.
	Caña fistula	½ to ¾	Pacific plains.
3	Caoba, (*Switenia mahogani*)	2 to 8	All parts of the Isthmus.
1	Caimitillo		Chimalapa region.
1	Caobilla, (*Croton lucidum*)	1 to 5	Atlantic plains.
1	Caracolillo, (*Phascolus cavacalla*)	1 to 2	Do.
2	Cascalote	¾ to 1	Pacific side; black, with reddish fiber, hard, heavy, tough, beautiful.
1	Costa rica	1 to 3	East of Coatzacoalcos; very durable.
2	Cedro fino, (*Cedrela odorata*)	1 to 4	All parts.
1	Cedro blanco, (*Cupressus thuyoides*)	1 to 3	Chimalapa region.
1	Cedro prieto	1 to 3	Do.
1	Ceiba	2 to 15	All parts; white, long fiber, soft, light.
	Chico zapote, (*Dysopyros obtusifolia*)	2	All parts; purple, hard, heavy, tough.
2	Ciprés, (*Cupressus semper virens*)	¾ to 2	Chimalapa region.

B.—Useful trees, plants, etc.—Continued.

No. of varieties.	Name.	Diameter of trunk in feet.	Location and remarks.
	Cucharita		Pacific plains; reddish, hard, tough, coarse-grained.
2	Ebano, (*Dysopyros lotus*)	1 to 2	Pacific plains; ebony, used for fuel in many places!
	El beoo		Pacific plains; gray, fine-grained, brittle, used for furniture and ornaments.
2	Cucina blanca, (*Juercus alba*)	1 to 3	All parts.
2	Cucina negra, (*Juercus virens*)	1 to 2	Atlantic side.
2	Emajagua	$\frac{3}{4}$ to $1\frac{1}{4}$	All parts; white, very light, tough, useful.
	Fresno, (*Fraxinus acuminata*)	$\frac{3}{4}$ to $1\frac{1}{4}$	Pacific slope.
	Frijolillo	$\frac{1}{2}$ to $1\frac{1}{4}$	Chimalapa; cherry yellow, lustrous silky grain.
	Gateado	1 to 2	Pacific plains.
2	Granadillo	$\frac{3}{4}$ to 2	Pacific plains; very useful, beautiful wood.
	Guamuchi		Pacific plains; pinkish, fibrous, tough, good for tensil strains, durable.
2	Guanacaste ?	1 to 3	All parts.
	Guayacan		All parts; the hardest Isthmian wood.
	Guayabo, (*Psidium pyriferum*)	1 to $1\frac{1}{4}$	Pacific side; reddish, hard, tough, heavy, fine-grained.
2	Guapaque, (*Ostrija Mexicana*)	$1\frac{1}{2}$ to 3	All parts; indestructible.
	Guichidani		Pacific side; black, hard, tough, heavy, yellow streaks.
	Gulabere ciá	1 to 2	Pacific side; yellow, long, tough grain, very useful.
2	Gulabere blando	1	Pacific side; dark, tough, heavy, forty feet high; produces a cherry, used for precipitating indigo from its solution. Gulabere blando, white flowers. Gulabere duro, red flowers.
	Gulabere duro	1	
1	Grisiña	$\frac{1}{2}$ to $1\frac{1}{2}$	Pacific side; the yellow rosewood, beautiful wood; tree forty feet high.
	Güiro, (*Crescentia cucurbitina*)	$\frac{1}{2}$ to 1	All parts.
	Hoja ancha		Pacific side; yellowish gray, fine-grained, tough.
	Hoja amarilla		Pacific side; like rosewood, with fine wavy grain.
	Huacillo	$\frac{3}{4}$ to $1\frac{1}{2}$	East of Coatzacoalcos.
	Huanacastle		All parts? olive color; indestructible; used for doors, counters, stairs, &c.
2	Jagua, (*Genipa Americana*)	1 to $1\frac{1}{2}$	All parts; very light.
	Jabi	1 to 2	Atlantic side; extremely durable.
3	Jobo, (*Spondias lutea ?*)	1 to $1\frac{1}{2}$	Atlantic side.
	Madre cacao		All parts? yellow, straight grain, resinous, tough, heavy.
	Llaga yushi, (sand-wood)		Yellow, superior to box.
	Leche de Virgen	$\frac{1}{2}$ to $1\frac{1}{2}$	Light, resinous, tough, coarse-grained, medicinal; Chimalapa.
	Lima		Whitish yellow, tough, compact.
	Macaya	1 to 3	All parts; said to petrify when cut.
	Mangle, (*Rhizophora mangle*)	1 to 2	Atlantic plains.
	Mata buey		Pacific plains; handsome wood, reddish brown, hard, tough, heavy.
	Mezquite, (*Acacia arabica*)	$\frac{3}{4}$ to 2	All parts; looks like cedar, smells like violets.
	Mora, (*Morus tinctoria*)		The mulberry tree.
3	Naranjo, (*Citras vulgaris*)	$\frac{3}{4}$ to 1	All parts; ash color, fine grain, light, tough.
2	Ocote amarillo, (*Pinus variabilis*)	1 to 3	Mountain regions.
	Ocote blanco, (*P. strobus*)	1 to $3\frac{1}{2}$	Chimalapas.
	Ocote colorado, (*P. translucens?*)	1 to 2	Do.
	Otate	1-12 to $\frac{1}{2}$	Central part; very useful for light constructions.
	Palma real, (*Oresdoxa regia*)	$\frac{3}{4}$ to $1\frac{1}{4}$	Both coasts, and on the table lands.
3	Palma de coco, (*Cocus nucifera*)	1 to $1\frac{1}{4}$	Do.
	Palma de coyor	$\frac{1}{2}$ to 1	Both coasts; Upper Coatzacoalcos.
	Palma vizcaya, (rattan)	1-12 to 1-6	All parts.
	Palma de sombrero, (*Chamærops?*)		Chimalapa.
	Palma yucateca, (*Chamærops humilis*)	$\frac{1}{2}$ to 1	Do.
	Palma cristi, (*Ricinus comunis*)		
	Palo blanco, (satin-wood)		Pacific slope; yellow, like box-wood.
	Palo mulato	$\frac{1}{4}$ to $1\frac{1}{2}$	All parts; light, smooth trunk, medicinal, used for floats, &c.
	Palo baria, (*Cordia gerascantoides*)	1 to 3	East of Coatzacoalcos.
2	Palo de rosa, (*Pterocarpus santalinus*)	$\frac{1}{2}$ to $1\frac{1}{2}$	Pacific plains; the red and black varieties.
	Pimentilla		Pacific plains; reddish purple, very hard, fine-grained, useful.
	Pimeinta	1 to $1\frac{1}{2}$	Pacific plains; like dark mahogany; large tree, with fine tough grain.
	Quiebra haeba, (*Hymenea*)	1 to $2\frac{1}{2}$	Atlantic plains.
	Roble blanco, (*Tecoma penlaphila*)	1 to $1\frac{1}{2}$	All parts; very tough and hard.
	Roble	1 to 2	Do.
	Sangre, (*Pterocarpus draco*)	$\frac{3}{4}$ to 1	All parts; like walnut, tough, silky grain.
3	Tamarinds, (*Tamarindus occidentalis*)	1 to 2	Central parts.
	Tepehuage	$1\frac{1}{2}$ to 2	Pacific side; like mahogany, tougher, more beautiful and durable.
	Yaachi		Pacific side; like walnut, but straight grained.
2	Zapote, (*Sapota mammosa*)	1 to $2\frac{1}{2}$	All parts.
2	Zapotillo	1 to $1\frac{1}{2}$	Pacific side; purple, hard, heavy, tough.
	Zopilote	1 to $1\frac{1}{2}$	Pacific side.

FRUITS AND MISCELLANEOUS PRODUCTS.

Name.	Varieties.	Location and remarks.
Anon, (*Annona squamosa*)	2	All parts; delicious, healthy.
Aguacate, (*Persea gratissima*)	2	All parts; alligator pear.
Ansubo		Atlantic side; like caimitillo.
Camote	3	All parts; sweet potato.
Chaymote		Atlantic side.
Caimito	2	Atlantic side; green and purple varieties.
Caimitillo	2	Atlantic side; green and purple; smaller varieties
Chico Zapote, (*Mesples*)	2	All parts; (*Dysopyros obtusifolia*.)
Chayote, (*Jatropha urens*)	1	Atlantic side; leguminous.
Chirimolla, (*Annona cherimolia*)	1	Atlantic side.
Chato bejuco, (*Coccoloba uvifera*)	1	Atlantic side and summit plains.
Cidra, (*Citras medica*)	2	All parts.
Ciruelas, (*Spondias*)	2	All parts; red and yellow varieties.
Coco de agua, (*Cocos muifera*)	3	Both coasts; cocoa-nut.
Corozo, (*C. crispa*)	2	Both coasts; small nut.
Coyor	1	Both coasts; small nut; pig food.
Granada, (*Punica granatum*)	2	Both coasts; small nut.
Guayaba, (*Psidium pomiferum*)	2	North slope; the white and red guava.
Guanabana	2	North slope; the sour-sap.
Higos, (*Opuntia*)		All parts; many varieties of figs.
Hicaco	2	Pacific side; used for preserves.
Lima, (*Citras limeta*)	2	All parts.
Limes	2	Do.
Limoncillo, (*Limonia trifoliata*)		Gulf coast.
Limon, (*Citras limonum*)		Many varieties of lemons.
Mamey colorado, (*Lacuma bomplandi*)	2	All parts.
Mamey Zapote	1	Do.
Mamoncillo, (*Melicocca bijuga*)	1	Do.
Mango, (*Mangofera domestica*)	2	Do.
Melon, (*Cucumis melo*)	×	All parts; great many varieties.
Nanche	1	Atlantic plains.
Naraja china, (*C. aurantium*)	1	All parts; best at Chimalapa.
Naraja agria, (*C. vulgaris*)		All parts; used as condiment.
Naraja silvestre		All parts; many varieties.
Ñame, (*Discorea alota*)	1	All parts.
Pajuil, (*Anacardium ?*)	1	Pacific side.
Papaw, (*Asamina triloba*)		Atlantic side.
Piña, (*Bromelia annanas*)		All parts.
Pinúa, or pinilla		Cactus fruit; very pleasant taste.
Platano, (plantains)		Great many varieties.
Guineos, (bananas)		Do.
Sandia, (watermelon)	3	Coatzacoalcos banks.
Tamarindo, (*T. occidentalis*)	2	All parts.
Tomato, (*Lycopersicum*)	4	Do.
Uvas, (very coarse grapes)	3	Both coasts, and San Juan Guichicovy.
Toronjas, (*Citras malus*)		Both coasts; coarse, large oranges, used for conserves.
Yuca, (*Jatropha manihot*)	2	All parts; excellent arrow-root.
Zapote negro, (*Dysopyros obtusifolia*)	1	All parts.
MISCELLANEOUS.		
Arroz, (*Oryza sativa*)		San Juan Guichicovy; all parts give a medium quality of rice.
Apio		Chimalapa—celery.
Cassia		Pacific plains.
Calabaza, (pumpkin)	2	All parts yield poor article.
Cacao, (*Theobroma cacao*)	3	Grows in all parts of excellent quality.
Café, (*Coffea Arabica*)	1	Would be excellent if properly cultivated.
Cana azucar, (*Saccharan officinale*)	Many	Varieties of superior quality.
Emajagno	2	Useful for cordage, paper, &c.
Frijoles, (beans)	Many	The chief food of the Isthmus.
Gengibre, (*Amonum zinziber*)	1	All parts.
Grana, (*Cactus coccinelifer*)	Many	Pacific side; excellent quality.
Hicara-Jicara, (*Crecentia cujete*)	2	All parts; induces extraordinary contractile powers in the uterus.
Maiz, (*Zea mais*)		All parts; around Tehuantepec it is said they raise a crop every 40 days.
Miel	Many	An excellent honey is obtained in great quantity in the Chimalapos, from a stingless bee.
Papas	Many	Quite inferior to Irish potatoes.
Pimiento, (*Myrtus pimento*)		Southern coast.
Tabaco de corral, (*Nicotina tabacum*)		Of excellent quality at the Chimalapas.
Tabaco cimarron		Poor everywhere.
Rhatany root		Potreros of Chichilua.
Cubeba canina		All parts.

TEHUANTEPEC CANAL SURVEY.

FRUITS AND MISCELLANEOUS PRODUCTS—Continued.

Name.	Varieties.	Location and remarks.
Guaco		All parts; used for snake-bites, cholera, &c.
Jachion		All parts; very abundant; medicinal.
Jacalote jaba		All parts; very abundant; medicinal.
Laurus sassafras		All parts; of excellent quality.
Liquorice-root		All parts; of excellent quality.
Parra		All parts; of excellent quality.
Sarsaparilla		All parts; many species of smilax.
RESINS, OILS,* GUMS, BALSAMS, ETC.		
Aguacate, (Alligator pear)	2	All parts; the fruit used also as cosmetic.
Balsamo del Perú, (*Myrospermum perniferum*)		Table-lands and Pacific slope; at least two species, one black.
Balsamo de malats		Chimalapas; used for healing wounds.
Cedro blanco, (*Cupressus thuyoides*)		Chimalapas; aromatic gum, healing wounds.
Ciruelas	Var. es.	All parts; medicinal gums.
Copal, (*Hedwigia balsamifera*)	3	Pacific plains; used for varnishes.
Guapinol, (*Catharto carpus*)	2	Table-lands and Pacific slope; frankincense.
Jaboncillo, (*Sapindo saponaria*)	2	Pacific plains, Chimalapa; used as soap.
Jaboncillo, (*Bejuco de*) (soap-reed)		Chimalapa; used as teeth-brushes.
Leche de virgen		All parts; fever antidote.
Liquid amber, (*Stryax officinalis*)		All parts; amber gum.
Mezquite, (*Acacia Arabica*)	3	All parts; gum-arabic, used in the manufacture of calicoes; remarkably aromatic, violet odor.
Ocosote, (*Arbor electrum ?*)	1	Central division; amber.
Palma de coco, (*Cocos nucifera*)	1	Both coasts; cocoa-nut oil, used for medicine and hair-dressing.
Palma cristi, (*Ricinus comunis*)	2	Atlantic plains; excellent oil.
Papaya, (*Caricu papaya*)	1	Atlantic plains; used also as cosmetic.
Pepita de melon, (melon-pits)		All parts; used for medicinal purposes.
Palo baria, (*Cordia gerascuntoides*)		Atlantic plains; used as glue.
Palo mulato		All parts; medicinal gum.
Petroleo		Pacific plains.
Trementina, pon, (*Grinis religiosa*)		Atlantic highlands; turpentine.
Sassafran, (*Laurus sassafras*)		Table-lands; yields balsam and oil.
Ule, (*Palode*) (*Siphonia elastica*)		The India rubber tree, which grows everywhere.
TANNIN, PICKLES, ETC.		
Bejuco amarillo	1	Pacific plain.
Guamuchi	3	Table-lands.
Guayabo, (*Pysidinum pyriferum*)	2	All parts.
Guluhero	2	Pacific plains; used to precipitate indigo.
Mangle blanco, (*Avisennia nitida*)	2	All parts.
DYES,† ETC.		
Aguacate, (Pepita de)	2	All parts; the pits used for marking clothing, &c.
Achiote, (*Bixa orellana*)	2	Pacific plains; dyes scarlet.
Aplysia depiluns, (Tyrean purple)	2	Pacific shores; much esteemed by the Zapatico women.
Anil cimarron, (*Indigofera citisoydes*)	2	Pacific plains; indigo.
Anil de Guatemala and chiapas, (*I. disperma*)	2	Pacific plains; indigo.
Azafran, (*Carthamus tinctoria*)	1	All parts; red or yellow.
Brasil, (*Cæsalpine crista*)	3	All parts; red.
Campeche, (*Hæmatoxilum campehianum*)	2	Pacific side; black or purple.
Cascalote	2	Pacific shore; black.
Ebano verde, (*Chloroxylum*)	1	Pacific slope; green.
Güisache		Table-lands; black.
Nopal, (*Cactus coccinelifer*)	Var. es.	All parts? cochineal cactus.
Palo amarillo, (*Morus tinctoria*)	2	All parts; yellow fustic.
Tuna de España	1	All parts; species of cochineal cactus.
Uale, (*Genipa Americana*)	1	All parts; black.
Vainilla, (*Vanilla aromatica*)	2	Table-land, in shady places; dyes brown; used as medicine.
CLOTH, CORDAGE, ETC.		
Algodon, (*Gonypium*)	2	All parts; fine, long fiber.
Achiote, (*Bixa orellana*)	2	All parts; excellent quality.
Ceibon, (*Bombax pentandria*)	2	Pacific slope; excellent quality.
Coco, cascara de, (*Cocos nucifera*)	Var. es.	Both coasts; bank paper has been manufactured from cocoa-nut rind.
Emajagua	Var. es.	All parts; extensively used as ropes, &c.
Yxtle, (*Bromelia sylvestris*)	3	All parts; superior quality.
Lino	1	Table-lands; excellent flax.
Pita, (*Furercea fœtida*)	3	All parts; excellent quality.
Pita maguey, (*Agave Americana*)	1	Table-lands; excellent quality.
Palma de sombrero, (*Chamarops humilis*)	1	Table-lands; medium quality.
Trunk of the plantain	Var. es	All parts; paper of a superior quality has been manufactured from this tree.

* The castor-oil bean is abundant, and of superior quality.
† There are many other dyes known to the Indians of San Miguel and Santa Maria.

ANIMALS.

QUADRUPEDS, ETC.

Mules, horses, cattle	All of inferior quality, through ignorance and neglect; abundant throughout.
Goats	Of Peruvian breed. The wild goat has a long bristly hair instead of wool.
Peccary, Jabali wild hog	Several species; very gregarious; meander in the mountains in immense herds; do not seem to be harmed by snakes, which they kill with zest; live on roots; flesh and lard much esteemed by natives; dangerous when wounded.
Deer	Are very numerous, especially in the Ostuta region.
Tejon, (*Nama rufa*,) Coatimondi, (*Nama rufa*)	Very gregarious, plantigrade, resembling a small brown bear; not unlike the raccoon, with a long snout; very active, novelty-seeker, (?) and stupid; they come down from trees to look at the coyote, who, making believe he is dead, waits until they begin to play with his body; they then fall easy victims of the coyote's cunning and their own curiosity; they live on fruits, nuts, and worms; flesh much esteemed by the natives.
Armadillo	Very common in the Atlantic plains; flesh relished by the natives.
Opossum	Very common in the Atlantic plains; flesh relished by the natives.
Hare	Innumerable, especially around La Venta de Chicapa; the natives are prejudiced against eating its flesh.
Rabbits, squirrels	Many varieties of both kinds.
Spider monkey, (*Ateles paniscus*)	Very abundant, gregarious, and sportive monkey, especially near Niltepec; cries angrily when met in the woods, and follows the traveler, throwing at him twigs, sticks, and often stones.
Preacher monkey, (*Micetes beelzebub*)	A ridiculous and more sedate brother, forever busy in outdoor preaching and emphatic gesticulation.
The howling monkey, (*Micetes ursinus*)	Makes a hideous, frightening noise, ringing through the forests like the howl of a powerful beast. After hearing its voice, the sight of its unimposing body induces a very pleasant disappointment.
Tapir, danta, anteburro	Not gregarious; inoffensive, though fearful and powerful when attacked; has many physical features in common with hog, ass, and elephant; tough, thick skin, with short, lustrous, steel-gray hair; head flatter, but like that of an elephant without tusks; strong, herbivorous teeth; feet three-cleft, with two rudimentary toes quite high on each limb; short, pig-like tail; is found throughout the Isthmus, but abounds in the Upper Coatzacoalcos. Its usual name among the natives is Anteburro, namely: before (it was) an ass.
Puma	The "American lion;" larger and of a darker color than the jaguar; voracious; cowardly.
Ounce	Improperly called "tiger;" very daring; voracious.
Ocelot	"Tigre chiquito;" smaller than the above.

Wild cat	Very troublesome to small game.
Fox	Very abundant north of Tarifa.
Porcupine	Rather scarce on the Isthmus.
Aquatic quadruped	Color, dark olive-brown; seen swimming on the Coyolapa River; round head; strong incisors; small ears; about eighteen inches long.

BIRDS.

RAPTORES.

Buzzard	Very common and domestic.
Hawk	Two or three species.
Owl	Several species.
Eagle, (white-headed)	Haliætus leucocephalus.
Eagle, (bald)	Seen at Salina Cruz.
Vulture	(Sarcoramplus papa,) polyborus.

PASSERINE.

Blue jay, crow, several species of blackbird, kingbird, scissor-tail, two species of robbins, several species of thrushes, magpies, humming-birds, orioles, larks, gold-finches, &c.

SCANSORIAL.

Several species of macaws; blue, red, and yellow, and yellow and green parrots; many parroquets; two species of toucans; lovies; woodpeckers, &c.

GALLINACÆ.

Two species of crested curanaws (Faican real and F. griton,) tinamous, wild turkeys, chachalacas, partridges, quail, several varieties of doves, pigeons, hens, &c.

GRALLATORIAL.

Sand-piper, terutero, bittern, curlew, heron, jacana, &c.

PALMIPEDES.

Pelicans, frigate-birds, zopilotes, gallareta, zamaragullon, ducks, geese, &c.

REPTILES.

Vampirus spectrum, extremely abundant at Santa Maria Chimalapa, and causing great damage to man and animals; tortuga, alligator, hicoteo, morrocoy, squana, lizards, chameleons, &c.

POISONOUS SNAKES.

Coral, coralillo, mano de metate, naviaca, bebe sangre, rattlesnake, sorda, vibora, aspid, anchan, nojaca, jicotea, culebra verde, azuleja cobriza.

FISHES.

Fishes are abundant in the ocean and the rivers. Speckled trout is most abundant in the upper part of Chicapa River and in the streams north and east of Santa Maria. The "bobo," a delicious fish, lives in immense numbers in the Upper Coatzacoalcos. It descends to spawn in the Gulf in the month of November.

INSECTS.

Insect-life has attained in the Isthmus an incredible development. The feathery, horny, and membranously winged tribes can be counted by the myriads.

The most troublesome to man and cattle are the mosquito, zancudo, chaquiste, gegen, rodador, broca, talaja, zangano, garrapata, pinolillo, nigua, (Pulex penetrans,) moyaquil, flea, comejen, and several kinds of ants, centipede, scorpion, gongoli, tarántula, migal, several kinds of. spiders, &c. There is no choice between them, all being trying and numerous. They appear at appointed hours, in succession, and with the precision of a watch. Insects constituted the greatest hardships met with in our explorations. Still, there is no field of inquiry that will prove more fruitful of discovery than the study of the variation of species in the insect-life of the Isthmus.

TEHUANTEPEC CANAL SURVEY.

TABLE OF BAROMETRICAL ALTITUDES.

NOTE.—The computations have been made with A. Guyot's tables. For corrections for the mean latitude of stations, see map No. 1. The reference-station is at Chivela 717.8 feet above the Pacific Ocean. Barometer's readings unreduced to freezing temperature.

Place of observation.	Greenwich mean dates.			BAROMETRICAL DATA.						ELEVATION—		
				On the field.			At Chivela.			Between stations.	Of cistern.	Above the sea.
	Month.	Day.	Hour.	Barometer, inches.	Thermometers.		Barometer, inches.	Thermometers.		Feet.	Feet.	Feet.
					Attached.	Detached.		Attached.	Detached.			
	1870.											
Tarifa	Dec	18	3.60	29.396	74.00	74.00	29.402	72.00	73.00	+ 10.9		
Do	Dec	18	4.00	29.390	76.00	76.00	29.404	75.00	75.25	+ 16.4		
Do	Dec	20	3.00	29.434	73.00	73.00	29.446	74.50	74.70	+ 10.4		
Do	Dec	20	4.00	29.438	74.50	73.70	29.454	74.50	74.75	+ 14.2		
Do	Dec	20	5.00	29.436	74.00	74.00	29.454	75.50	75.75	+ 14.6		
Do	Dec	20	6.00	29.424	75.00	75.00	29.433	76.00	76.25	+ 11.1		
Do	Dec	20	7.00	29.405	76.00	76.50	29.420	77.00	77.00	+ 13.6		
Do	Dec	20	8.00	29.387	76.50	76.50	29.400	77.50	77.75	+ 13.5		
Do	Dec	20	9.00	29.374	78.00	77.00	29.382	78.00	78.00	+ 17.5		
Do	Dec	21	11.00	29.388	72.00	71.50	29.413	74.00	74.50	+ 19.1		
Do	Dec	22	2.00	29.410	68.00	68.00	29.427	68.00	71.00	+ 16.5		
Do	Dec	22	3.00	29.422	68.50	69.00	29.442	69.20	71.00	+ 17.1		
Do	Dec	22	5.00	29.406	75.50	71.00	29.430	72.00	72.00	+ 17.1		
Do	Dec	22	7.00	29.369	72.75	72.50	29.394	75.00	75.00	+ 21.4		
Do	Dec	22	11.00	29.362	73.50	73.00	29.377	74.00	74.00	+ 13.3		
Average										+ 15.1		732.9
Summit of Sierra Blanca	Dec	19	4.00	28.903	76.05	77.00	29.360	76.00	76.00	+ 451.3	+ 63	1,232.0
Chichihua River, near Corozo Bank	Dec	19	9.00	29.343	83.50	80.00	29.260	78.00	78.75	— 71.2		643.6
Monetza River, west cave	Dec	21	6.00	29.578	70.00	69.50	29.463	74.50	75.25	— 112.0	+ 5	600.8
San Miguel Chimalapa, at Don Martinas's adobe house near the Chicapa River.	Dec	23	11.00	29.896	60.50	61.00	29.567	64.50	64.75			
	Dec	23	12.00	29.922	61.00	61.50	29.576	62.00	62.00			
	Dec	24	8.00	29.940	61.50	61.50	29.616	66.00	67.00			
Average				29.919	61.00	61.30	29.586	64.10	64.50	— 321.6	+ 3.0	399.2
Chicapa River at Palmar rancho	Dec	25	8.00	29.503	70.00	69.50	29.524	66.50	67.00	+ 24.8		742.6
Chicapa River at Ultimo rancho	Dec	26	4.00	29.310	66.75	66.75	29.604	65.75	66.00	+ 278.3		
Do	Dec	26	5.00	29.312	67.75	67.50	29.600	66.50	66.50	+ 272.4		
Average										+ 275.3	— 3.0	993.1
Rosetta Hill	Dec	26	7.00	28.224	66.50	66.50	29.540	67.00	67.00	+1,296.1		2,013.9
Chicapa River, at the rancho of Mr. L. Scarce.	Dec	27	5.00	28.878	74.50	73.50	29.512	67.25	67.25	+ 633.6		
	Dec	27	7.00	28.832	76.75	76.00	29.430	69.00	69.00	+ 614.1		
	Dec	27	8.00	28.784	77.50	80.00	29.400	69.60	69.50	+ 630.2		
	Dec	27	9.00	28.769	75.00	76.00	29.334	69.50	70.00	+ 619.7		
	Dec	27	10.00	28.759	73.50	73.50	29.383	69.50	70.00	+ 623.3		
Average										+ 624.3	—36.0	1,378.6
Providencia Brook, Camp 1	Dec	31	2.20	28.806	62.00	63.00	29.527	65.60	66.00	+ 703.5	+36.0	1,457.8
	1871.											
Aguas Nuevas Brook, Camp 2	Jan	1	2.00	28.154	64.25	65.50	29.563	65.00	66.00	+1,375.8		2,093.6
Point P on the transit-line	Jan	1	5.20	27.078	64.00	66.00	29.565	66.00	67.00	2,471.5		3,189.3
Atravesado Mountain, Camp 3	Jan	1	10.20	26.236	64.50	60.00	29.455	70.00	70.00	+3,245.0		3,962.8
Atravesado, highest peak of	Jan	2	5.00	25.584	69.50	67.00	29.522	68.00	68.00	+4,060.3		4,778.3
Atravesado, Camp 5	Jan	3	11.00	28.604	70.00	68.50	29.550	65.50	66.00	+ 924.4		1,642.2
Niltepec, house of Don Antonio Sesma	Jan	5	4.00	29.972	77.50	77.50	29.514	66.00	66.75	— 400.9		
Do	Jan	5	5.00	29.956	79.50	79.00	29.502	67.00	67.75	— 404.4		
Do	Jan	5	6.00	29.930	81.50	81.00	29.474	67.50	67.25	— 402.7		
Average										— 402.6	+ 3.0	312.2
Ostuta River, behind the house of Don Cisareo Lopez.	Jan	7	4.00	29.992	81.50	80.00	29.532	67.25	68.00	— 405.4		
	Jan	7	5.00	29.984	81.50	80.00	29.526	67.00	68.00	— 408.3		
	Jan	7	6.00	29.960	83.00	81.50	29.500	68.00	68.50	— 407.5		
	Jan	7	7.00	29.924	82.50	81.00	29.466	69.25	69.75	— 410.1		
Average										— 407.8	+20.00	290.0
Ostuta River, Camp 6	Jan	10	10.35	29.606	78.50	78.75	29.385	73.00	73.00	— 203.6		514.8
Ostuta River, Camp 7	Jan	12	2.00	29.532	59.00	61.00	29.352	70.00	70.75	— 200.0		517.8
Ostuta River at the highest point explored.	Jan	12	6.00	29.526	80.00	78.00	29.336	74.00	73.50			
	Jan	12	7.00	29.498	80.00	79.00	29.390	76.00	74.75			
Average				29.512	80.00	78.50	29.318	75.00	74.10	— 176.1		541.7

TEHUANTEPEC CANAL SURVEY.

TABLE OF BAROMETRICAL ALTITUDES—Continued.

Place of observation.	Greenwich mean dates.			Barometrical Data.						Elevation—		
				On the field.			At Chivela.			Between stations.	Of cistern.	Above the sea.
	Month.	Day.	Hour.	Barometer, inches.	Thermometers.		Barometer, inches.	Thermometers.		Feet.	Feet.	Feet.
					Attached.	Detached.		Attached.	Detached.			
	1871.											
Copadia Huts	Jan	18	11.00	29.918	64.50	65.50	29.478	67.50	68.20	+ 532.6		1,250.4
	Mar	3	2.00	29.170	67.50	68.50	29.408	74.00	74.25			
	Mar	3	3.00	29.198	69.75	70.00	29.440	74.00	74.27			
	Mar	3	4.00	29.225	70.25	70.50	29.475	74.50	74.75			
	Mar	3	5.00	29.227	71.50	72.00	29.479	74.50	74.75			
Santa Maria Chimalapa, at the municipal house.*	Mar	3	6.00	29.210	73.00	73.00	29.460	76.00	76.25			
	Mar	3	7.00	29.196	75.25	75.50	29.436	79.00	79.00			
	Mar	3	8.00	29.190	76.50	76.50	29.416	78.75	78.75			
	Mar	3	9.00	29.185	74.00	74.00	29.408	78.00	78.00			
	Mar	3	10.00	29.198	71.00	71.00	29.432	74.50	75.50			
Average				29.200	72.08	72.33	29.439	75.91	75.72	+ 224.0	+ 6.0	947.8
Corte River, north of Santa Maria	Feb	2	5.50	29.898	75.75	75.00	29.503	75.75	75.75	− 384.2	− 3.0	336.6
Corte River, at Capepac Bank†	Feb	19	8.00	29.906	66.50	66.00	29.590	68.00	68.50	− 298.0		419.8
Summit of Blanco Ridge	Feb	20	3.45	28.454	66.25	64.00	29.622	66.50	67.25	+1,134.1		1,851.9
Blanco River, at foot of Blanco Ridge	Feb	20	6.20	29.568	73.00	71.00	29.581	68.00	69.50	+ 26.3		
Do	Feb	20	7.20	29.538	70.50	70.00	29.553	70.00	70.25	+ 26.6		
Average										+ 26.4	− 6.0	738.2
Corte River, Camp 1	Feb	20	8.50	29.582	69.50	69.00	29.513	69.50	70.00	− 56.5	+ 0.5	660.8
Corte, Camp 1	Feb	21	2.20	29.586	69.25	66.50	29.494					
Do	Feb	21	2.50	29.593	69.00	67.75	29.502	67.00	68.00			
Do	Feb	21	3.20	29.590	70.75	68.50	29.508					
Do	Feb	21	3.50	29.591	72.50	69.75	29.513	67.25	68.50			
Do	Feb	21	4.20	29.584	72.75	70.50	29.515					
Do	Feb	21	4.50	29.580	75.50	72.25	29.515	68.50	69.00			
Do	Feb	21	5.20	29.574	79.50	74.50	29.502					
Do	Feb	21	7.50	29.478	77.00	73.50	29.415	71.25	71.50			
Corte, Camp 1	Feb	21	8.20	29.462	77.00	73.50	29.397					
Do	Feb	21	8.50	29.458	77.50	73.00	29.382	71.25	71.77			
Do	Feb	21	9.20	29.446	75.50	73.50	29.374					
Do	Feb	21	9.50	29.443	73.50	71.75	29.370	72.00	72.00			
Means				29.532	73.98	71.37	29.457	68.75	70.75	− 55.1	+ 0.5	662.2
Corte, Camp 1	Feb	22	2.10	29.476	66.25	60.50	29.402	66.50	68.00			
Do	Feb	22	2.30	29.486	67.00	66.50	29.406					
Do	Feb	22	3.00	29.492	70.00	67.50	29.401	68.50	69.00			
Do	Feb	22	3.30	29.490	71.50	68.25	29.416					
Do	Feb	22	4.00	29.490	73.75	70.25	29.421	71.80	72.50			
Do	Feb	22	4.30	29.491	78.25	74.00	29.418	.50				
Do	Feb	22	5.00	29.486	80.50	76.00	29.414	72.50	72.50			
Do	Feb	22	5.30	29.482	82.00	77.00	29.399					
Do	Feb	22	6.00	29.453	81.50	77.00	29.387	74.50	74.25			
Do	Feb	22	6.30	29.430	81.50	70.00	29.367					
Do	Feb	22	7.00	29.408	82.00	81.00	29.349	75.50	74.75			
Means				29.471	75.84	72.79	29.399	71.50	71.83	− 58.6	+ 0.5	658.7
Corte, Camp 2	Feb	22	11.00	29.999	74.00	73.50	29.268	77.50	77.25	− 40.89	−0.0	676.9
Do	Feb	23	2.56	29.407	69.00	70.50	29.376	72.00	72.50			
Do	Feb	23	3.26	29.415	71.00	72.25	29.380					
Do	Feb	23	4.00	29.412	73.75	74.00	29.384	73.75	73.75			
Do	Feb	23	4.30	29.406	74.50	75.00	29.383					
Do	Feb	23	5.00	29.396	75.75	77.00	29.383	74.00	74.00			
Do	Feb	23	5.30	29.384	78.50	78.00	29.370					
Do	Feb	23	6.00	29.370	80.75	80.00	29.356	75.50	75.00			
Do	Feb	23	6.30	29.352	83.50	83.00	29.339					
Do	Feb	23	7.00	29.343	85.75	85.50	29.320	75.75	75.00			
Do	Feb	23	7.30	29.316	82.50	85.00	29.306					
Do	Feb	23	8.00	29.300	81.75	85.00	29.291	76.50	77.75			
Do	Feb	23	8.30	29.291	81.75	80.00	29.282					

* Raining at Santa Maria and very disturbed weather at Chivela; norther at both stations.
† Unsettled weather at both stations; hourly differences variable.

TABLE OF BAROMETRICAL ALTITUDES—Continued.

Place of observation.	Greenwich mean dates.			BAROMETRICAL DATA.						ELEVATION—		
				On the field.			At Chivela.			Between stations.	Of cistern.	Above the sea.
	Month.	Day.	Hour.	Barometer, inches.	Thermometers.		Barometer, inches.	Thermometers.		Feet.	Feet.	Feet.
					Attached.	Detached.		Attached.	Detached.			
	1871.											
Corte, Camp 2	Feb	23	9.00	29.278	84.60	80.60	29.274	76.75	76.00			
Do	Feb	23	9.30	29.276	81.25	80.00	29.273					
Do	Feb	23	10.00	29.270	77.75	77.09	29.274	77.00	77.00			
Do	Feb	23	10.30	29.273	75.50	75.50	29.281					
Means				29.343	78.53	78.86	29.329	75.15	78.84	− 5.00	+ 4.0	708.8
Camp 3, Corte River	Feb	24	4.30	29.364	71.25	71.50	29.389					
Do	Feb	24	5.00	29.359	73.60	73.00	29.387	76.25	76.25			
Do	Feb	24	5.30	29.359	82.00	76.75	29.376					
Do	Feb	24	6.00	29.324	80.00	78.50	29.356	77.25	77.25			
Do	Feb	24	6.30	29.302	80.00	77.50	29.334					
Do	Feb	24	7.00	29.288	81.00	78.75	29.319	78.50	78.00			
Do	Feb	24	7.30	29.262	81.50	78.50	29.300					
Do	Feb	24	8.00	29.250	81.50	79.50	29.290	79.50	79.00			
Do	Feb	24	8.30	29.230	81.00	79.75	29.280					
Do	Feb	24	9.00	29.222	80.00	79.00	29.267	80.00	79.75			
Do	Feb	24	9.30	29.212	79.00	78.00	29.263					
Do	Feb	24	10.00	29.208	78.00	77.25	29.261	81.50	80.00			
Do	Feb	24	10.30	29.210	77.50	76.00	29.263					
Means				29.276	78.90	77.24	29.314	78.66	78.37	+30.71	−14	734.5
Camp 3, Corte River	Feb	25	1.59	29.349	62.00	60.50	29.373	75.50	75.75			
Do	Feb	25	2.30	29.354	63.00	63.25	29.380					
Do	Feb	25	3.00	29.354	65.00	64.50	29.388	76.50	76.75			
Do	Feb	25	3.30	29.356	66.00	66.00	29.391					
Do	Feb	25	4.00	29.352	69.00	68.25	29.396	77.50	77.50			
Do	Feb	25	4.30	29.346	71.50	70.00	29.389					
Do	Feb	25	5.00	29.334	73.00	72.25	29.385	78.00	78.00			
Do	Feb	25	5.30	29.326	76.50	76.00	29.370					
Do	Feb	25	6.00	29.306	79.00	79.00	29.353	78.75	78.75			
Do	Feb	25	6.30	29.290	81.50	79.75	29.336					
Do	Feb	25	7.00	29.276	82.00	80.25	29.332	79.75	79.25			
Do	Feb	25	7.30	29.262	84.50	83.25	29.306					
Do	Feb	25	8.00	29.248	86.50	85.75	29.292	80.50	80.00			
Do	Feb	25	8.30	29.234	84.00	84.60	29.281					
Do	Feb	25	9.00	29.222	82.75	82.50	29.271	80.50	80.60			
Do	Feb	25	9.30	29.212	81.00	80.75	29.264					
Do	Feb	25	10.00	29.210	79.00	79.00	29.259	80.50	80.00			
Do	Feb	25	10.30	29.206	79.00	77.25	29.257					
Means				29.291	77.50	75.12	29.334	78.61	78.55	+33.40	−14.00	737.2
Camp 3	Mar	1	3.00	29.478	68.50	70.00	29.463	68.25	69.00			
Do	Mar	1	4.00	29.464	73.75	73.75	29.469	69.50	70.00			
Do	Mar	1	5.00	29.440	75.25	75.50	29.450	70.75	71.00			
Camp 3, Corte River	Mar	1	6.00	29.398	76.75	77.00	29.416	72.25	72.25			
Do	Mar	1	7.00	29.374	77.25	77.50	29.386	74.00	74.00			
Do	Mar	1	8.00	29.362	78.50	78.50	29.358	74.25	74.52			
Do	Mar	1	9.00	29.328	79.00	78.50	29.323	74.75	74.75			
Do	Mar	1	10.00	29.326	77.60	77.00	29.306	75.00	75.00			
Means				29.389	75.71	75.93	29.396	72.34	72.53	− 15.41	−14.00	719.2
Camp 4	Feb	28	6.38	29.528	69.00	75.50	29.546					
Do	Feb	28	7.00	29.512	68.25	71.50	29.520	71.50	71.75			
Do	Feb	28	7.30	29.490	68.25	73.50	29.514					
Do	Feb	28	8.00	29.475	69.50	73.25	29.496	71.75	72.00			
Do	Feb	28	8.30	29.464	68.50	71.50	29.484					
Do	Feb	28	9.00	29.450	69.00	72.00	29.474	71.75	72.00			
Means				29.486	68.75	72.25	29.507	71.60	71.91	+ 12.60	− 5.00	725.4

N. B.—The above calculations were performed on the field without access to tables for reducing the height of the barometer to the freezing point, but, of course, the reduction was effected by Guyot's Table II.

TABLE OF NUMBER OF INHABITANTS, HORNED CATTLE, ETC.

POPULATION.

In the absence of reliable statistics, the following tables of the number of inhabitants and horned cattle, &c., in the Isthmus, are given as mainly copied from the accounts furnished by Dr. Pedro de Garay. His statements were based upon his own estimates, the census of 1831, and information received from the district prefects. I have modified them to some extent whenever the information received from the different town presidents or municipal records warranted the corrections made.

SOUTHERN DIVISION OF THE ISTHMUS.

Name of the town.	Census.	Remarks.
San Catalina Mistequilla	247	1843.
Tehuantepec	14,000	Garay estimated 8,934.
Tlacotepec	300	Garay estimated 282.
Santiago Laollaga	152	Garay estimated in 1843.
Chihuitan	400	Garay gives 532 in 1843.
Comitancillo	500	
San Geronimo	2,060	Garay gives 805 in 1843.
Iztaltepec	1,200	Garay gives 1,546 in 1843.
Aspinal	400	Garay gives 504 in 1843.
Juchitan	11,000	Garay gives 4,567 in 1843.
Huilotepec	60	Garay gives 185 in 1843.
San Mateo del Mar	600	Garay gives 1,500 in 1843.
San Maria del Mar	300	Garay gives 148 in 1843.
San Dionisio del Mar	888	Garay gives in 1843.
San Francisco del Mar	287	Garay gives in 1843.
Zanatipec	500	Garay gives 336 in 1843.
Venta de Chicapa	150	
Tarifa	50	
Santiago	10	
Chivela	70	
Palangana, Xochiapa, and Sarabia, huts	150	
San Miguel Chimalapa	400	Garay gives 318 in 1843.
Santa Maria Chimalapa	1,030	Garay gives 524 in 1843.
Petapa, (San Maria)	1,447	Garay gives in 1843.
Petapa, (Santo Domingo)	700	Garay gives 626 in 1843.
El Bario	1,200	Garay gives 999 in 1843.
San Juan Guichicovi	3,000	Garay gives 5,000 in 1843.

Plantations and huts in the southern division of the Isthmus.	Horned cattle.
Mal Paso, in the year 1843	250
San Nicolas, in the year 1843	1,000
Zuleta, in the year 1871	800
Jicaras, in the year 1843	1,000
Salazar, in the year 1843	125
Nisabiti, in the year 1843	300
Cienaga, in the year 1843	60
Guigo Chani, in the year 1843	50
Rio Grande, in the year 1843	800
San Cruz and Clano, in the year 1843	Unknown.
Nanches, in the year 1843	150
Santo Domingo, in the year 1871	1,800
Petapa district, (5,000 miles are said to be owned by the Guichicovi Indians,) in the year 1871	2,530
Guichilona, in the year 1843	200
Chicapa, Tarifa, Santiago, and Chivela, in the year 1871	14,000
Cipinal, in the year 1843	3,000
Mezquital, in the year 1843	200
Los Cerrillos, in the year 1843	400
Paso Lagarto, in the year 1843	700
Huasuntlan, in the year 1843	80
Piedro Grande, in the year 1871	4,000
San Barbara, in the year 1843	100
La Chilana, in the year 1843	100
Comitancillo, in the year 1871	300
Juchitan, in the year 1871	14,000
San Francisco del Mar, in the year 1871	9,000

TOWNS, PLANTATIONS, AND HUTS IN THE NORTHERN DIVISION OF THE ISTHMUS.

Name of the town.	Inhabitants.	Oxen.	Horses.	Mules.
Acayucam, town, census of 1831	1,902	267	249	50
Sayultepec, town	1,206		249	
Tesistepec, town	2,132		88	
San Juan Oluta, town	659		88	
Soconusco, town	1,611		46	
Jaltipan, town	1,302	88	239	
Cosoliacaque, town	1,595	303	52	
Joteapa, town	1,665	16	40	
Mecayapa	736		55	
Minsapam, town	773			
Chinameca, town	779	3,679	906	45
Oteapan, town	857	147	33	
Ishuatlan, town	497	500	21	
Molvacan, town	624			
Minatitlan, town, census in 1871	1,200	150		
Coatzacealcos, town, census in 1871	80			
Almagres, town, census in 1871	503	40		
Súchil and La Puerta, town, census in 1871	100			
Michapa, hut, census in 1831	325	230	160	
Encinal, hut, census in 1831	382		35	
Coyote, hut, census in 1831				
Guellapan, hut, census in 1831				
Jalapa, hut, census in 1831	450			
Cosaguilapa, hut, census in 1831				
Lechonal, hut, census in 1831				
Pedregal, plantation, census in 1831	20	100		
Calabozo, plantation, census in 1831	63			
Santa Catalina, plantation, census in 1831	210	1,000	10	2
San J. Ba. Nopalapan, plantation, census in 1831	435	30,000	4,000	180
Guatotolapan, plantation, census in 1831	716	19,000	4,000	285
La Malota, plantation, census in 1831	287			
Corralviego, hut, census in 1831	81			
Paso de San Juan, hut	264			
Los Quemados, hut	254			
Camahuacapa, hut				
Correa, hut	165	513	73	
Carasviejas, hut				
Solenautla, plantation	123	5,000		
San Catalina Ortizes, plantation	133	1,300	360	18
San Felipe, plantation				
Los Almagres, plantation	49	2,200	200	8
San Antonio, plantation	9	400	90	4
San José Teposapa, plantation	7	2,400	10	2

SUMMARY OF THE ABOVE STATISTICS.

Division.	Inhabitants.	Horned cattle.	Horses and mules.	Sheep.
Southern division	40,811	54,915	18,000	1,500
Northern division	22,191	67,103	11,260	200
Total	63,002	122,018	29,260	1,700

B.

REPORT

OF THE

HYDROGRAPHIC SURVEYS ON THE ATLANTIC COAST

IN CONNECTION WITH

A SHIP-CANAL ACROSS THE ISTHMUS OF TEHUANTEPEC.

BY

NORMAN H. FARQUHAR, LIEUTENANT-COMMANDER, U. S. N.

UNITED STATES STEAMER KANSAS, (4th rate,)
Off Minatitlan, Mexico, April 15, 1871.

SIR: On the 25th of November, 1870, at 2.30 p. m., I proceeded with the Kansas, under my command, to the mouth of the Coatzacoalcos River, to inaugurate the surveys, &c., directed by you to be made, in your instructions to me of the 12th of November.

On the following day I made several reconnaissances, with a view to select a suitable place for a base-line, which was finally located on the western shore, just without the mouth of the river.

Our work, once commenced, was carried on with all the energy and intelligence we were capable of, and nothing but bad weather was suffered to interfere with it.

I append a general order I issued.

It affords me much pleasure to say that all the officers took a lively interest in the surveys, and were ever ready and anxious to take part in them.

The work of the day was plotted on the same evening, and all bearings, observations, &c., which did not seem to plot well were at once rejected, and the work gone over again the next day.

In this way all doubt was removed, and I can safely say that all the work is perfectly reliable, and its accuracy beyond question.

The lines of soundings of 5, 7, and 10 fathoms off the Gulf shore were run by the Mayflower, Master Henricks commanding.

I desire particularly to commend Lieutenant Commander Hoff, executive officer of this vessel, who notwithstanding his many duties on board ship, found time to take a prominent and valuable part in the surveys.

Master E. W. Henricks, commanding the Mayflower, and Master James W. Miller, of this vessel, were particularly zealous, (as was also my clerk, Mr. N. F. Clark,) and the practice these officers have had in this important part of their profession will make their services always valuable to the Government, the more so now.

The watch officers, Lieutenant Impey, Midshipmen Ludlow, Milliman, and Ellery took such parts as they were enabled to do when off watch.

The charts were made by Mr. E. Somers, the accomplished draughtsman of the Expedition.

With each chart you will find such notes, data, &c., as may be useful.

I am, very respectfully, your obedient servant,

N. H. FARQUHAR,
Lieutenant Commander, Commanding.

Captain R. W. SHUFELDT, U. S. N.,
Commanding Tehuantepec and Nicaragua Surveying Expedition.

GENERAL ORDER.

1. Shore party, and to survey Tierra Nueva and La Barilla, Lieutenant Commander Farquhar, Master Miller, and captain's clerk, Clark.

2. The bar and soundings, including tidal observations, Lieutenant Commander Hoff, in charge, assisted by all the officers.

3. Astronomical party to determine latitude, longitude, variations of the compass, &c., Master Miller in charge.

4. The crew will breakfast early, so that the parties may be in readiness to leave the ship by 6.30 a. m. or latest 7 a. m.

5. Work will be stopped, when practicable, at 11 a. m., and recommenced at 2 p. m.

6. The executive officer will see that all boats are supplied with water, and anchor, lead line and compass; the crews to wear straw hats.

7. The commanding officer would impress upon the officers the necessity of being very precise and accurate in their work and observations, and he directs that no doubtful or uncertain work be recorded.

N. H. FARQUHAR.

United States Steamer Kansas,
Off Coatzacoalcos, Mexico, November 25, 1870.

CHAPTER I.

THE BAR.

The bar and harbor of Coatzacoalcos were surveyed during the months of December, 1870, and January, 1871. The topography is by myself, assisted by Mr. N. F. Clark, captain's clerk, and Mr. E. Somers, draughtsman.

The hydrography by Lieutenant Commander Hoff, assisted by Lieutenant Impey, Master Allibone, and Midshipmen Milliman, Ludlow, and Ellery.

The latitude, longitude, and variations of the compass were determined by Master J. M. Miller.

The light-house was the station at which the observations were made. The variation of the compass is decreasing, and if we regard that determined in 1848 by the party under the command of Lieutenant Commanding Leigh, of the United States brig Stromboli, as correct, the annual decrease will be about $17'$. The French chart of 1861 would give $8'$, which latter result is more in conformity with that given by the chart of this coast recently issued by the Hydrographic Office in Washington.

A parallel to the base-line was staked out on the level beach, then carefully measured several times with a chain which had been adjusted, and the results of the various measurements differed not more than a very small fraction of a link. This was frequently verified by measuring between the different stations with a tape-line, and in every case the measurements by our chart agreed with that given by the line, a gratifying result.

The azimuth compass belonging to this vessel was used exclusively for measuring the various angles; the readings were taken from the azimuth circle, and the bearings also by compass. I regard this instrument as much superior to the sextant or the ordinary surveyor's compass, for such purposes, for the instrument levels itself, the angles read are always horizontal ones, and the instrument does not get out of adjustment.

The steam-launch was used principally in running the lines of soundings; bearings were taken at each end of the lines, and a uniform speed maintained. The soundings were taken at regular intervals.

To obtain the eastern and western extremities of the bar, I caused the launch to anchor at these places, and took bearings on it, from both ends of the base-line, thus checking the bearings taken from the boat at the same time, and locating these very important points with great precision and beyond all doubt.

The soundings are all for low water, and develop the fact that fourteen feet may cross the bar with safety, and by arranging buoys fifteen feet. Buoys should be placed at the eastern and western extremities of the bar.

The bottom is everywhere a stiff clay, with a very thin coating of sand; no rocks or hard sand have been encountered.

The tides are of the diurnal type. The time of high water at full and change is at 4 p. m.; the greatest rise and fall two feet; mean rise and fall, one foot.

It is to be observed that the tides are very much affected by the winds and the current of the river, a norther usually causing very high water, and a southwest wind the contrary.

The winds also affect the times of high water, and render it almost impossible to find the time of high water by any of the known methods of calculation.

The best anchorage is abreast the town, in about seven fathoms of water, or, if you expect a norther, above the town, under the lee of the woods; the holding-ground is good, and no danger of dragging the anchor, with an ordinary scope of chain.

Vessels are generally uneasy at their anchors during a norther, on account of the strong current and the wind across it. To avoid this, let go another anchor under foot, or moor ship with an anchor up and down stream; if close to the weather shore, a hawser made fast to a tree will answer the purpose of another anchor.

The light-house is an old Spanish vista or watch-tower, on the highest bluff on western shore, with an iron frame-work on top. The illuminating-apparatus at present consists of a steamer's mast-head light, and, under favorable circumstances, is visible ten or twelve miles. It is the intention of the Mexican government to replace this light with a better one.

At the mouth of the river the shore on the eastern side is green and bushy to the water's edge; on the western, a red bluff, nearly bare.

SAILING DIRECTIONS.

To cross the bar, bring the light-house to bear by compass south or south one-fourth east, and stand in on this course till you deepen the water to three fathoms; then haul up for the middle of the river, or close Point Picho by red bluff on western bank, and stand in.

Except in case of an emergency, I would not advise strangers to cross it at night. Should the light be made, bring it to bear south, and stand in on that course until you strike seven fathoms of water, and anchor; good holding-ground of sand and clay will be found.

The pilots are very ignorant, and know nothing about handling a vessel; they simply know where the best water is, and masters of vessels must work their ships themselves. These pilots come out in a boat as far as the bar, if the usual signals are made.

It is a well-established fact that this bar has changed very little, if any, for many years. From this fact, and the character of the bottom, I have no hesitation in saying that it may be dredged to any depth, say 20 feet, and it would remain at that depth without filling up.

The current coming down the river first strikes on the eastern shore, and there deposits most of the debris; then, turning slightly to the westward, deposits what may be left on the western bank, thus leaving the channel on the bar clear.

The position of the light-house, as determined by Master J. M. Miller, is: Latitude 18° 08′ 15″ N.; longitude 94° 21′ 42″ W. Longitude in time, 6^h 17^m $26^s.8$; fixed light, 125 feet above the level of the sea, visible 12 miles; variations of the compass 6° 49′ E.

CHAPTER II.

THE COATZACOALCOS RIVER, FROM BAR TO MINATITLAN.

This river was surveyed during the months of January, February, and March, 1871.

Topography by myself, Masters Henricks and Miller, and captain's clerk, Clark.

Hydrography by Lieutenant Commander Hoff, Masters Henricks and Miller.

The base-line measured for the bar was the starting-point of this survey. The river was triangulated the entire distance, and soundings taken between all the stations, as well as between all other points of interest.

This survey proves the inaccuracy of the several charts now in use, viz:

Sketch made by order of Commander Perry, in 1847, and that by the French in 1861.

The banks of the river are low throughout, except at Paso Nuevo, and during the freshets are, with this exception, entirely overflowed.

The bed of the river is mud, except at the shoal water below the Sugar rancho, and at the extremities of the islands of Diablo and Guerrero, where sand and gravel are found.

There are but two places where twenty feet of water cannot be carried—one abreast the upper end of the Island of Guerrero, and the other above the mouth of the Uspanapa River. To get this depth at these places it will be necessary to dredge only about 25,000 cubic feet at each.

The channel which has been marked on the chart "Kansas Channel" was discovered by us on the other side of the rock, is of great importance, and very easy of navigation, and nowhere in it is found less than twenty-four feet of water.

This channel is better than the old one, because it has more water, is wider, and more definitely marked.

I believe that the Kansas is the first vessel of any size that has ever gone through it. I have, therefore, named it the Kansas Channel, and I predict that as soon as the chart of it is published it will be exclusively used.

SAILING DIRECTIONS.

1st. To the Rio Tierra Nueva, keep the western bank close on board; then to go through the old channel at the "Rock;" arriving at the north point of the Tierra Nueva, haul gradually toward the middle of the river, and when a little above the mouth of this river a large tree will be seen some distance ahead on high ground; steer for it, keeping the most easterly green mound astern. This will take you clear, and in not less than fifteen feet of water. The "Rock" will be passed when abreast of the point where the grass on the eastern shore meets the trees.

To go through Kansas Channel, keep close to the western shore till the passage between the two islands of Pajaritos is well opened; then steer for the point on the eastern shore, on a course of S. S. E. to S. E. by S., approaching this point; keep that shore close on board until you have passed the junction of the trees and grass, and you will be all clear, and have carried not less than twenty-four feet water.

Going down the river, when abreast of the Rio Stapa, haul in toward the eastern bank, and keep about one hundred feet from it until you have rounded the point before mentioned, when two remarkable mounds will be seen ahead—one sandy and bare, the other green—bearing about N. N. W.; steer for them till you open the passage between the islands of Bajaritos.

2d. When above the "Rock," keep in the middle of the river until abreast of Devil's Island, when take the eastern shore until you pass the town at Paso Nuevo; then the western shore until abreast the upper end of Guerrero Island; then cross over to the eastern bank, which keep until you reach the rancho, a short distance below the Uspanapa, where the middle of the river contains plenty of water.

From September till January the tides in this river are not well defined, the current being so strong from the continued rains that the flood-tide cannot overcome it, and the only difference this tide makes is, perhaps, to lessen the current a little and swell the waters.

The latter part of February the dry season commences, and then the tides are more regular, and only affected by the winds. The greatest rise and fall observed at Minatitlan was two feet, and the least nine inches. Time of high water, full and change, April, 1871, 3.30 p. m.

The tides are of the diurnal type.

CHAPTER III.

COATZACOALCOS RIVER, FROM MINATITLAN TO THE ISLAND OF TACAMICHAPA.

This survey was made by Lieutenant Commander Hoff, in the month of March, 1871.

I inclose his report. I am of the opinion that this river cannot be used for canal purposes beyond the Island of Tacamichapa.

As the river is quite wide, I can see no difficulty in dredging a channel of sufficient width and depth, the effect of which will only be to narrow the river, for the volume of water will be sufficient to fill such a channel.

UNITED STATES STEAMER KANSAS, (4TH RATE,)
Off Minatitlan, Mexico, March 25, 1871.

SIR: In obedience to your order of the 18th instant, directing me to verify the chart of the Coatzacoalcos River, known as "Tehuantepec Survey, Barnard, 1851," I have the honor to make the following report:

I proceeded as far up the river as I could, finding invariably less water than is put down on the chart. With the exception of leaving out a small island, the river, as laid down upon the chart, is correct. I was able to ascend the Apotzongo branch of the Coatzacoalcos River to within three and a half miles of Almagres. Here I was stopped by three feet and a half water, sandy bottom, banks quite low and shelving. The tide ascends to beyond this point, with about four inches rise and fall this season.

Finding I could not reach Almagres, I returned and entered the Brazo Mistan by the northern mouth. In this branch I found generally more than is put down on the chart. The river, however, is laid down perfectly, and proved most excellent to run by. I was stopped by shoal water in this branch about one sea mile above the village of Galeras. The tide also ascends beyond this point, with about five or six inches rise and fall. Above the branching of the Coatzacoalcos River are many snags, sand-bars, and rocks (generally under water or just awash) of limestone, covered with clay.

Inclosed are the courses, (magnetic,) depths of water, and distance run, with remarks necessary to plot a chart. I also inclose a cross-section of the river at the highest point reached in each, branch, and a tracing of the map, with a few remarks.

My thanks are due to First Assistant Engineer John Purdy, and Midshipman F. Ludlow, U. S. N., for valuable assistance during the reconnaissance.

Very respectfully,

WM. BAINBRIDGE HOFF,
Lieutenant Commander, United States Navy.

Lieutenant Commander N. H. FARQUHAR,
Commanding United States Steamer Kansas.

CHAPTER IV.

THE COACHAPA RIVER.

This river was surveyed in the month of December, 1870, by a party consisting of Lieutenant Commander N. H. Farquhar, commanding Kansas, Master J. M. Miller, First Assistant Engineer John Purdy, and captain's clerk, N. F. Clark.

The survey was made by means of the patent log and compass, steaming at a uniform rate of speed, noting the courses and the times run on them, checking these from time to time by observations on shore. The soundings were also taken at regular intervals.

We left the Kansas at the bar December 11. At Minatitlan we were delayed two days, securing the services of a pilot, and in completing our preparations.

Leaving Minatitlan December 14, at 9.15 a. m., in the steam-launch, we proceeded up the Coatzacoalcos a distance of 3 miles, to the mouth of the Coachapa, which we entered at 9.56 a. m. on a course southeast one-half east, the width of the river at this point being about two hundred feet.

Proceeding up the Coachapa a distance of $5\frac{1}{4}$ miles, we arrived at the rancho of Doña Clotilde Baldwin, situated on a series of quite high bluffs, on the right bank of the stream. Here we tarried a short time, and obtained what information we could bearing upon the survey.

We then continued our course up stream, passing, first, San Cristobal, the largest village on the river, $5\frac{1}{2}$ miles from Doña Clotilde's; next, $1\frac{1}{4}$ miles farther on, the village of Amasquite, and reaching in the evening the rancho Capalapa, on the right bank of the river, $21\frac{1}{2}$ miles from its mouth. Here we remained over night.

Up to this point we found the river from 150 to 200 feet wide, and, with a few exceptions, the water from 10 to 18 feet in depth, no very short bends, but few snags, and very little debris or drift.

Leaving Capalapa at 7.15 on the morning of the 15th, we began to experience some difficulty in our movements up the stream; snags and sawyers were encountered all day, and also several bars, on which the water was but $3\frac{1}{2}$ to $4\frac{1}{2}$ feet in depth.

The river also became very winding and circuitous, and in many places the bends were so short that it would be impossible for even a small vessel to pass around them. The convex sides of all these bends were observed to be invariably sand-banks.

In many places we found snags and fallen trees extending from the banks out into the stream, and generally considerable debris and drift were accumulated around them. This debris was for the greater part composed of pieces of decayed trees, underbrush, &c.

At a distance of $9\frac{1}{2}$ miles from rancho Capalapa, the river divided. Proceeding up the left branch a distance of nearly one mile, the water became so shallow, and we encountered so many bars, that we were compelled to turn back.

We then entered the other branch to the right, and soon found that it was the main one. Our progress was slow, however, and very much interrupted on account of the snags, sawyers, and fallen trees we encountered, and we had not proceeded more than a mile when we came to a point where the channel was obstructed by a large fallen tree, which it would be necessary to cut away in order to make a passage for the steam-launch. It now being rather late in the afternoon, we built a camp, and remained in it over night.

The next day (16th) we made a reconnaissance in a canoe up the river to the mouth of the Rio Coahuapa, distant about a mile from the camp. In the meantime we had one man at work cutting away the fallen tree and clearing the channel.

This being accomplished, we left our camp on the morning of the 17th, in the launch, and continued our course up stream, passing the Coahuapa coming in from the left, which was in a very low stage—too low, in fact, to enter it with the launch.

With considerable difficulty we reached a point $11\frac{1}{2}$ miles above the Coahuapa, or a distance of $44\frac{1}{2}$ miles from its confluence with the Coatzacoalcos.

Here we found the river completely obstructed, several large trees having fallen into the stream, and extending entirely across, both under water and above the surface.

Not deeming a further exploration of the stream of sufficient importance to warrant us in undertaking the removal of these obstacles, which would have been attended with no little delay, as we had only limited means and facilities at hand, I decided to terminate our reconnaissance at this point.

In some places the banks of the river rise to a considerable height, forming bluffs, and in these localities rocks and large sandstones were observed. But with these comparatively few exceptions, the banks on either side are low, and the general appearance of the stream resembles a canal rather than a natural river. The rise and fall of the water is considerable, being in many places as much as 18 to 20 feet. At San Christobal, for instance, where we found from two to two and a half fathoms of water, we were told by the natives that in the dry season it falls to the depth of 7 feet, while marks on the banks and trees gave evidence that during the time of freshets it rises some 12 feet higher than our soundings.

Our pilot informed us, also, that up as far as Coahuapa, the river is at times so low that even canoes cannot pass up, and are frequently hauled overland for some distance.

In the times of a freshet the river overflows its banks, and the whole country is more or less inundated.

On our way down the river we visited a remarkable cave, petroleum lakes, and salinas, (salt springs,) all near the villages of Amasquite and San Christobal, and about a mile from the river. They were also visited by Surgeon J. C. Spear, the naturalist of the Expedition. I leave it to him to report upon them.

We reached Minatitlan, on our return, on the evening of the 19th of December.

CHAPTER V.
THE USPANAPA.

On the morning of March 9, 1871, Lieutenant Commander N. H. Farquhar, commanding Kansas, with Surgeon J. C. Spear, naturalist, Master E. W. Henricks, Second Assistant Engineer George Caire, and N. F. Clark, captain's clerk, left the ship in the steam-launch, to make a survey and exploration of the Rio Uspanapa.

It was surveyed on the same plan as the Coachapa.

At 10.5 a. m. we entered the Uspanapa; width at mouth, about 300 feet; banks on either side; low and marshy. Uspanapa Island, three miles from mouth, has a channel on either side. Proceeding up stream a distance of 11¾ miles, we reached the mouth of the Rio Chichigapa, coming in from the westward, and having a width of some 50 feet. We made a reconnaissance up this stream about three miles, and found the banks low and marshy, and lined with a thick growth of underbrush and trees. Beyond, a distance of one mile, we found no current at all, the stream resembling a lagoon rather than a river. The water was very muddy, and was from two to four fathoms in depth.

Returning to the Uspanapa, we continued on our course up that stream, arriving at 5.48 p. m., at the rancho " De la Concepcion." Here we passed the night.

On the following morning, at 6.57, we took our departure, with a pilot and guide on board, named Claudio Ramos.

A short distance above rancho " De la Concepcion," on the west bank of the river, is the site of a French colony settled in 1828. Up to this point the banks of the river on both sides are generally low, and become inundated in the time of floods.

Above the French settlement the banks on the right become higher, and generally increase in height, and on reaching " Santa Maria del Cármen," a small village on the east bank, 12 miles above rancho " De la Concepcion," they become quite high and steep, being composed of clay and soft stone of sandy formation.

At 11.05 a. m. we reached the rancho of José Maria Rosali, situated on the east bank of the river, 14½ miles above the rancho Concepcion. Here we stopped a short time for the purpose of taking observations.

Starting again at 12.22 p. m., we continued on our course up stream. We had proceeded a distance of but two miles, when we ran aground at a point where the river is very wide. At such places we invariably found the water very shallow.

We were two hours in getting off, and finally found a channel at the east side, with from 6 to 8 feet of water.

We now began to encounter snags and bars, and proceeded on our way with considerable difficulty and frequent interruptions. At 6.55 p. m. we again ran aground. Distant from rancho Concepcion 23 miles, or from the mouth of the river 42½ nautical miles, and about one-fourth mile below " Playa del Tigre."

At this point the river is very wide, (from 500 to 600 feet;) the water very shallow, (from 2 to 4 feet,) with sandy bottom, which is continually shifting. Here we passed the night on board the launch.

On the next day, the 11th, we worked all day long, endeavoring to get off the bar on which we had run the night previous, but the sandy bottom shifted to such an extent and so rapidly that we accomplished but little, and at night found ourselves still aground, having moved but a short distance. During the day we sounded in our canoe, and found there was not by any means sufficient water to enable us to proceed any further up the river in the steam-launch. This was confirmed by natives passing down the river in canoes.

On the 12th we continued our efforts with renewed energy, and finally, at 4 p. m., got fairly started down stream, and at 5.30 p. m. reached the rancho of our new pilot, José Maria Rosali, where we passed the night.

On the forenoon of the 13th we made a reconnaissance in canoes up the Rio Tecuanapa a distance of two miles. This small stream flows into the Uspanapa from the eastward a short distance from the rancho, and has its source in a lagoon of the same name, about three miles from the Uspanapa Island. Our object was to visit this lagoon, but we were unable to do so, even in our small canoe, on account of the shallowness of the water and great number of fallen trees we encountered. The Tecuanapa, (so called from the fact that a celebrated Indian chief, Tecuan, was killed upon its banks by a tiger,) is a very small stream, its width being not more than 10 to 20 feet, and depth from 2 to 4 feet, with many very shoal places.

We returned to rancho Rosali, and took our departure in steam-launch at 2 p. m., arriving at 5.50 p. m. at rancho Concepcion, where we passed the night.

On the morning of the 14th, at 6.35 a. m., we started on foot to make a reconnaissance of the lagoon Mexcalapa, the source of a stream of the same name flowing into the Uspanapa from the eastward.

The lagoon is about one league distant from the rancho, and a walk of forty minutes, through a magnificent forest, brought us to its shores. It is a beautiful sheet of water, having a length of about two miles and a width of one and a half miles.

We returned to the launch, and at 9 a. m. were under way for Minatitlan, which place we reached at 3 p. m.

There was little or no débris or drift observed in the river as far as our survey extended, except where the river was unusually wide and shallow.

The flood-mark measured on the trees and bushes along the banks was 13 feet above the stage of water we found, and where the banks are low the whole surrounding country is inundated during the wet season.

From the mouth of the river up to rancho del Carmen, thirty-two miles, the soundings show from five to ten fathoms; above that point they gradually decrease, and in many places 5 to 7 feet was the deepest water obtained.

The map known as Barnard's Survey of this river, made in 1851, is very correct, and the only exception I can make is that nearly all of the high land is represented too high; but the turns, directions, ranchos, and arroyas are faithfully laid down.

I was very much disappointed in not finding the river navigable to a greater distance, having been led to suppose that there would be no difficulty in ascending at least one hundred miles in the steam-launch; but the truth is that the river, from its great width and clear water, has deceived those who have only traversed it in canoes. Of course, during the season of high water or freshets, the launch would no doubt be able to go fifty miles further.

The soil is very rich, and adapted to the cultivation of the fruits, vegetables, &c., of these parts.

The extent of the tides depends upon the season of the year. We experienced them as far as we went, but this was the commencement of the dry season; during the wet season the tide is not perceptible.

Where the water was shallow, the bottom was found to be of a sandy nature, which changed into mud as the water deepened.

CHAPTER VI.

SEA-COAST FROM TONALA TO BARILLA.

The shore-line was surveyed in the month of January, 1871, by Master E. W. Henricks and J. M. Miller. The whole distance was chained, and the courses taken by a surveyor's compass.

The lines of soundings were run by the United States sloop Mayflower, Master Henricks, commanding, in the month of February, 1871.

These lines were plotted by means of cross-bearings from established points and from the courses run by compass.

On all the charts I have consulted, including the last one of this coast issued by our Hydrographic Office in Washington, the position of Tonala is put down too far to the eastward; many of the merchant vessels have complained of this, and two of them to my knowledge mistook Tonala for Coatzacoalcos on this account.

This survey has developed the fact that the position of Tonala has been laid down nine miles too far to the eastward of its proper position on the chart.

The currents are quite variable, and depend much upon the prevailing winds; a norther creating a strong easterly current, and before a norther or with a southerly wind, a westerly current.

I append the reports of Masters Henricks and Miller.

UNITED STATES STEAMER MAYFLOWER, (4TH RATE,)
Coatzacoalcos River, Mexico, January 24, 1871.

SIR: We have the honor to report that, in obedience to your verbal order of the 18th instant, we have run the coast-line from the mouth of the Coatzacoalcos River to the west bank of the river at Tonala.

Inclosed is a table of the courses run and the distances on each, in feet. The line was run at nearly high-water mark. The beach runs back about 120 feet from this line, and from this a line of hills rises about 30 feet, covered with a thick growth of bushes.

We found six streams of water: the Colorado, 120 feet wide; Gavilan, 148 feet; Rabon, 78 feet, and the Tortuguero, 15 feet. The others were merely rivulets, without names.

They are all open to the northward, but, after running back about 100 feet, turn to the eastward, and run parallel to the coast. The larger ones might be useful for watering ships, but only in very smooth weather, as the breakers are too heavy, even with a moderate breeze, for a boat to get in.

With a moderate breeze there are lines of breakers the whole length of the beach, extending about a quarter of a mile from shore.

There is 9 feet of water on the bar at Tonala at low water, with a rise and fall of tide about 3 feet.

The river at Tonala, measured between stations 48 and 49, is 589.2 feet wide.

The total distance from No. 1 to No. 50, is 16 miles 1,129 yards. Station 46 is just abreast of the wreck of the Cromwell.

Very respectfully, your obedient servants,

E. W. HENRICKS, *Master.*
JAS. M. MILLER, *Master.*

Lieutenant Commander N. H. FARQUHAR, U. S. N.,
Commanding United States Steamer Kansas, and Senior Officer Present.

UNITED STATES STEAMER MAYFLOWER, (4TH RATE,)
Coatzacoalcos River, Mexico, January 26, 1871.

SIR: We have to inform you that, in obedience to your orders, we have run the coast-line from the mouth of the Coatzacoalcos to the east bank of the Barilla. Inclosed is a table of the courses run, and the distance on each, in feet.

The coast is much more abrupt than from Coatzacoalcos to Tonala.

The hills rise to about the same height, but for some distance from the coast there is no vegetation except on the banks of the streams.

There are quite a number of small streams running back from the coast, but all so small as to be of no use for any purpose.

As you approach Barilla, the hills are much nearer to the water, leaving a beach of only about 60 feet.

We found 4 feet of water on the bar at low water, the rise and fall of tide about 2 feet, though we had no means by which to determine it accurately.

The river Barilla runs from the coast nearly west, but about three-quarters of a mile from its mouth it bends to the northward; its course then is about northwest by west.

Running from the mouth of the Barilla is a bayou, which runs nearly parallel to the coast for two miles, when it ends very abruptly in a fresh-water stream, about four inches deep; up to this point the water is from 1 to 2 fathoms deep, and is salt. It is called "the old mouth of the Tierra Nueva."

There is about a fathom of water at the mouth of the Barilla, but it shoals very rapidly to the turn, where there is only 6 inches.

The natives informed us that at high water a canoe might get through to the Coatzacoalcos, but they could not take us.

The width of the river at its mouth is about 400 feet. The whole distance from station 1 to station 56 is 12 miles 754 yards.

Very respectfully, your obedient servants,

E. W. HENRICKS, *Master.*
J. M. MILLER, *Master.*

Lieutenant Commander N. H. FARQUHAR,
    Commanding United States Steamer Kansas, and Senior Officer Present.

CHAPTER VII.

NORTHERS.

The season of these much-dreaded winds commences in October and ends in April, being most frequent in the months of January and February. The interval between successive ones is from four to ten days.

These winds, I think, are not as dangerous in these parts as is generally supposed, nor are they enough so to warrant the high rate of insurance charged.

In my opinion, most of the vessels that are lost are so on account of bad management; for the wind itself, which is never more than north by west, and more often northwest, together with a current setting to the eastward, enables any ordinary vessel to get over to the Campeachy Banks, where the sea is smooth, the wind does not blow so hard, and a good anchorage in as little as three fathoms if necessary.

The proper thing, then, to do if caught in a "norther," if it is not considered prudent to cross the bar, is to stand to the east on the *port-tack*, until a sufficient offing is reached; then heave to on that tack, or run over to Campeachy and anchor, and on no account to heave to with the ship's head to the westward, for the current and leeway will certainly set the vessel on shore.

The barometer is the most reliable indicator of a norther, and so certain as it falls, so certain will there be a norther during these months; nor is it necessary for the barometer to fall very much—a tenth or two is sometimes all it falls for the heaviest northers.

The time which elapses between the northers and the commencement of the falling of the barometer varies from twenty-four to forty eight hours, which ought to be sufficient warning. Do not be deceived by supposing that the falling of the barometer is due to the southerly wind, which may be prevailing at the time, for this wind is almost invariably followed by a norther. The range of the barometer in good weather is between $30^{in}.10$ and $30^{in}.20$; when it falls below the former, look out for a norther. It frequently falls to $29^{in}.80$, and during the norther rises as high as $30^{in}.50$.

I have not been able to connect the intensity of the norther with the fall of the barometer, for the wind has been just as strong with the barometer falling on to 30 as when it fell to $29^{in}.80$; but I have observed that the duration of the norther may be comparatively known by the fall of the barometer; when it falls slowly, and a great deal, you may expect the approaching norther to last at least three days; so when it falls rapidly, and only a tenth or two, the norther will most likely last not more than twenty-four hours.

Just before the norther comes the barometer ceases to fall; and when it has reached its height it ceases to rise, and as the wind and weather moderate it assumes its normal stand.

Among the signs of an approaching norther are Mount San Martino perfectly clear and its outline sharply defined, birds, such as buzzards, flying unusually high, and a fresh south wind.

During the winter months the northers are accompanied with much rain, and the weather very disagreeable.

C.

REPORT

OF THE

HYDROGRAPHIC SURVEYS ON THE PACIFIC COAST

IN CONNECTION WITH

A SHIP-CANAL ACROSS THE ISTHMUS OF TEHUANTEPEC.

BY

ALFRED HOPKINS, LIEUTENANT COMMANDER, U. S. N.

UNITED STATES STEAMER CYANE, (3D RATE,)
San Francisco, California, June —, 1871.

SIR: I have the honor to transmit herewith the charts, field-book, remark-book, &c., &c., of work performed by the officers of this ship, in accordance with your instructions, given last February.

The survey of the Upper Lagoon occupied a longer time than I had anticipated, as it was impossible to work during the time a norther was blowing, and about two weeks were lost from that cause.

I hope the results will be satisfactory, though I fear that the plan of making a harbor in the Upper Lagoon will be impracticable on account of the expense, a vast amount of dredging being required before it could be accomplished.

South and west of the islands in the lagoon is a large basin, with from 18 to 21 feet of water. The bottom is soft sand and mud, and could be readily dredged out to any required depth, provided, of course, that the soft sand is deep, and not merely a thin deposit over a rocky bottom. The latter appears to be probable, from the character of the surrounding country and of the islands, but we had no means of ascertaining.

A serious objection is the difficulty of making an entrance into the lagoon. The natural entrance, the Boca Barra, is utterly impracticable. The current is very swift, so rapid that boats could do nothing in it, and the sea breaks a mile from the beach in moderate weather, sending in a surf that was impossible to work in. No perceptible tide was found to exist in the lagoon, or in the Chicapa River, the only stream which was running, a description of which will be found in the remark-book of the Expedition. The bay of Ventosa I consider entirely unfit for an exit for the proposed canal. It is entirely exposed to any wind from east to west by the southward, and moreover is rapidly filling up with sand, as I was informed by persons acquainted with the coast.

The shore-line is now very different from that given by Mr. Trastour in 1850, the bay having become much less deep than it was. I was unable, from the want of provisions, to remain on the coast long enough to make a thorough survey of the bay of Ventosa, or of any points to the eastward.

The bay of Salina Cruz appears to me better adapted for an exit than any other point in the vicinity. True, it is not by any means a harbor, and has no protection from any wind but the northers, but the holding-ground is good, the best I have found on this coast, being a fine sand and mud, into which an anchor soon sinks.

During the time the Cyane was in Salina Cruz Bay—over two months—we had no wind from the southward strong enough to require a second anchor let go. I was informed that during the rainy season, *i. e.*, from May to November, it sometimes blows strongly from the south-southwest, and occasionally heavily from east-southeast, the latter lasting only a few hours, the gales, however, being more of the nature of squalls.

It would be, in my opinion, perfectly practicable to build breakwaters that would make the bay entirely safe as an exit for the proposed canal, and also a safe harbor for shipping to await their turn for making the passage.

A curved or half-moon breakwater, from the rocky western point of the bay (marked H on the chart) to a point a little south and east of the buoy, would be a protection against winds and sea from south-southwest; and, if thought necessary, a short breakwater, extending south-southwest from the eastern point, would afford shelter from east-southeast squalls. The latter I consider hardly necessary, as there is never much swell from that direction. During the two months the Cyane was in the port, there was a long swell from south to south-southwest, and this is the only swell that ever becomes important, according to my own observations and information from natives.

There are not so many soundings on the chart of Salina Cruz as I should like to have taken, but I had lost all boats but one, and, being very short of provisions, was obliged to leave the work unfinished as it should have been done.

The chart will give an accurate idea of the place, and the missing soundings may be safely filled in from those plotted by the distance from the land, for the bottom is very regular.

The expenses of the survey were greater than I supposed they would be, but we were entirely at the mercy of the rascally natives, and equally rascally persons who claim to be "American citizens," in transporting boats, &c., and also in sending provisions to the party.

During Holy Week it was almost impossible to get a cart to take absolute necessaries, and then only at a perfectly scandalous price.

I was careful to be as economical as possible, but I fear you will be surprised at the amount remaining due to Paymaster Colby. I assure you, however, that it was as small as it could be made under the circumstances.

I beg to call your attention to the zeal displayed by Master C. B. Gill, Ensigns F. P. Gilmore and U. Sebree, and Master T. H. Stevens, in carrying out to the best of their ability your instructions. Though I fear the work may not be quite so satisfactory as you desire, it is to be attributed to want of time rather than to any neglect on their part.

I think, indeed, they are entitled to great credit for having done so much and so well with the instruments they had to work with, and under the difficulties of climate, &c., that they were obliged to encounter.

Ensign F. P. Gilmore was the draughtsman of the charts, which would have been copied in ink but for want of paper and also for the want of time.

I am, sir, very respectfully, your most obedient servant,

ALFRED HOPKINS,
Lieutenant Commander.

Captain R. W. SHUFELDT, U. S. N.,
Commanding Tehuantepec Surveying Expedition, Washington, D. C.

UNITED STATES SHIP CYANE, AT SEA, MAY 10, 1871,
Latitude 15° 17′ north, longitude 110° 04′ west.

SIR: I have the honor to report that the survey of the lagoons, according to instructions, is finished, and I herewith transmit to you the chart, field-book, journal of soundings, and remark-book.

It is evident, from these records, that it will require an immense amount of dredging to make "an artificial harbor of the upper lagoon," for vessels of twenty feet draught. The soundings show, generally, a sand or mud bottom; but the volcanic origin of these lagoons make it a very possible fact that neither the sand or mud extend to any great depth, being the deposits of the various streams which flow into the lagoon during the rainy season.

About Cerro Poigetoe, and the islands to its westward, and south of these islands to within a thousand yards of San Dionisio Spit, there is from 18 to 20 feet of water. In no other part of the lagoon did we find any extensive soundings of more than 15 feet.

Examined the Chicapa River "as to tides;" found no change in height at a thousand yards from the mouth. The slight rise and fall nearer the mouth was the result rather of the changes in the direction and force of the wind than of any tidal influence. This river is a most sluggish stream at this season. I found by cross-sectioning the volume of water passing per second, to be 3,379 cubic inches. At most any point along the narrow strips of land separating the lagoon from the sea, cuts for the canal can easily be made, the land being all low and sandy.

The sea-coast from the Boca Barra to the Bay of Ventosa presents no natural qualifications for a harbor, and this bay is fast filling up with changing sands; and, not considering this obstacle, a very extensive breakwater would be necessary to make this bay a snug harbor.

A line of soundings from the canal of St. Teresa to the Boca Barra, show a depth varying from 6 to 16 feet, and at the Boca Barra the shifting sands, strong current, and heavy surf, make this proposed outlet of the canal very unfeasible.

The zeal and efficiency of the officers of this ship associated with me in the severe labor of this survey, deserve the highest commendation.

Very respectfully,

C. B. GILL,
Master, United States Navy, Commanding Surveying Expedition.

To Lieutenant Commander ALFRED HOPKINS,
Commanding.

MINATITLAN, MEXICO,
Tuesday, April 25, 1871.

SIR: In obedience to your instructions I have to report that I proceeded from La Chivela to Tehuantepec, to be present during the time the survey of the Pacific lagoons was being carried on by the officers and men of the United States sloop Cyane, ordered to report to you for that duty.

A party, consisting of Master C. B. Gill, (in charge,) Ensigns F. B. Gilmore, U. Sebree, and Thomas H. Stevens, and eighteen men, with two boats and necessary instruments, left Salina Cruz Bay on the 2d of March, for La Punta de Agua, the western point of the upper lagoon, the boats being transported by land in carts. Commencing their labors at that point, they were carried on around the northern shore, crossing the land at Santa Teresa, and connecting their lines at La Punta de Agua on the 10th of April, embracing a line run across the lower lagoon to the Boca Barra, with tidal observations of that channel; also a line running through the narrow Tilema Lagoon. I made it my object to be present with the working party, to see that your instructions were carried out, and to inform myself, as fully as possible, of the nature of the lagoons, and as to the practicability of running the ship-canal from the line of the Chicapa River through the upper lagoon, to connect with the Pacific at the Bay of Salina Cruz, the latter being, in my opinion, the only part of the isthmean coast where it would be feasible to form a harbor and a port of entry; and then only by the means of breakwaters, for which ample materials are to be had in near proximity, the holding-ground being excellent, in 7 to 12 fathoms of water, and at distances of one to three miles from the beach.

The bay is perfectly protected from the strong northerly gales; and though during the stay of the Cyane at this port there occurred no southeast gales, it is my opinion that breakwaters would afford sure protection to vessels anchored under their lee. The tidal current sets east and west, along the coast, the strength not yet having been determined.

The superior, or upper lagoon, embraces an area bounded by a dry-season coast-line of fifty-one miles, (nautical,) similar to an immense flat covered by the sea-water, and separated by narrow and low sand-spits from the ocean itself, and receiving the waters from numerous rivers and streams traversing the Pacific plains, and receiving, besides, the quicksands and deposits from those streams. The upper lagoon is intersected from east to west for nearly two-thirds of its length by a chain of islands, the continuation of a range of hills to the eastward, and among them was found the deepest water, 19 feet. Bottom, generally, of mud and soft sand; on the south shore, rocky. A line through Santa Teresa Canal gave a channel of 17 feet, but forming a bar in the lower lagoon, with 4 feet of water. The Bocca Barra Channel, with its rapid currents, its bottom of quicksands, and the impassible barrier of surf-lines, render it useless for navigation. Between Bocca Bara and Salina Cruz lies the deserted Bay of Ventosa, which receives the deposits from the Tehuantepec River, so that, from observations made, Salina Cruz seems to be the natural terminus, if the upper lagoon can be used. This survey was carried on during the dry season, but the high-water line could easily be traced, showing that in the season of rain there must be an increased depth of 3 to 4 feet.

I would beg leave to state that the work was carried on by the Cyane's officers under many local difficulties, such as the scarcity of fresh water, the strength of the winds, both from the north and from the south, raising such a sea that at times it was impossible to venture out in their boats, and even one of those was lost by being swamped, exposed to the sea.

Master C. B. Gill will forward, through Lieutenant Commander Hopkins, commanding Cyane, complete records of the work, and a detailed report, upon the arrival of the vessel at San Francisco.

I am, very respectfully, your obedient servant,

PHILIP H. COOPER,
Lieutenant Commander, United States Navy.

Captain R. W. SHUFELDT,
Commanding Surveying Expedition to Tehuantepec and Nicaragua.

D.

REPORT

ON THE

GEOLOGY, MINERALOGY, NATURAL HISTORY, INHABITANTS,

AND

AGRICULTURE OF THE ISTHMUS OF TEHUANTEPEC.

BY

JOHN C. SPEAR, SURGEON, U. S. N.

July 15, 1871.

Sir: I have the honor, in obedience to your order, to submit herewith a report on the work assigned me last winter, in connection with the exploration of the Isthmus of Tehuantepec. It is an account of the geology, mineralogy, climate, diseases, and inhabitants of that region; and, in addition, contains other information of a practical bearing on the proposed interoceanic ship-canal at Tehuantepec.

Very respectfully, your obedient servant,

JOHN C. SPEAR,
Surgeon, United States Navy.

Captain R. W. SHUFELDT, U. S. N.,
Commanding United States Tehuantepec and Nicaragua Surveying Expedition.

CHAPTER I.

GEOLOGY.

The Sierra on the Isthmus of Tehuantepec takes an east and west direction, and is at this point both very low and narrow. The highest peaks have an elevation of less than 3,000 feet, and the table-lands and mountain-passes about 800 feet; and the width of the range, including the table-lands, is, at its narrowest part, perhaps twenty-five miles. Owing to this depression in the Cordillera, the geological formation of the Isthmus presents but little variety—probably much less than is found in the same range to the east or west, where the elevation is greater. This also explains the scarcity of mineral substances, which is certainly one of the marked features of the Isthmus.

Running nearly parallel with both the Atlantic and Pacific shores, and much nearer to the latter, are two limestone-belts; the one to the south forming the Masahua Range, and the other the Majada Range. Between them there is the usual synclinal valley, which constitutes the table-lands or mesas of Tarifa and Chivela. The Masahua Range seems to be the continuation of the Cordillera, and forms the true dividing-ridge between the two oceans. The nucleus of these ranges is, in its composition, blue mountain limestone, which forms everywhere the summits of the dividing ridges and the highest peaks. It has been upheaved through a formation of shale and gneiss, which now constitute the foot-hills on either side. The gneiss rock is, however, rarely exposed, except in the dry beds of the deep arroyos, and in other low places. The superficial shaly formation is traversed in almost every direction by narrow veins of milk-quartz, and in many localities, where the shale has been disintegrated and washed away by the rains, the quartz, in the form of small pebbles, is thickly strewn over the surface of the hills.

The southern limestone-ridge becomes abruptly depressed or broken at the Cerro Rineconchapa on the Pacific plains, just at the outlet of the Pass of Tarifa; and the northern ridge, from Mount Timbon in its course to the eastward, becomes gradually depressed until, along the Arroyo de Tarifa, at the hacienda of the same name, it dips so low as to disappear altogether; but it reappears abruptly in the Cerro Convento, which borders the eastern limits of the plain of Tarifa, and then continues again its easterly course along the valley of the Monetza. In relation to the construction of the interoceanic canal, it is a very fortunate circumstance that both these limestone-belts of the Cordillera are thus depressed at the same point. Indeed, they apparently disappear altogether on the table-lands of Tarifa and in the pass of the same name, while along the Chivela, Masahua, and San Miguel routes they crop out in many places. This geological formation of the country crossed by the Tarifa route suggests at once that we have here the lowest point in the divide, and the level gives positive proof of it.

The general strike of the Cordillera is about north 35° west; and the dip for the most part is nearly perpendicular; in some places, however, it is 60° to 70° to the southwest. The shale in Tarifa Pass strikes southwest by west, and the gneiss, in the same locality, north 10° west, with a dip of 75° to the southeast. On the whole, it appears that the dip and strike of the rocks in this locality do not follow any very uniform rules, so far as we were able to judge.

The accompanying geological plan of the Isthmus exhibits at a glance the different rock formations, and shows the extent and locality of each one in a much better manner than it is possible to do by any written description.

The oldest portion of the Isthmus evidently began its super-aquatic existence at a comparatively recent period, geologically speaking. The limestone ridges of the Sierra were probably upheaved during the cretaceous period—certainly not previous to it; the proof of which is to be found in the fact that certain deposits of chalk in the Chivela Pass rest on the mountain limestone, and *has its inclination*, which, of course, was given to it at the time of the upheaval. This chalk is rather coarse, of a yellowish color, and exhibits, under the microscope, after having been treated with nitro-muriatic acid, minute spicules of sponge, which establish its cretaceous origin. We failed to find any other sort of fossil in it. It is, therefore, evident that during the cretaceous period when this chalk was forming at the bottom of the sea, the waters of the two oceans joined at this point.

At a later period the great level plains on either side of the Cordillera were formed, the part nearest the foot of the mountains being the oldest. This is evident from the belt of modern lime, deposited in horizontal strata, and probably of the eocene period, which skirts along the foot of the Sierra on the Pacific side from Tehuantepec to the Chicapa River. Farther down on the plain this formation disappears, and a later one, composed of loam and shell-marl, comes into view. Here we pass through extensive tracts where the surface-soil is a dark loam, in which a certain fresh-water shell, the *Ampularia Cumingii*, in a fossil state, is met with in abundance. The same shell is found alive in the stagnant fresh-water ponds of small extent which are occasionally met with at the present day on this plain. It therefore appears that the Pacific plain, now so dry and parched, was, not very long ago, partially covered with fresh-water lakes or ponds of considerable extent.

Bordering the lagoons, the surface-soil, to the depth of 2 or 3 feeet, is filled with species of fossil *Turritella*, *Ostrea*, and *Trigona*, and the same is the case in the bottom-lands about the mouth of the Tehuantepec River. These shells, all of which belong to the salt-water variety, are still found alive in great abundance in the waters of the lagoons and the ocean. This, then, proves that the lagoons, at a recent period, covered a larger area than they do at the present time. Indeed, we were told by the natives that, previous to the year 1820, the lagoons covered a much larger tract of country than they do now, and in that year, by some convulsion of nature, they were reduced to their present limits. However correct or incorrect the date may be, it is quite evident such an event has taken place and at a comparatively recent period.

We noticed a great many bowlders scattered about the elevated section of the Isthmus. Generally they rest quite on the surface, and many of them are on the summits of hills or ridges 100 feet or more above the surrounding country. The largest ones are 20 to 30 feet square, and all of them in composition correspond to the rocks that form the peaks or high ridges in their immediate vicinity. On the hill where the village of Santa Maria Chimalapa stands there are, in a space not larger than half an acre, twelve large bowlders from 4 to 15 feet in height, and generally globular in shape. Most of them are ranged in a well-marked line, the direction of which is south 30° west; and to the southwest there is a high mountain-ridge, between which and the location of the bowlders the deep valley of the Milgro intervenes. There is other evidence of glacial action on the Isthmus, but a full account of it is foreign to the purpose of this report.

In making a canal-cut across the Pacific plain, sand, loam, and shell-marl will be encountered, and near the foot of the Sierra a belt of modern lime, quite soft and pliable, will be met with. Though this portion of the Isthmus is arid, with a sandy soil very permeable to water, we found the wells in the month of February contained water at an average depth of 28 feet below the surface. February is about the middle of the dry season here, and the inhabitants assured us that even as late as May, which is the close of the dry season, the water in the wells does not fall much below the point where we saw it. In Tarifa Pass shale above and gneiss below will be encountered in the cut, and possibly below these, in a few places, compact limestone. On the table-lands the surface is loam and clay, which, judging from the banks of the arroyos and gulleys, we estimated extends to the depth of about 25 feet on an average. Below this there is shale and gneiss. The Atlantic plain is composed of alluvial deposit, often 40 feet in thickness, with here and there a few unimportant upheavals of soft talc, rotten sandstone, and limestone, none of which are likely to present any difficulties for a canal-cut.

On the narrow strip of sandy country along the Pacific shore, from La Ventosa to Boca Barra, the road crosses from time to time gulleys ten to twenty feet deep, and twenty-five to fifty feet wide, which, at first sight, we supposed were formed by the action of water during the rainy season, but in a few hours a norther began to blow, and the manner in which these singular cuts are made was quite apparent. The violent wind plowed up the loose sand, and carried it along like drifting snow, forming by this process deep cuts, which cross the country in a direction from north to south.

MINERALOGY.

On the Coachapa River, twelve miles from its mouth, there are several extensive deposits of petroleum and asphaltum, the two principal deposits or springs of which we took occasion to visit and examine. One is on the right bank of the river, about three miles in the interior, in an easterly direction from a ranch called Santo Cristobal, and is reached by a bridle-path through a dense forest. The land is rolling and heavily timbered where this deposit is located, and we estimated that the surface of the spring was at least fifty feet above the Coachapa River. In a space of about half an acre we counted ten springs of various sizes, from four to ten feet in diameter, and on the surface quite distinct from one another; but the ground between the several springs is, in many places, soft and spongy, and on treading on it, it gives the impression that it is resting on a liquid mass. One of our party, while busily engaged in collecting some specimens of the purest petroleum, gradually sunk into this spongy earth to the depth of two feet or more before he was aware of his situation, and it required a vigorous effort to extricate himself. The substance found in these springs, when unmixed with earth or dried leaves, is black, and is about as thick as molasses. In order to examine the depth of the deposit, we cut poles twenty-five feet long, and pushed them down several of the springs the entire length of the pole without touching any bottom. There is no evidence of any considerable overflow of these springs, nor is the temperature of their liquid contents increased by internal heat so far as we were able to ascertain. Heavy forest trees are found growing abundantly on the half-acre in which the springs are located, and, indeed, these trees are quite as numerous and large as in any other locality in the surrounding wood. Even the underbrush grows as in any other part of the forest, except in the very tarry openings themselves. We observed about these springs a great many tracks of the wild Mexican hog, and our guide assured us that these animals come here to drink of this substance. Crude petroleum being an excellent application to free the body of the myriads of insects which annoy the animals in this region, it is possible that these wild hogs wallow in it for this purpose.

The other deposit is on the left bank of the river, half a mile in the interior, and perhaps a mile above Santo Cristobal. It is located in an open potrero, which is subject to the annual overflow. Both to the south and the north of it there is a small range of hills, perhaps fifty feet high, and a mile or more away. The range to the north is composed of limestone, and the one to the south contains some deposits of sulphur in a very pure condition, so we were credibly informed. We estimated that the extent of the surface covered with pure asphaltum is about five hundred square feet, and it is in the form of several irregular patches. The soil of the potrero, for several hundred yards in all directions, is also impregnated with this substance, but not in quantity sufficient to prevent the growth of the wild camalote, which covers this open plain, growing luxuriantly even to the very borders of the pond of pure asphaltum. The surface of this pond is hard, and one can walk all over it. There are, here and there, in the upper crust, cracks of considerable size, into which we inserted sticks, and at the depth of three feet found the mass to be quite soft, having the consistency of dough. This pond of asphaltum resembles, in several respects, the famous pitch-lake in Trinidad.

From both of these localities we obtained specimens, and they have been examined by Dr. Henry T. Slemmer, a gentleman who has had a great deal of experience in refining petroleum. He informs me that the specimen from the right bank of the river contains about fifty per cent. of what is known in the market as heavy oil of petroleum, which will make a good lubricating-oil. It contains neither benzine, gasoline, nor the light oil of petroleum—the common burning oil of the shops—having lost these usual ingredients of crude petroleum probably through volcanic heat; and this is rendered the more likely from the fact that the specimen contains a great deal of sulphurous matter. It is possible to make from this heavy oil a burning-oil, by treating it repeatedly with sulphuric acid, and subjecting it to several distillations; but this would be very expensive, and probably render a refined burning-oil obtained from the Tehuantepec petroleum twice as costly as that distilled from the common crude petroleum found in Pennsylvania. The specimen from the other deposit is mineral pitch, or Jews' pitch, and contains no petroleum in any form, and is of no commercial value, except as asphaltum.

There is an abundant supply of common salt found on the Isthmus, and it is obtained either from the salinas or from salt-water springs. Along the Pacific sea-shore and on the borders of the Laguna Superior there are, at certain points, extensive natural deposits of salt mixed with the earth, and these places are called salinas. Such deposits are found in low bottoms, which are separated from the sea or the waters of the lagoon by narrow ridges of sand. It is evident that these salinas were at a very recent period a part of the sea, from which they have been cut off by the beach, which is continually advancing and encroaching on the sea along this shore. In the salinas, the soil, to the depth of many feet, is saturated with salt, and during the rainy months these low bottoms become filled with fresh water, which gradually abstracts the saline matter from the soil, and when the water is all evaporated in the dry season, the surface is left covered with a deposit of pure salt, in many places as much as three inches in thickness. Laborers are set to work, generally in the month of February, to collect the salt. They gather it up with their hands and make large piles of it, after which it is put into ox-carts and hauled into the nearest town, where it is sold, a considerable quantity of it being purchased to supply the interior of Mexico. There are a great many of these salinas in this vicinity, and some of them have an area of a hundred acres or even more, and they are altogether, if judiciously managed, capable of yielding a very large quantity of excellent salt, which, owing to its cheapness, might become a profitable article of export as soon as there is convenient transportation for it to a good market. On the Coachapa River we found a spring of salt-water, from which the mulattoes residing there manufacture enough salt to supply the neighborhood by evaporating the salt-water over a fire. The humidity of the atmosphere is generally so great at this point, and the rains are of so frequent occurrence, that it is hardly practicable to manufacture salt by solar influences alone.

There are, on the Isthmus, several deposits of what may be called "brown coal." One is on the Coatzacoalcos River, another on the Puerta River, and still another has been discovered near the sea-shore, west of the Coatzacoalcos. This material is light, rather soft, without luster, and, in general appearance, closely resembles cannel-coal. It takes fire on holding it in the flame of a candle, and burns with a bluish flame, but, unlike cannel-coal, small attached fragments do not continue to burn longer than a few seconds. While burning, it emits a slightly bituminous odor, and it does not melt. A sufficient quantity of this coal was not collected with which to make a proper trial of its burning qualities in the furnaces of one of the steamers; a few lumps, however, were burned in a small forge, under the observation of the chief engineer of the Kansas, but the experiment was, for several reasons, unsatisfactory. A canoe-load of it was brought down the river and thrown on the bank near Minatitlan, where the Indian women found it, and used it all in a short time, (burning a little wood with it,) on the small fires they make in the open air to cook their food. Of course, all the specimens we saw were from the out-crops, and probably inferior to that further below the surface.

We found several small veins of specular iron-ore, from three to four inches in width, in veins of quartz, in the Chivela Pass. This ore is black, and in appearance closely resembles plumbago. In the brook at Tarifa there are masses of red hematite; and it is said other varieties of iron-ore are found in certain localities on the Isthmus.

During the last twenty years the Isthmus of Tehuantepec has been extensively explored for gold by American miners of considerable experience in California. They washed the sand in the beds of various rivers, and discovered some gold in several places, but never in sufficient quantity to pay. The best washings were found in the Malatengo River, but even these were abandoned after a short working, and considerable sums of money were lost in the operation. One of these miners is still pursuing his explorations for gold—" prospecting," as he calls it—and is now located on the Chicapa River, far up in the mountains, beyond the limits of the habitations of the Indians. He informed us that he succeeded in getting a few dollars' worth of gold-dust every year, hardly enough, now, to pay his expenses, but he fully expects to find, some day, a rich pocket, when his fortune will be made. No attempt has ever been made, so far as we can learn, to search for gold as it occurs in the rocks, in the hills, and mountains, but all the operations of the miners have been conducted in the sands and alluvial deposits along the courses of the rivers. On the Isthmus there is a very common belief that rich deposits of gold exist in the bed of the Uspanapa River, high up in the mountains. At the highest point we reached, on this river, about fifty miles from its mouth, the sand on its bottom and along its banks contains an abundance of yellow mica in the form of minute scales, but we did not observe any traces of gold.

ROCKS FOR CONSTRUCTING MATERIAL.

There is an abundance of this material on the Isthmus, and there are many varieties of it, among which the engineer will find all that he requires for the construction of the proposed interoceanic canal, with the single exception of hydraulic lime; and even this, there is some probability, will be found in one of the many different varieties of limestone in the mountainous section of the Isthmus. As a general rule, this material is conveniently located along the proposed route, but this is not always the case.

Beginning on the Pacific shore at Salina Cruz, the hills, in the form of a semicircle about this harbor, are composed of granulite, a rock closely allied to granite, and it will make an excellent stone for general building purposes, as well as for constructing a breakwater. The bold, jutting bluffs on either side of the harbor, composed of this rock, show, at a glance, how well it has resisted for ages the disintegrating action of the surf. The surface-layer of this formation is stratified, which will render the quarrying of it comparatively easy. But from the nature of the rock, it is hardly probable that the stratifications extend very far below the surface. The supply of it, at this point, is practically inexhaustible; and it is also found in abundance at La Ventosa, where, however, it is not of so fine a quality. Some of the hills about Huilotepec are composed of this rock, which may possibly be found a more convenient point to quarry it for a portion of the route. Unfortunately, there is no limestone in the coast-range, but the soft tertiary lime is met with three miles northwest of the city of Tehuantepec, and, two miles further on, the hard limestone occurs. The natives use the former for building purposes and for whitewashing, &c., preferring it to the hard variety, on account of the comparatively small amount of heat necessary to reduce it to quicklime. The small hills about Tehuantepec, and several isolated ones on the plain near San Geronimo, as represented on the geological chart, are composed of syenite, or rather there are veins of it running through them, from which good building-stones can be quarried.

In the mountainous section of the Isthmus compact limestone, blue and white marble, and gneiss, are abundant, and all of them are found at convenient points along the proposed route. In the Chivela Pass, Masahua Pass, the Cerro Convento, and in several localities along the valley of the Monetza, we observed extensive formations of white marble.

On the Atlantic plains no good constructing material was discovered, though it is probable that in the sandstone regions of this section, a little below the surface, the sandstone becomes less coarse-grained and not so friable as that found on the surface. On the Coachapa and Jaltepec Rivers, and near the village Jaltipan, there are limestone formations, from which the natives burn quicklime of an excellent quality.

The trachyte which forms the bed of the upper Coatzacoalcos can be easily quarried along the little streams that flow into the main river from the south, and this, with the compact limestone in the valley of the Milagro, will furnish sufficient material at convenient points for the construction of the proposed feeder. Along the banks of the larger rivers, on both sides of the Isthmus, as well as on the table-lands, there is an abundant supply of sand well adapted for building purposes.

THERMAL SPRINGS.

There is on the Pacific plains, half a mile from the Sierra and midway between the passes of Tarifa and Chivela, a hot spring, which has an extensive reputation in this section of the republic as a remedy for rheumatism, scrofula, syphilis, and cutaneous diseases. A quantity of this water, which we collected for the purpose of making an analysis, was unfortunately lost in transit on the Isthmus. The spring is circular in form, with a rim of calcareous tufa surrounding it, and is about six feet in diameter and two feet in depth. The water bubbles up through several small openings, and just at these points it is so hot that it burns the hand, but the general temperature of the spring is about 94° Fahrenheit. The water has a slight saline taste, and occasionally a faint odor of sulphureted hydrogen is perceived. As it bubbles up from the interior of the earth, it brings with it small pieces of gravel and sand, mixed abundantly with minute calcareous shells. The rock formation in this vicinity is limestone. We observed small fish swimming about in the spring, and the cattle grazing near it came and drank of its waters while we were there. Several hundred yards from this spring there is a similar one, situated on a limestone cliff fifty feet above the plain. The view of the Pacific plains, the lagoons, and ocean from this point, is exceedingly fine.

In La Chivela Pass, at a point in the course of the Rio Verde, a short distance above the ford, where the river flows between high perpendicular walls of limestone, there are several remarkable thermal springs. As yet, so far as we are aware, they have not been resorted to by invalids, and it is therefore impossible to make any assertions as to their medicinal value. The temperature is 98° Fahrenheit, and the water has a sulphurous taste, and the rocks in the vicinity are blackened by the escaping sulphureted hydrogen. We caught little fish in the springs, and although they are the same species found in the cold waters of the Rio Verde, their colors are less bright.

EARTHQUAKES.

In the Cordillera of the Isthmus there are no evidences of very recent volcanic action, and there are no extinct craters, which were once active volcanoes, of any considerable extent. Sharp, rugged peaks of compact limestone and crater-like precipices of the same material are frequently met with, but in no place did we find the cones of scoria, lava, &c., so characteristic of long-continued volcanic action. San Martin, a detached peak near the shores of the Gulf, and not belonging to the Cordillera, is a small volcano, and is occasionally active, but it was not so during our stay on the Isthmus. It is as much as forty miles distant from the nearest point of the proposed canal, and more than one hundred miles from the part where the constructions most liable to injury by volcanic action or earthquakes will be built. The singular freedom of this region from volcanoes, both active and extinct, and, in consequence, the less probability of violent earthquakes, is certainly an important consideration in favor of the Isthmus of Tehuantepec as a location for the interoceanic ship canal. It is not true, however, that no earthquakes occur here, for they do; but they seem to be less violent and not so frequent as at many other points in the volcanic regions of Central America. When we were at work in the mountains, it was no uncommon thing to experience slight shocks of earthquakes, and on the 6th of February a severe one passed across the Isthmus. From all the reports we received, it seems that the shock was more violent in the Chimalapa region, where we happened to be, than at any other point, so far as we could learn. There the doors and window of the house we occupied were unhinged, a section of the adobe wall over the window was broken in, portions of the plastering and some of the thatched roof were thrown down, our animals were thrown on their knees and were unable to regain their feet, and the old house, with its long grass roof, near which we had been sitting, shook like a load of hay passing over a stony road, which, indeed, it much resembled. It was exceedingly difficult to stand erect, and we found it necessary, in order to maintain this position, to hold fast to an old stone wall which happened to be near. The shock, which lasted sixty-four seconds, came from the east and passed to the west, and was preceded by a loud rumbling noise. The motion was wholly of the vibratory or horizontal sort. It happened at seven o'clock and twelve minutes in the evening of a day which had been remarkably clear and calm for that locality. There was an indescribable gloomy appearance about the sky and the sunset, which was noticed and remarked upon by the chief engineer of the exploring party only a minute or two before the occurrence of the shock. It certainly seemed to us that twilight was unusually prolonged that evening, but unfortunately no specific observations were made on this point. Five hours later we experienced "the return wave," as it has been called, which, however, lasted only a few seconds, and was not nearly so violent as the first shock. We could not learn that this feature of this particular earthquake was felt at any other point on the Isthmus. On inquiry, we ascertained that about a year before this shock a similar one was experienced on the Isthmus, and still other well-known shocks are mentioned. Owing to the peculiar construction of the houses, but very little damage has ever been done them, but the large stone churches have been from time to time materially injured.

CHAPTER II.

CLIMATE.

In the three natural divisions of the Isthmus, the climate is essentially different, so that a separate account of each is necessary.

On the Pacific plains, the rainy season begins late in June, and ends in September. During the remaining nine months of the year there is no rain whatever. The soil by the last of November is dry, and vegetation soon becomes parched and scanty. From November until June, the corn-patches or milpas have to be supplied with water by irrigation. Some plants and certain sorts of timber, as the indigo and the acacia, flourish in this dry soil, but the general character of the vegetation covering this plain is small and stunted. Along the banks of several rivers, and near the lagoons, there is occasionally an exception to this rule, and the timber there is large and valuable. Many of the rivers of this plain, some of them considerable streams, become quite dry by the beginning of March. The northers, which are so common in the winter season, never bring with them rain, as they generally do on the Atlantic slope and on the table-lands, but, instead, clouds of dust and drifting sand are caught up by these violent winds, and are driven across the plain in a southerly direction, and finally fall into the Pacific Ocean. Oftentimes, standing at the foot of the Cordillera when a norther is blowing, you can see dense rain-clouds, less than eight hundred feet above you, deluging the elevated table-lands of Tarifa and Chivela, and the adjacent mountains; but the instant these clouds are driven over the dividing range into the dry atmosphere of the Pacific plains they are absorbed and melt away, not a drop of rain falling where you are. A rainbow is often seen in such clouds, the whole affording a singularly interesting and beautiful phenomenon, and illustrating in the most forcible manner the marked difference in the humidity of the atmosphere in two contiguous sections of the Isthmus. The temperature is relatively higher than on the Atlantic plains, and this is especially the case in the winter season, for the prevailing north wind, having lost its moisture in the form of rain on the Atlantic side, is considerable warmer when it reaches this point; and, in addition, the Pacific plain has a direct southern exposure, with the sierra forming a high natural wall to the north. We found many days, even in December and January, very warm when exposed to the midday sun, the thermometer often standing in the shade above 80°. May is the warmest month, and December is the coldest. The plain is covered with a stunted growth of timber and other vegetation, generally not higher than twenty feet, which is just high enough to keep off the breeze, and not high enough to afford any shade along the roads or bridle-paths, and the traveler, therefore, not unfrequently finds these dusty roads exceedingly hot. Persons belonging to the European races residing here rarely expose themselves to the midday sun, but perform their journeys or out-door labors in the mornings and evenings, and at night. But of course we could not follow this practice, and it is not believed the health of any of us suffered in consequence. Except in the rainy season there are very few cloudy days. There is nothing enervating in this climate, which is so apt to be the case in tropical regions not elevated. The extreme dryness of the atmosphere, like that of Egypt, induces insensible perspiration to a very marked degree, and the body is in this way kept cool, and no disinclination is felt to physical exertion, as is sure to be the case in a damp climate where the temperature is as high as it is here.

On the elevated table-lands and the mountainous district the rainy season begins early in June and ends in November, except in the Chimalapa and Guichicovi regions, where it rains more or less until March. On the plains of Tarifa and Chivela it occasionally rains a little as late as February. The rain after November generally comes with the northers, which are then called "wet northers." The temperature of this division of the Isthmus is considerably cooler than on the Pacific plains, and the difference is even greater than the ordinary change due to elevation, for this would be less than 3° Fahrenheit, while the actual difference in the winter months ranges from 5° to 10°. The contiguous high mountain ranges of vast extent on either side to the east and the west, and the increased velocity of the Isthmus wind-currents, where they pass through the narrow break in the Cordillera, are undoubtedly the cause of the temperate climate found in this portion of the Isthmus. The pine and the oak of the temperate zone are the most common trees in all exposed localities; while at the same elevation, in spots of small extent, well protected by hills or spurs of mountains from the wind-currents, the tropical vegetation of the plains is found. This condition is best seen in Masahua Pass, which, although quite as elevated as Chivela Plains, possesses the flora and fauna of the lower regions. During a norther the thermometer sometimes falls as low as 60°, and the piercing wind, at the same time, makes it seem much colder. Thick woolen clothing and a pair of heavy blankets are needed in this region during the winter months.

On the Atlantic plains the rains set in about the 10th of June, and continue until November; and after this, throughout the winter, perhaps half the northers are accompanied with rain, and nearly all of them with cloudy weather. At Súchil it rains more than at any other point on the Isthmus. The climate of this portion of the Isthmus is damp, except for two months, April and May, which time is the most pleasant part of the year. In consequence of the abundant supply of rain and the tropical temperature, vegetation attains an excessive growth, presenting in this respect a striking contrast with the stunted vegetation of the plains on the Pacific side. The rains which occur after October do not seriously interfere with out-door work any more than the usual autumnal rains in the United States. It is rather cooler than on the Pacific plains, and the thermometer occasionally falls 20° in the course of a few hours when a norther is coming on. Thin woolen clothes are the most comfortable, as well as the most wholesome, for the greater part of the year.

The general direction of the neck of land forming the Isthmus of Tehuantepec, runs from east to west, and the Cordillera here is very low and narrow. On the Atlantic side there are lateral ranges of mountains, which form on the Isthmus a sort of funnel, with the large end toward the north. Through this passage the north wind, so prevalent in the Gulf of Mexico in the autumn and winter, rushes, increasing in velocity the nearer it approaches the narrowest part of this funnel-like passage, until, when it reaches the plains of Tarifa and Chivela, it is blowing a furious gale. It often happens that a gentle north wind at Minatitlan is a severe norther at Tarifa. The high, dense forests of the Atlantic plains break very much the force of the northers, so that a few miles from the Gulf coast up the Coatzacoalcos, ships at anchor are perfectly protected at all times from these winds, and the growing crops are not injured by them. On the Pacific plains, at some points, it is found to be necessary to build thatched fences, to protect the gardens and fields, so great is the force of the northers there. But it is on the elevated and exposed table-lands about Tarifa and Chivela where these winds are most violent. We recollect that, on one occasion, in the month of January, a severe norther continued for fifteen days without any intermission. They would, no doubt, occasionally cause some delay and additional expense for ships passing through a canal here. Vessels bound to the Atlantic side would have to make their way across the exposed table-land for a distance of twenty miles or more, directly in the face of these very strong winds. In the summer the prevailing wind is from the south, and it rarely blows with any great violence.

Frost is never seen on the Isthmus, and none of the mountain peaks in sight, from any point, have snow on them, even in the winter. The temperature in the summer never rises very high, rarely above 90°.

The scenery in the mountainous regions, and from elevated localities overlooking the Pacific plains, is, at many points, exceedingly fine.

HEALTH, DISEASES, ETC.

In a tropical region like the Isthmus of Tehuantepec, and especially in those sections of it where the temperature is high, the rain-fall abundant throughout the year, and the land low and swampy, one must expect to meet with malarious fevers.

Intermittent and remittent fevers occur in all parts of the Isthmus. On thé Pacific plains, and on the elevated plateaus of the Central Division, they rarely originate except in the months of August, September, and October, although it is not an uncommon thing to find even here, at any season of the year, cases of these fevers, the seeds of which were probably contracted during the unhealthy season, or in some other portion of the Isthmus. Here these diseases are generally of a mild type, and yield readily to the ordinary quinine treatment. We were, however, credibly informed that in several localities on the Pacific side, and especially near the lagoons, malarial fevers were prevalent even in the dry season. As a rule, neither intermittent or remittent assumes any peculiar symptoms, as is often the case with these fevers in tropical countries, except, perhaps, that the irritability of the stomach is more constant and more marked than is ordinarily the case; and this is equally true for all other parts of the Isthmus.

On the Atlantic plains these fevers prevail throughout the year, being, of course, more numerous and of a worse type in the summer and autumn. As a general rule, with unacclimated persons, the intermittent fever of this region does not yield readily to quinine or any other medical treatment. This was certainly the experience of the medical officer who treated a great many cases on board the two ships-of-war belonging to the Expedition, and engaged in hydrographic surveys at the mouth of the Coatzacoalcos, along the Gulf-coast line, and in the rivers on the Atlantic plains. The United States steamers Kansas and Mayflower, with about two hundred officers and men, and the land-exploring party, consisting of nine naval officers and two civil engineers, arrived at Minatitlan on the 11th of November, when all were in good health and excellent spirits. From the accounts we had already received of the healthfulness of the Isthmus at this season of the year, it was not deemed necessary to adopt any unusual sanitary measures. The land exploring party left the ship the same day we arrived, and found quarters at the hotel, which is situated near the river-bank, and overlooks a low swamp, reeking with filth and decaying matter, both animal and vegetable. After remaining in Minatitlan seventeen days, adjusting instruments and preparing the outfit, the land party started for the interior of the Isthmus in canoes, but before doing so we were joined by a party of five sailors from the Kansas and Mayflower, all of whom, up to that time, had been living on board; and when they started with us, all of them were apparently in good health. Before we reached the mountains, which we did on the thirteenth day after leaving Minatitlan, all the sailors had been attacked with fever, one case being severe remittent, and the others intermittent. On the other hand, all the officers and civil engineers remained perfectly well, except two, who had the fever, but in both cases it had appeared before we left Minatitlan, and was no doubt due to severe exposure in a norther while making a passage to Vera Cruz. The food, shelter, labor, and exposure of the officers and sailors, from the day we left Minatitlan, were precisely the same. It is quite certain that the seeds of the disease were received into the systems of these sailors while they were on board their ships; and the remarkable absence of fever among the land party, who quitted the ships for quarters on shore, is probably due to the fact that at the hotel there was a better supply of food, and more complete protection against the insects. On board the ships three or four days had elapsed before any means could be devised for protecting the sailors from the mosquitoes, which were so numerous that, in the absence of a proper netting, no one could sleep for an instant in the night-time. This circumstance was, no doubt, enough to lower the vitality of the system, and render it less able to ward off the malaria in the very beginning. Both intermittent and remittent fevers began to appear on board these vessels about three weeks after entering the river, and continued until every person on board, save fifteen, had been attacked. Nearly all of them suffered from relapses quite regularly at intervals of two or three weeks. In this way it not unfrequently happened that half the ship's company was on the sick-list at the same time. All the sailors of the land party and one of the officers suffered from relapses while in the mountains, from time to time, whenever much exposed in the sun or rain. Indeed, we had expected, that on reaching the cooler and purer atmosphere of the elevated plateaus, a permanent cure would be speedily effected, with the aid of remedies, but such unfortunately was not the case. There were two deaths from remittent fever on board the ships of war, and in both instances the disease was contracted on the Isthmus. The inhabitants, both of the European and Indian races, suffer a good deal from fever; but with them, it was noticed, relapses are not nearly so common as with unacclimated persons. It is quite true that the unacclimated sailors, belonging to the merchant ships loading with mahogany in the Coatzacoalcos River, were not attacked with the fever in the same proportion as our naval crews, but this was probably due to the fact their stay was shorter and their sleeping-apartments better. We do not believe a person in good health is more liable to contract the fever here than in many malarious districts in the Western and Southern States in the months of August and September, but on the Isthmus of Tehuantepec, or rather on the Atlantic plains, one is liable to be seized with it at any season of the year. Here the malarial poison, once fairly in the system, remains with remarkable tenacity. There is no frost, the great destroyer of malaria, both in the human system and out of it, and so the disease often runs on from month to month, inducing chronic disease of the liver and spleen, chronic diarrhœa, or pulmonary consumption. It therefore becomes a matter of the greatest importance to ward off the first attack, and it is believed a great many unacclimated persons can do so by strictly adhering to a few simple sanitary rules. The first thing after rising in the morning, a cup of tea, coffee, or chocolate, and something to eat, if nothing more than a piece of bread, should be taken; flannel should be worn next the skin, and woolen clothing always after sunset; the use of distilled liquors should be avoided altogether, but light wines and fermented drinks are, so it seemed to us, often beneficial; great care should be taken to protect the person from the bites of the myriads of different insects that infest this region; daily bathing in the clear streams is advisable when a norther is not blowing; over-fatigue and long exposure in open boats to the mid-day sun or rain-storms should be carefully avoided; a liberal supply of nourishing food should always be taken; and sleeping on the ground or passing the night without the protection of a tent, or a temporary house, should never be done. On the high table-lands and on the Pacific plains in the dry season, for persons who have not already been exposed to malaria or attacked with the fever, some of the above sanitary precautions may not be strictly necessary. To a ship's company, or a large number of unacclimated persons employed on the Atlantic plains in the summer and autumn, it would be, no doubt, advisable to issue a daily ration of quinine.

Congestive chill, or pernicious fever, occurs on the Atlantic side occasionally, and even as late as January, but from all we could learn concerning this fever, as it occurs here, we formed the opinion that it is probably less frequent and not more fatal than in some parts of the Mississippi Valley in the summer and autumn.

It is the boast of the inhabitants of the Isthmus that yellow fever has never visited them, although at Vera Cruz, only one hundred and twenty miles distant, it rages as an epidemic nearly every summer, or rather it has done so until the last two years. It is further stated that the residents of Minatitlan have been in the habit of constantly visiting Vera Cruz when the worst epidemics are raging, and not only escape the disease themselves, but never introduce it into their own district. On the other hand, it is well known that the Mexicans who live in the elevated table-lands, as at Puebla and the city of Mexico, for instance, are almost sure to be attacked with yellow fever whenever they go down to Vera Cruz during the prevalence of this disease. The comparative freedom which Vera Cruz has enjoyed from this terrible scourge for the two summers just passed is due, no doubt, to the fact that the city now gets its water-supply from another and better source, good modern water-works having been introduced. It is, therefore, reasonable now to predict that in the future Vera Cruz will enjoy as great freedom from yellow fever as any other tropical sea-board of the same size and equal foreign commerce.

The water used for drinking purposes in the town of Minatitlan is obtained from springs, and is very good. The river-water, too, was found to be wholesome, and was used on board one of the ships; while, on the other one, distilled water was used for drinking, but without any apparent advantage in a sanitary point over the river-water.

On the Pacific plains in the month of January, we met with two cases of dysentery among the natives, but none of our party suffered from this disease. In many localities on the Atlantic slope, where the climate is damp and subject to sudden changes of temperature, rheumatism and pulmonary diseases are quite common.

In the towns of Santa Maria Chimalapa, San Miguel Chimalapa, San Juan Guichicovi, as well as several places on the Pacific side, near the foot of the mountains, a singular leprous skin disease, called *pinta* or *tania*, affects perhaps more than one-half of the inhabitants, nearly all of whom are Indians. White or blue spots, many of them as large as a silver dollar, appear about the face, hands, and body, and occasionally an individual is met with whose face or hands are quite changed from their natural copper-color to a white or blue. Later in life this diseased surface often becomes covered with a scaly substance, in which unsightly ulcerated fissures appear. We saw one unfortunate old woman whose back and legs were so changed, that her skin resembled that of an alligator more than a human being. The affected parts are not swollen, nor are they painful, and the toes and fingers do not fall off, as in the West India leprosy. The skin is often contracted, which generally gives the face an idiotic expression, but we have no reason to believe that the mind is really affected in this disease. It never incapacitates any one for work, nor is it ever fatal, so far as we could ascertain. Probably it is contagious, and the natives regard it as being so themselves, but in order to contract it, it is necessary to live in very close relations with an affected person, and adopt more or less the filthy habits of the natives. It is not often any one belonging to the European races takes the disease, but there is one case, well known on the Isthmus, of a Frenchman who was unfortunate enough to contract it, and after trying in vain all the native remedies, went to France, where he was cured. He returned to the Isthmus, contracted the disease a second time, when he became so disgusted with his unsightly person that he committed suicide. Persons affected with pinta are exempt from military duty, and it is said the men often endeavor to catch it on that account. The women, on the other hand, take great pains to ward it off and to cure it, in neither of which do they seem to be very successful. "Have you a remedy for my disease?" is generally the first and only question these poor afflicted women ask a stranger. There are no physicians here, nor has any intelligent effort ever been made by the government or private charity to stamp out this disgusting malady, which rests like a curse on not less than five thousand souls on the Isthmus of Tehuantepec, descending from father to son.

The following information, kindly furnished by Dr. H. N. Beaumont, passed assistant surgeon, United States Navy, is a synopsis of the aggregate daily sick-reports of the United States steamer Kansas, (4th rate,) from November 11, 1870, to April 19, 1871, which embraces the period of service of this vessel on the Isthmus with the Surveying Expedition.

Diseases.	No. of cases.	Diseases.	No. of cases.
Intermittent fever	288	Rheumatism, acute	2
Remittent fever	15	Paronychia	1
Colic	18	Orchitis	1
Diarrhœa, acute	24	Syphilis, primary	2
Diarrhœa, chronic	1	Syphilis, secondary	1
Inflammation of the liver	5	Contusions	2
Jaundice	3	Hernia	1
Inflammation of the spleen	1	Sprains	1
Bronchitis, acute	1	Wounds	4
Hypertrophy of the heart	1	Total	381
Hypochondriasis	1		
Neuralgia	1		
Abscess	1	Number of deaths	2
Boils	4	Average number of persons on board	130
Ulcers	2	Daily average number of sick	16

Upon the arrival of the Kansas in the United States, 61 persons of her crew of 130, were invalided to the naval hospitals, and 12 more, greatly debilitated and subject at short intervals to paroxysms of fever, were considered by the surgeon of the vessel unfit for active service. Of these seventy-three invalids, all except two were suffering from malarial fever or its sequela, contracted on the Isthmus. In this connection it should be stated that this ship was not provided with sufficient berthing-room of the proper kind for the crew, and, besides, the ventilation of the berth-deck was unusually bad.

TROUBLESOME INSECTS, REPTILES, SERPENTS, ETC.

Of the many hardships the members of our party encountered in exploring the Isthmus, none were so trying as the bites of the numerous insects which infest this region. Both the covered and uncovered parts of the body were attacked, and each by a different class of insects; nor did the day-time or night-time afford any certain relief. There is no doubt that the loss of sleep which these troublesome insects cause, and the irritation of the system induced by their bites, which sometimes become large sores, are often strong predisposing causes of the malarial fevers of the Isthmus.

The mosquitoes, "zancudos," are, for the most part, confined to the Atlantic plains, but in the rainy season they are met with on the Pacific side, and even on the high table-lands. Near the Atlantic rivers there is no season of the year when one can sleep at night unless protected by a mosquito-net. The exploring party was supplied with the ordinary netting used in the United States, which a little experience proved to be entirely worthless in this region, for the mosquitoes penetrated it with the greatest ease. We had to resort to the netting used by the natives, which consists of ordinary thin muslin. This, although it affords protection against the mosquitoes, cannot be commended for the ventilation it allows the sleeper. The Indians, however poor, invariably have their rude beds protected by a mosquito-net.

When the Kansas and Mayflower arrived at Minatitlan, the officers and men attached to them were unprovided with mosquito-nets, and for several days, until a supply could be obtained, not a person on board closed his eyes at night. The officers, driven from their cabins, betook themselves to the deck, where they walked and smoked the whole night long. The sailors wandered about the ship like madmen, now climbing up the rigging and resting for awhile in the tops, and then descending again to the decks, but no relief was to be found anywhere. There was one member of our party who, after partaking of a hearty dinner, fell asleep, and neglecting to put down his mosquito-bars, the next morning he found his legs and feet so badly bitten and so much inflamed that he was unable to wear his shoes, and was in the hands of the surgeon for several days. This insect is so annoying to the horses and cattle, that it constitutes a serious obstacle to raising herds on the Atlantic slope. Toward the close of the dry season they become much less numerous, but they never disappear altogether.

The rodadors, called by the natives "mosquitoes," are little dark and green flies, about one-third as large as the common house-fly, which they somewhat resemble in the general outline of their bodies, although, of course, the rodadors are a great deal smaller. This insect is confined to the Atlantic side and to portions of the central division of the Isthmus; it is, however, not found on the Atlantic plains near the sea-coast. Ascending the Coatzacoalcos, one first encounters it a few miles above Almagres; and on the Uspanapa we found it first about twenty miles above the mouth of the river. It therefore seems probable that this insect does not exist within a belt thirty or forty miles wide along the sea-shore. They are not found on the plains of Chivela, but they are numerous at Tarifa. Being very indifferent flyers, they are unable to attack when one is in rapid motion, as in riding or walking fast. In deep ravines and in the fastness of the forest they are most abundant. They do not bite when it is dark, and even in a dark room in the day-time they are quite harmless. When we were obliged to keep a bright light burning at night to prevent the vampires from attacking us, we noticed that the rodadors would occasionally bite. The sting of a rodador is followed by a minute speck of extravasated blood, which lodges just beneath the epidermis, the opening being apparently too small to allow the blood corpuscles to escape. At first it is not painful, but in the course of twenty-four hours the flesh surrounding the bite becomes red, hard, and swollen, resembling a boil; and is attended with an intolerable itching, all of which symptoms subside in the course of three or four days. With some persons the bite of this insect is not followed by any swelling or irritation, and such seems to be uniformly the case with the natives, whose naked bodies are often speckled with the minute red spots characteristic of the sting of the rodador. It is, therefore, probable that foreign residents would soon become accustomed to this insect. They bite the horses and mules until they make large raw surfaces, especially between the legs and under the belly. At Santa Maria Chimalapa, where they are exceedingly numerous, they annoyed our animals so much that they would quit the fields, where they were put to graze, and gallop at full speed into the town. We found a cerate of carbolic acid an excellent application to prevent the insect from biting, as well as to mitigate the inflammation and itching following the bite.

The ticks, "garrapatas" and "pinolillos," do not differ from the same insects found in our own forests in the summer season, except that on the Isthmus they are much more abundant. They are found in all parts of the Isthmus, but fortunately not at all seasons, being limited to the dry months. In the uninhabited regions, where domestic animals do not range, there are no ticks. They annoy animals much more than men, and it is no uncommon thing to see horses and mules that have had their ears eaten off by the "garrapatas." It is the common practice among the residents, after a ride on the plains or a walk in the woods, in order to free themselves of pinolillos, which are the very smallest ticks, to bathe the whole person in aguardiénte, the native rum, which has the effect of detaching the insects entire. If it is attempted to pick them off, the head is often left buried in the flesh, and causes a great deal of irritation. Sponging the person in a weak solution of carbolic acid was found to answer the same purpose.

The nigua is a small black insect, which resembles a flea. It burrows slowly under the skin, without producing any pain, and deposits there several hundred minute white eggs, about which a sack forms. In the course of a week the sack, with its contents, has attained the size of a pea, and can be seen slightly protruding from beneath the skin, and at this stage is generally attended with a slight itching. By inserting the blade of a knife between the sack and the surrounding flesh, the former can be easily enucleated entire, after which the cavity heals rapidly. If, however, the sack is broken, and some of the minute eggs escape into the surrounding tissue, they may continue to multiply, producing oftentimes ulcers which are troublesome to heal. The nigua, like the tick, is troublesome only in the dry season, and is, therefore, most abundant on the Pacific slope. The Indian boys are very expert both in finding and extracting them; and it is a good plan to have one's feet, for this is the part where they are generally found, examined once a week, or oftener.

Fleas are found in all parts of the Isthmus, but they are most abundant on the Pacific side. Fortunately they are limited to the towns and Indian huts, and one is not much troubled by them when living in the woods or in camp. Two of our party had their bodies covered with large suppurating sores, which were caused by the repeated bites of this insect.

The moyaquil is a worm which grows in the flesh, and the Indians say it originates from an egg deposited under the skin by a certain fly. The presence of the worm is not noticed until it has attained a considerable size, an inch or more in length, when suddenly the attention is called to it by the flesh near it becoming swollen and inflamed, and exceedingly painful. The Indians are very expert in extracting it, which they do by applying to the head of the worm, which is visible just under the skin, some resin found in the forest. This is allowed to remain two or three hours, when it is removed, and the worm is found to be dead, and is easily extracted by manipulating and squeezing the flesh. We met a lady who, having suffered from one of these worms in the forehead, now never ventures out of her house without having her face closely veiled. The moyaquil is not very common, and is, we believe, confined to the Atlantic slope.

Tarantulas are very numerous, especially on the table-lands, and they are generally very large. Since they never bite except when pressed upon, they are not troublesome. None of our party was bitten, although it was no uncommon thing to find a large tarantula in the tent, or even between the blankets in the morning. We were unable to learn of any deaths or severe injuries among the Indians from the bite of this insect; and we took some pains to make inquiries on this point. No doubt these people are frequently bitten, for they constantly go about the plains and through the forests barefooted, and must occasionally tread on the tarantulas. Horses not unfrequently step on them in the fields, and, if they are not crushed, they bite the frog of the foot, and the animal is often lame for a number of months, for the hoof falls off.

Scorpions are met with quite frequently, but they are generally small, and not very poisonous. Several of our party were stung, but the pain in every case was very slight, and there was no swelling.

We expected to encounter a great many serpents on the Isthmus, and each person, therefore, went fully prepared with the means for applying an antidote at a moment's notice, should he be bitten; but during our residence there we saw only a very limited number of serpents, the most of which belong to species that are quite harmless. No one of the party was bitten, nor even attacked, notwithstanding the fact that our explorations led us into the densest forests and the most unfrequented regions. We saw two cases where Indians had been bitten by venomous serpents, both of which were followed by the entire destruction and sloughing of the parts; in one instance a foot, and the other a fore-arm. We also heard of several deaths that had resulted from the bites of serpents. But these cases are very rare, probably not more frequent than similar occurrences in our own forests. It was a matter of general surprise and constant remark that we should see so few snakes. We traveled in a canoe for nine days, ascending the Coatzacoalcos, passing within an arm's length of the river-bank, which is covered with rank vegetation, and is apparently the very home of serpents and the like, but we saw, during all this time, only one snake, a harmless water species. The annual fires that sweep over the whole of the uplands destroy a great many serpents, with their young and their eggs, and the yearly overflow of the low-lands has a similar effect. The vultures and the peccaries also kill a great many of them.

Alligators infest the large rivers and lagoons on both sides of the Isthmus, but none are found in the central division. The rancheros told us that the alligators destroy a considerable number of young cattle. Shooting these ugly reptiles afforded tolerable sport; and so numerous are they that one person might easily dispatch a dozen or more in a few hours. It happened that on one occasion we came upon a huge alligator, some distance from the water, in an open space, and in chasing him, in order to get near enough for a good shot, we discovered, much to our surprise, that he ran as fast as we could, and for a part of the way his course was up hill.

Sharks abound along the coast, on both sides of the Isthmus, and we occasionally saw them as much as sixty miles up the Uspanapa and Coatzacoalcos Rivers. They do not seem to be very voracious, for we saw the Huave Indians standing waist-deep in the water, a considerable distance from the shore, at the mouth of the Tehuantepec River, with hundreds of large sharks swimming leisurely along quite near them.

Iguanas and small lizards, of many different varieties, are exceedingly numerous, and are often very tame, inhabiting houses and running about the streets. The iguana is highly esteemed for food by the Indians, being preferred to beef or chicken. The larger and more esteemed sorts are found along the banks of the unfrequented rivers, high up in the mountains. When we were fifty miles up the Uspanapa River, we met six Jaltipan Indians in canoes, who informed us that they were on their way to the headwaters of the same river to hunt the iguana, as was the custom of their tribe. They catch this reptile in traps, and also chase it into its hole in the earth, and then dig it out. These Indians purposed remaining up the river a month, when they expected to return with as many as two hundred iguanas, which are kept alive, and sold in Jaltipan and Acayucam for about fifty cents each.

In some parts of the Isthmus vampire-bats, (*Phyllostoma spectrum,*) of which there are several varieties, are found in considerable numbers. One sort is as large as a half-grown chicken, and its wings, when extended, measure across from two to three feet, while another sort is not larger than a meadow-lark, and whose extended wings do not measure more than eight or ten inches. We found them most troublesome in the Chimalapa region, where they attacked our animals nearly every night, inflicting oftentimes two or even three bites on the same horse. The opening they make in the skin is round, with clean-cut edges, and about a quarter of an inch in diameter, and does not penetrate much below the true skin. It is not uncommon to find blood oozing from the opening several hours after the bat has left. The neck of the horse or mule is the part most generally attacked. Observing this, one night, for the purpose of protecting a horse which was always bitten more than the rest, we covered his neck and body with a blanket, but the next morning, greatly to our disappointment, we found that he had been bitten on the hind leg. Two of our servants were bitten about the feet. They said they did not feel the bat until it flew away, which waked them; they also said the wound was slightly painful, but they did not complain of feeling weak from the loss of blood. In one of them, to arrest the hemorrhage, it was necessary to apply a small compress to the opening. The horses appeared to be somewhat exhausted from the repeated bites, but not nearly so much as we supposed they would be. We noticed that when there was a bright moonlight, the animals outdoors were not attacked, for the vampires, disliking the light, entered the houses and other dark places for their victims. A candle was kept burning in the room we occupied, and although the vampires were seen to enter, finding a light, they quickly flew out again. The natives close their houses as well as they can in order to keep out the vampires, and they also find it necessary to put the pigs and mules into houses built for this purpose. An old Indian assured us that two bites of a vampire the same night generally proved fatal to an infant.

We repeatedly watched, in order to ascertain the exact manner in which the vampire depletes his victim, to see whether he keeps his wings in motion while he bites, &c., but we were never fortunate enough to see one in the act of biting, though they were whirling through the air about our heads constantly. Horses are bitten a great deal more than mules, and we had reason to believe that animals, after some experience, contrive to keep off the vampires in a great measure.

The comején, or wood-louse, is an insect which resembles an ant, and is often called the white ant. It is rather larger than the common red ant, has a white body and a reddish head. It makes its nest on the trees, or on the tops of the houses, and always connects it with the ground by dark lines or ridges, which are hollow, and afford the comején a covered passage-way to and from its nest; indeed, it never exposes itself for an instant to the open air, but always keeps under cover, either in its nest or in its covered passage-ways, or in the wood it is boring. The nest reminds one of the hornet's nest, but its composition seems to be more earthy. This insect owes its chief importance to the fact that it is very destructive of certain kinds of timber used in construction. It enters a piece of timber unobserved, by a small concealed opening, and eats out the interior, grinding it to a powder. In this way rafters and sills, and the like, are often quite destroyed before the presence of the comején is even suspected. The softer sorts of wood are those usually attacked. It seems to be particularly fond of white pine, for instance; but yellow pine is either too hard for its inroads, or the taste of the wood is not acceptable. Mahogany, red cedar, zaphote, and many other native timbers are free from its ravages. It is readily destroyed by putting arsenic in its nest.

The teredo-navalis, or navy-worm, is exceedingly destructive all along the Atlantic coast, and in the spring and early summer months it ascends the rivers with the salt water as high up as the town of Minatitlan, where it is so destructive that mahogany or cedar logs, if left in the river during these months, are completely honey-combed. The mahogany shippers, therefore, if they have any rafts of timber left over from the last shipping season, which is during the winter months, are obliged to float them higher up the streams, to a point where the water is always fresh, and therefore free from the teredo. On the Coatzacoalcos River, this point is found a short distance above the mouth of the Coachapa.

CHAPTER III.

AGRICULTURE.

Only a very small portion of the land on the Isthmus is cleared and under cultivation. Here and there patches of an acre or two in some fertile valley, or small cultivated fields in the vicinity of towns and villages, show at a glance the limited extent of the agriculture of the Isthmus. The roads and bridle-paths lead for miles and miles through unbroken forests, or across plains covered only with wild grass. Of late years agriculture has materially declined, and it is a very common thing to meet with deserted ranches, and sugar and indigo plantations that have been abandoned. The Indians perform all the labor in the fields, either in their own small patches, or as hired laborers on the estates of the wealthy proprietors. The clearing of the forest, as now done, is a laborious and tedious process, for the Indians possess no other tools to do it with than rude axes and machetes. A very common price for clearing an acre of forest-land is eight dollars. The ordinary farm laborers receive about twenty-five cents a day as wages.

As might be expected, the dry, level plains of the Pacific side, the high table-lands in the central division, seven hundred feet above the sea-level, and the Atlantic slope, intersected with large rivers, and abundantly supplied with rain, all materially differ from each other in agricultural products as well as vegetation in general.

The Pacific plains are covered with scrubby-looking timber, such as lignum-vitæ, Brazil-wood, acacia, rosewood, and cactus, with occasional clumps of palm. From some elevated point in the dividing-ridge, the whole plain, stretching from the foot of the Cordillera to the Pacific, is distinctly visible. Its variegated tropical vegetation, and here and there a solitary hillock rising like a pyramid on the level plains, and the boundless blue ocean for a background, all combine to render this one of the most beautiful landscapes we have ever seen. Once fairly on the plain the sandy roads wind through the scrubby forests, and the traveler rides on for hours unable to see more than a few yards in advance of himself, meeting with neither fences, nor cleared fields, nor habitations.

The soil is either sandy or a light loam, with occasional deposits of shell-marl on the surface, or near it. After September there is no more rain until June, and the whole country becomes parched and sterile, and only such vegetation as is suited to a very dry soil flourishes at all. For corn and beans, and so forth, necessary for the wants of the inhabitants, sufficient land is irrigated, but the water-supply for this purpose being obtained from the small rivers of the plains, is very scanty, and, indeed, toward the close of the dry season, most of the rivers become quite dry. From October until April northers blow from time to time very violently across this plain, so that the gardens and growing crops require thatched fences or strips of timber land to protect them from the violence of the winds. The soil is no doubt fertile, but the want of rain and a water-supply sufficient for irrigation on an extensive scale, as well as the destructive northers, are all natural drawbacks to an improved and diversified agriculture in this section of the Isthmus.

In the central division the country is rolling land, level plateau, or fertile valley, all covered with wild grasses, with here and there forests of palm, pine, and oak. Some of the soil is a dark loam, a sort of bottom-land, and is very fertile; the remainder is gravel and sand, and is generally barren. Wild grasses, well adapted for the grazing of horses and cattle, grow luxuriantly in the fertile portions. Once a year these lands are set on fire, and the whole surface is burnt clean, at which time millions of insects and their larvæ, so troublesome to the herds, are destroyed. Were it not for this annual wholesale destruction of these insects, it is doubtful whether herds could thrive at all. On the whole, the rain-fall is sufficient to meet the wants of the cultivator of the soil; but the northers are even more violent and destructive here than on the Pacific plains, and will always constitute a serious drawback to the development of a flourishing agriculture. It is true that there are many sheltered localities to which this does not apply.

The soil on the Atlantic plains is a rich alluvial deposit, often twenty feet in depth. This region is generally heavily timbered, but occasionally open, grass-covered plains are met with; and in the vicinity of the large rivers there are vast open meadow-lands, subject to an annual overflow, and are called potreros. On these potreros the wild "camalote," a coarse grass, grows in great profusion, affording excellent pasturage for herds in the dry season. The soil is remarkably fertile, and, if cleared and cultivated, would yield abundantly all the agricultural products adapted to this latitude and climate. The north wind is not violent enough to be a serious drawback to the cultivation of this plain; but the myriads of troublesome insects, which attack both man and beast, and the prevalence of malarial fevers during the entire year, are two great natural obstacles in the way of the agricultural development of this region.

Indian corn is the great staple, and grows in all parts of the Isthmus and at all seasons. It is possible to grow four crops on the same piece of land in one year, for in three months from the time the seeds are planted the corn is matured, but for obvious reasons it is but seldom that so many crops are taken from the same soil in so short a time; it is, however, quite the common practice to have two crops in the same year. It is very fortunate that in this climate it is possible to renew so often this crop, so indispensable as an article of food, because very soon after the corn is gathered it is attacked by the weevil and ground to a powder, in spite of all the natives can do to protect it. They sometimes smoke the ears until they are quite black, but even this does not afford absolute protection. The corn grown on the Pacific side is indifferent, and the ears are nothing more than nubbins, and the best yield does not exceed fifteen or twenty bushels to the acre. On the Atlantic plains the ears are large, and the yield quite as abundant as that of our own fields. The price of corn is variable, but on the whole it is probably a little less than in our own eastern markets. In constructing a canal, the animals and some of the laborers will have to be subsisted on the native Indian corn, which can, no doubt, be grown on the Isthmus, under the direction of intelligent farmers, quite as cheap as on the western prairies of the United States.

No wheat is raised on the Isthmus, nor in any part of Mexico adjacent to it. It probably requires a higher elevation and a cooler atmosphere than are to be found on any of the land susceptible of cultivation on the Isthmus. Several attempts have been made to grow it on the elevated table-lands, but all of them have been unsuccessful. This is certainly a great misfortune, for owing to the great expense of transporting flour on pack-mules from distant parts of Mexico, and the various state and town duties it is subject to in transit, a barrel of inferior flour costs at Tehuantepec or Minatitlan, $25; and the duty on foreign flour is so heavy that it cannot be imported and sold for a less sum.

Rice, at present, is produced in only very small quantities, but as soon as there is a demand for it the central division and the Atlantic plains will be found capable of producing it in any quantity that may be desired. The aborigines greatly prefer their own indigenous maize, and have, therefore, paid but little attention to the cultivation of rice.

Many of our garden vegetables grow very well in all parts of the Isthmus. The ants are very troublesome to the young plants, and in some instances to the vegetables themselves, when they are matured. We recollect having seen an okra patch, where these little insects ate the vegetables as fast as they ripened, leaving the plants, which here grow to the height of twelve feet, uninjured. Some of our vegetables, as the cabbage and carrot, for instance, grow very well, but they do not go to seed, and it is, therefore, necessary to get a fresh supply of seed from abroad for each planting. We saw lettuce, radishes, tomatoes, string-beans, beets, and onions growing in the gardens, and the quality and yield of these vegetables, considering the rude manner in which they are cultivated, did not seem to be inferior to the same in our gardens at home. The ginger and the chile, or vegetable-pepper, are found growing wild. It seems that the bean has found here a soil and climate particularly well adapted to its growth, for some of the varieties of this vegetable have a superior flavor not found out of Mexico. There is a small black bean—the common frejole of the Isthmus—which Abbe Clavigero informs us came originally from France, where it is still found, and is so unsavory that it is eaten only by the peasantry; but the soil of Mexico has so improved it, that both strangers and natives regard it as one of the most savory dishes of the country. So highly is it esteemed by those who are acquainted with it, that the inhabitants of Havana import it in large quantity from Mexico. It grows in all parts of the Isthmus, and yields abundantly, a single pod often containing as many as twenty beans. The Irish potato does not flourish here, but fortunately there is an excellent substitute for it in the chyote, or one-seed cucumber, which grows on a vine, and is to be had at all seasons of the year. There is a coarse sort of sweet potato, called, in Mexico, camote, which yields abundantly, and the quality of it could doubtless be improved, or better varieties might readily be introduced.

Sugar-cane grows in all the several natural divisions of the Isthmus, but the high ridges on the Atlantic slope are best suited to its cultivation. It is said that a cane-field here produces as long as thirty years without replanting, when properly managed; and we saw ourselves several deserted plantations on the banks of the Coatzacoalcos, where the cane was large and very sweet. The Indians told us that these cane-patches had been there a great many years. The culture of sugar was formerly of considerable importance on the Isthmus, but of late years it, like most agricultural ventures, has greatly fallen off, until at present little more than enough to supply the wants of the inhabitants is produced.

Coffee of a good quality grows on the Atlantic slope and in the central division. The Indians pick it, and bring it into the towns, and sell it often as low as five cents per pound. A small quantity is also cultivated. Not enough is collected to supply the inhabitants of the Isthmus, and a considerable quantity is brought from other parts of Mexico. From what we saw of the coffee-tree growing in the woods and in the gardens, we came to the conclusion that the soil and climate of the Isthmus are very well adapted to its cultivation. We were all surprised to find the Mexican coffee of so fine a flavor. It is rather milder than the Java coffee, but in flavor is not inferior.

The cacao, from which chocolate is manufactured, is grown in small quantity. The soil on the Atlantic slope, where alone cacao flourishes, seems to be admirably suited to its cultivation. We saw several small plantations of this tree on the Uspanapa River, which belong to mulattoes who came to the Isthmus from Tabasco, where the cultivation of cacao is very well understood. There are hundreds of acres of uninhabited lands along the Uspanapa, where the soil is a light alluvium, which our guide, who was familiar with the cultivation of cacao, commended in the highest terms as well adapted to growing this valuable product. We saw a wild variety of cacao growing in the forest in this locality, but it is said to be greatly inferior to the cultivated. It is necessary to protect the cacao-tree from the scorching rays of the sun, and the coral-tree, or "madre de cacao," as it is called, is planted with the cacao for this purpose. The cacao-tree does not begin to bear the cacao-bean until about the sixth year after planting, and then continues to produce two crops a year for forty or fifty years. About two hundred trees are planted on an acre, and a fair yield for which, at each crop, is about two hundred pounds of cacao-beans, worth on the Isthmus about $45. A cocao plantation does not require much labor, nor a great deal of care, but considerable capital is necessary for an undertaking of this sort. The chocolate found on the Isthmus is often very good and sometimes very inferior, which is doubtless owing to the different manner in which it is manufactured from the bean. There can be little doubt that this beverage, indigenous to the country, and found in common use among the natives at the time of the Spanish conquest, is very healthful and nutritious for foreigners residing in this climate, as well as for the native inhabitants, who prefer it to coffee, and use it to a much greater extent.

The best tobacco found in Mexico grows on the Isthmus of Tehuantepec, on the Atlantic plains west of the Coatzacoalcos River. It is extensively cultivated by the Indians belonging to the towns of Jaltipan, Acayucam, and Chinameca. The same people also manufacture from this tobacco very good cigars in considerable quantity, for exportation, the best of which the smokers of our party declared to be but little inferior to first-rate Havana cigars. The best brands cost in Chinameca only fifteen dollars a thousand at retail.

There is a plant belonging to the genus agave, and called on the Isthmus ixtle, or pita, of which there are several varieties. From the long, large leaves of this plant a very superior quality of hemp is obtained. Although in appearance it is similar to the well-known sisal-hemp of commerce, upon a close inspection the ixtle or pita is found to be a much finer fiber, and some of the varieties have a silky texture. The plant grows wild, and is also cultivated, which is said to improve the quality of the fiber. It is planted in rows about four feet apart, and at intervals of two or three feet. The leaves, which are of a bluish color, grow from a fleshy bulb like a pine-apple, and are from two to five feet in length, and about three inches in width, tapering to a point which is capped with a long thorn. The outer leaves, being the oldest and largest, are cut off from time to time, as they mature. At Santa Maria Chimalapa, it is a very common thing to see two or three rows of this plant surrounding the houses, within a few feet of the walls. Cords, cloth, hammocks, and thread are manufactured from it. It is probable that the best varieties would, owing to the fineness of the fiber and its silky texture, be found very well adapted for the fabrication of certain sorts of fine dress-goods. At present they have no means of dressing and cleaning it, except by a tedious and expensive hand-process, and this circumstance, so it is said, renders the collection of this very excellent fiber unprofitable when undertaken on an extensive scale. A German blacksmith in Minatitlan claims to have invented a machine for dressing the pita, but we had not an opportunity to witness it in operation.

The most important article of export cultivated on the Isthmus is indigo. Its cultivation is confined entirely to the Pacific side, in the light soil and dry atmosphere of which this plant seems to do remarkably well. Owing to intestine wars and other political causes, the production of indigo has greatly declined in the last fifteen or twenty years, but under favorable circumstances the cultivation of this valuable article of commerce could be easily revived. The plant (*Indigofera disperma*) which yields the indigo of commerce resembles in general appearance a small asparagus plant after the branches have formed, but the leaf of the indigo-plant is not like that of the asparagus, for it resembles very closely the leaf of the common locust. It is planted in rows two feet apart, so as to allow the earth to be hoed. New land yields the best crop, and is therefore generally selected. One planting lasts four years, and one crop is gathered each season. The yields of the second and third years are always the best. About forty pounds to the acre is considered a good crop. The indigo grown and manufactured by the rude process used by the Indians is sold in Itztaltepec for about seventy-five cents a pound; but an intelligent American, engaged here for several years in the cultivation of indigo, informed us that he always sold his crops in England, where he obtained as much as two dollars and a half a pound, which rendered his occupation a very profitable one. To extract the indigo, the whole plant—leaves, stock, and branches—is soaked in water for a certain period, generally less than twenty-four hours, when a sort of fermentation takes place, and the indigo is extracted and held suspended in the water. This is then drawn off, and is agitated by stirring with poles or paddles until the indigo curdles, and precipitates in flaky masses to the bottom of the vat or vessel, after which the water is drawn off. The indigo is then dried and pressed, and packed in bales containing one hundred and ninety pounds each. It is all sent across the Isthmus to Minatitlan, where it is shipped, generally to England.

Cattle are found in all sections of the Isthmus on the ranches or cattle estates. We did not see any wild ones. The best herds are found on the high table-lands and along the narrow strip of land between the Tilema Lagoon and the Pacific Ocean. In the latter locality there are here and there fine stretches of bottom-land, which afford good grass in the dry season, and fortunately, owing probably to the proximity of the ocean, the insects are not at all numerous. On the whole, the animals attain a good size, and may be said to be in fair condition. The beef is lean, but it is remarkably tender and juicy, and we all agreed that it was superior to any tropical beef we had ever eaten. The natives rarely preserve it with salt, but, instead, cut it in strips like pieces of rope, and dry it in the sun for two or three days, when it is cured. It is then called "tasájo," and being easy of transportation on mules or on the backs of Indians, is very valuable for exploring parties. If it be well pounded and then broiled or roasted, it is quite palatable. The usual price for a good bullock is about fourteen dollars. Many of the steers are large enough for cart-oxen, and on the Pacific plains a good deal of the hauling is now performed with them. A sufficient supply of cattle, both for beef and for hauling, to meet the immediate requirements in constructing an inter-oceanic canal, will be found on the Isthmus, and the supply can be readily increased to any amount in the course of a few years. A large number of calves are destroyed by the tigers every season. So troublesome to the herds are these animals, that every ranch maintains a hunter and a pack of dogs for the exclusive purpose of hunting and killing them. We could not learn that any form of cattle disease has ever made its appearance on the Isthmus.

The horses are numerous, but they are generally small and of an inferior breed. The average price for a young horse is about thirty dollars. A much superior breed of horses is found about Oaxaca. Mares are rarely used for the road, and a Mexican gentleman will not be seen mounted on one of them.

Mules are relatively much superior to the horses, and command about double the price. Indeed, they are quite equal in size and in endurance to the mules found in the United States.

We noticed several flocks of sheep on the plains of Chivela, but they were small, and it was very apparent that they did not thrive well. Hogs do very well, and their flesh is esteemed beyond any other by the Indians. Turkeys, chickens, ducks, and geese are all abundant, and of good quality, being greatly superior to any fowls we have ever eaten before within the tropics. The insects do not trouble the fowls and the birds, and the whole region seems to be admirably adapted to the growth of all the feathered tribe. In the meanest Indian hut one can always purchase a good chicken and fresh eggs.

FRUITS.

Oranges grow in all parts of the Isthmus, but those of the Atlantic plains and the central division are the best. At Santa Maria Chimalapa this fruit is particularly fine, and there are two crops yearly, but not always on the same trees. "La primera fruta," the first crop, is always the best, and is ripe in December and January; and "la segunda fruta" is ripe in February and March, and in size is not inferior to the first, but it is less sweet. The soil in which these fine Chimalapa oranges grow is peculiar, being a very clean white sand, the same that the earth-eaters of this region partake of, and it is on account of this peculiarity of the soil, no doubt, that the fruit is so unusually fine. On the banks of the Coatzacoalcos there is an orange-grove of about ten acres, planted by an American, where the fruit is equal to the best Havana oranges. We measured a large basket-full taken indiscriminately from the trees, and found the average circumference of the oranges to be $9\frac{17}{20}$ inches. We estimated that the ripe crop we found on this deserted and untilled orange-grove was as much as one hundred and fifty bushels to the acre. On the Isthmus of Tehuantepec there is no frost to blight this crop, as there is occasionally in Florida and Louisiana; nor hurricanes to destroy it, as in the West Indies; nor are the northers violent enough on the Atlantic plains to materially injure it. Oranges of the very best quality can be readily grown along the banks of the Coatzacoalcos and Uspanapa in quantity sufficient to supply the markets of the United States, and, if they are shipped by the way of New Orleans, will be subject to less than three days of sea transportation, which is always found to be so injurious to the best American oranges. Bitter oranges and "la naranja del monte" are found growing in the woods in many localities.

There are as many as fifteen well-known varieties of the banana, some of which are of a very superior quality. The manzána variety is the most delicious of all, and, as its name indicates, has the flavor of the apple. Like the orange, the best bananas are found on the Atlantic plains and in the central division, and they are ripe at all seasons of the year. Plantains are met with everywhere. The natives prefer them to the bannana, and for these people they constitute, after Indian corn, the most important article of food. We found no native dish so palatable as the fried plantains. Limes and lemons are often seen growing wild. The pine-apple is of good size and fine flavor, and the best that we saw were grown on the Pacific slope. The mango is found all about the country, and this fruit is a favorite with the Indians. The tree which produces it is the most common shade-tree in their towns or about their dwellings. We did not meet with the aguacate, or alligator-pear, except in the gardens at Minatitlan, where the tree attains a large size and the fruit is said to be delicious. It is not ripe until June. The papaya, a large pear-shaped fruit, is very plentiful, and is highly esteemed by the natives. The stalk which bears the fruit is about 10 feet high when it attains its full growth, which it does the fifth year. It begins to bear about the fifth month, and continues to do so, always having ripe fruit on it until the stem dies. The black sapote, a delicious fruit, resembles the apricot, except that its skin is of a rusty color, and the central seed is very large and black. The white sapote is a larger fruit, but is inferior to the other variety in flavor. The tamarind, mamey, pomegranate, and guava were constantly met with. The cocoa-nut palm was seen growing about the towns and in gardens, but we did not observe it in the woods, though the forests abound in many other varieties of the palm.

There is a native grape of a black color, a very tough skin, round, and rather larger than our Concord grape. It grows wild in great abundance, and, considering that it is unimproved by cultivation, is quite eatable and very juicy. At San Andrés a wine is made of it, which is said to resemble claret, and competent judges declare it to be very good.

We were constantly in the habit of eating these fruits during our stay on the Isthmus, and never had any reason to believe any of them unwholesome.

MEDICINAL PLANTS, DYES, GUMS, ETC.

The *Epidendrum vanilla*, from which the vanilla-bean of commerce is obtained, grows wild in the woods in many localities, and in the Chimalapa region especially it is very plentiful. Often, when riding through the forest, our attention was arrested by the agreeable and well-known odor of vanilla. Here the plant flowers in February and the bean is ripe in May and June. A small quantity is cultivated by the Indians, and they also gather some in the woods. Its cultivation is very easy and might be made profitable. In size, these beans are inferior to those obtained from Guatemala, but we can state from personal observation that the flavor, both in quality and quantity, of some specimens of the Tehuantepec vanilla, is greatly superior to the sort usually found in the shops. The Palma Christi, the plant which bears the castor-oil bean, grows wild along the river banks on both sides of the Isthmus. The natives are acquainted with the medicinal value of these beans, and collect them in small quantity for domestic use only, though the plant is so abundant that a large amount for exportation might readily be gathered.

Sassafras, liquorice-root, annotta, logwood, and Brazil-wood are the most important products of this class, and all of them are found on the Isthmus. Several years ago there was a great demand in Europe for the red dye the Brazil-wood yields, and the price of the wood here suddenly trebled, and in consequence a large quantity of it was cut, but in a short time the price declined, and a great deal of the wood is still on hand waiting shipment.

Sarsaparilla abounds along the headwaters of the Atlantic rivers. This plant is so plentiful along the upper course of the Puerta that it is the common belief that the waters of this stream are rendered medicinal by it. The palo-mulato, a conspicuous forest-tree, with a red, smooth bark, and generally destitute of leaves, is highly esteemed by the natives for its medicinal properties. They make a decoction of the bark, and use it in the treatment of the malarial fevers, and from this circumstance we supposed, of course, it contained some bitter principle, but, on tasting it, we found it contained nothing of the sort, but, instead, was very rich in mucilage, to which it probably owes its medicinal value, if it really possesses any. The tree which the Indians call copalchí is abundant on the Pacific plains, where its scarred trunk, stripped of its bark, constantly attracts the notice of the traveler. It is of medium size, with long spreading branches and scanty foliage, and the bark is a light gray color, very bitter to the taste, and slightly aromatic. This is not cascarilla, as some have supposed. The Indians use it in the form of a decoction of the bark in the treatment of intermittent fever, and there can be but little doubt of its efficacy in this complaint.

The Ule, or India rubber tree, abounds on the Atlantic plains and in some localities on the elevated table-lands. The tree here is never large, its trunk being rarely more than one foot in diameter, and it is easily distinguished in the forest by its large coarse leaf, which somewhat resembles that of the multicaulis, or Chinese mulberry. At the present time only a small quantity of the gum is collected, but owing to the large number of trees in this region and the increasing demand for this substance, the day is probably not far distant when this valuable gum will be gathered here in large quantities for exportation.

There are many varieties of the agave, but the one which yields pulque, the famous Mexican drink, does not flourish in this part of the republic. The Indians make a drink from the bulbous portion of the wine-palm, which is found growing everywhere in the forest.

The mata-palo, or tree-killer, a singular vine, which finally becomes a tree, is constantly met with on the Atlantic plains, and is of sufficient interest to merit a brief notice. It starts as a little vine not thicker than a watch-cord, and either ascends the tree it is to destroy, or grows as a parasite on one of the branches, establishing, after awhile, its connection with the earth by sending down roots. Increasing in size, it finally envelops the trunk of the tree and its branches with huge coils, which by this time have grown to be a large mass of wood, and the original tree is quite concealed save a few limbs, perhaps, which have escaped. We noticed several royal-palms on the banks of the Coatzacoalcos, whose tall, straight trunks were completely enveloped by the tree-killer, but the graceful branches of the palm were seen towering above the tree-killer, and apparently ingrafted upon it. It always destroys the tree it attaches itself to, and then shortly dies itself. And finally, the famous tree-fern, so full of interest on account of its being the sole living representative of a class which in past geological ages formed dense primeval forests everywhere, is seen growing in profusion in the shady groves, where it often attains a height of thirty feet.

TIMBER FOR CONSTRUCTION.

Good timber, suitable for purposes of construction, is exceedingly plentiful on the Isthmus. Fortunately there are many varieties of it, quite sufficient in number to supply the various requirements pertaining to the building and operating of the proposed interoceanic canal. Most generally it is found growing on the unoccupied public lands, and can therefore be obtained at very little original cost.

In the Chimalapa region, along the banks of the Upper Coatzacoalcos and on the Rio Blanco, white pine, pitch pine, white oak, cypress, mammee-sapote, and chico-sapote abound. Many of the pines are of large size, and very tall and straight. On the plains of Tarifa the pine appears first at an elevation of about nine hundred feet above the sea, and in the Chimalapas they are first met with at a height rather more than this. On the high ridges in many places these gigantic trees form extensive forests, quite free from underbrush or shrubs or trees of any other sort. In these beautiful groves the earth is covered with a growth of green grass which, combined with the agreeable fresh odor of the pine and a bracing atmosphere, renders these pine-groves exceedingly enjoyable after a sojourn in the swamps and on the rivers. The oak found here is inferior to the same tree in the United States, but it is nevertheless of considerable value as timber for construction. The mammee-sapote resembles the chestnut-tree. It is not attacked by insects, and has been already extensively used in this vicinity, so we are informed by an engineer, for cross-ties on the railroad now in the course of construction between Vera Cruz and the city of Mexico. The chico-sapote wood is dark, and resembles black walnut, but it is tougher and the grain is finer.

These valuable timbers of the Chimalapa region can be floated down the Coatzacoalcos and its tributaries to some convenient point, whence they can be transported wherever needed on the

Isthmus. The numerous rapids on this river afford at almost any point abundant water-power for sawing lumber.

On the Atlantic plains mahogany, cedar, (*Cedrela odorata, L.,*) macaya, guapaque, mammee-sapote, and piqui, or iron-wood, are abundant, and all of them are well adapted for building purposes. Both the mahogany and the cedar are sawed into boards at Manatitlan, and are used in building houses there. The Indians use these two woods for making their canoes, or dug-outs, and it is said the cedar is slightly preferred to the mahogany for this purpose. One of these dug-outs, if properly taken care of, last twenty years, or even more, which gives one a very good idea of the durability of these woods when exposed in this climate. The macaya, guapaque, and iron-wood are hard and durable, and since they are indestructible by insects, are, like the mammee-sapote, well adapted for railroad cross-ties, spiles, and the like.

On the Pacific plains lignum-vitæ, rosewood, calabash, and ebony are the most common and most valuable woods for construction. They are all small and very hard. Along the lagoons and near the water-courses there is a small quantity of mahogany, mammee-sapote, and guapaque.

The cciba is the most conspicuous forest-tree seen on the Atlantic plains. It is of great size and spread, and has huge roots above the ground, which, in their arrangement, resemble somewhat the knees of a ship, and serve as natural supports to the trunk. On the Pacific side the ceiba is not very common, but the hammatti-tree, which closely resembles it, is frequently seen. The latter has a larger leaf than the cciba, and its foliage is more abundant and of a deeper green color. These huge trees possess no value as timber, for the wood is very soft, and decays in a short time; and they are also of very little importance as fuel. The swamp-willow is found growing along the banks of the Atlantic rivers, but this tree here is always small, rarely more than a foot in diameter.

ROADS, TRANSPORTATION, AND CANOE NAVIGATION.

The roads on the Pacific Plains are very good, considering the small amount of labor and money expended in constructing them and keeping them in repair. They are passable for the rude ox-carts of the country, and are considerably used in transporting timber and produce. There is not sand enough in them, as might be expected, to render hauling difficult, but in the dry season they are very hot and dusty. No bridges of any sort are found here, and the same is true for all other parts of the Isthmus. The streams have to be forded, which, however, is readily done, even in ox-carts, except for a few days toward the close of the rainy season, when the rivers are so flooded as to be quite impassable. The soil and topography of this part of the Isthmus are of such a nature that excellent roads may be constructed in any direction at very little expense. These good roads do not, however, extend much beyond the limits of the Isthmus, even on this side of the Cordillera, for the road leading from Tehuantepec to Oaxaca is hilly, rocky, and quite impassable for wheeled vehicles of any sort, all the merchandise which passes over it being carried on pack-mules. The Cordillera, on the Isthmus of Tehuantepec, is pierced by five passes, through all of which, except the Masahua Pass, there are traveled roads or bridle-paths. The one in La Chivela Pass is the best known and most used, and was constructed about twenty years ago by American engineers; but it has fallen into decay, the bridges are all destroyed, and deep cuts and washes render it generally impassable, except for mule-trains and persons on horseback. With great difficulty, however, light carts are occasionally forced up this road, so we were informed. At Tarifa Pass we found the best natural opening through the Cordillera. Here the road makes no windings, nor ascents and descents, but penetrates the dividing-ridge in nearly a direct course, and by an ascent which, for the most part, is very gradual, reaches the elevated plains of Tarifa, and the entire length of the passage cannot be more than three miles, for we passed over it, our horses walking slowly, in one hour and ten minutes. Upon the level, open plains of Tarifa and Chivela, the roads are good and suitable for ox-carts. Further to the north, proceeding across the Isthmus, the roads become mere paths, which wind over hills and plains and through dense forests; crossing from time to time rivers, which are always fordable on horseback, except for a few weeks in the height of the rainy season. North of the Jumuapa or La Puerta River the roads are but little used, on account of the mud and water, and the canoe navigation begins there and takes their place. There are roads from La Puerta and Súchil to Minatitlan which are passable for mules and horses in the months of March, April, and May, but even then they are little traveled, the natives preferring to make the passage in their canoes. It is not only in crossing the Isthmus canoes are employed, but nearly all the transportation and traveling on the Atlantic plains, in various directions, is done by this means. These canoes are made out of a solid stick of mahogany or red cedar by the natives, and are of all sizes, from the light traveling-canoe, capable of holding two persons, to the large cargo-canoes, which carry six tons of merchandise or produce and half a dozen passengers. Many of them are nicely finished, with seats and row-locks, and have fine models, which is highly creditable to the builders, considering they have no other tools than rude axes and machetes. Toward the stern a section is roofed over, by bending small sticks and fastening them to the side of the canoe as sort of rafters, upon which a shingling of green oba-leaves is tied with the bijuco-vines. This is called the casa, or house, and is set apart for the accommodation of the passengers, and affords sufficient protection from the sun and rain. Three Indians compose the crew. The most experienced one takes his seat in the stern, and steers with a paddle, and is called the captain or patron, and all his commands are promptly obeyed. The others, who call themselves palenqueros, push the craft with long poles, to the end of which a forked piece of very hard wood is lashed. These fellows, standing in the bow, plant their poles on the bottom of the stream, or against a log or the limb of a tree, and then push the canoe forward, walking aft as she goes until they reach the after-part of the vessel, when they withdraw their poles, march forward again to the bow, and plant them for another push, going through each movement with the precision and uniformity of a military drill. The skill these people display in managing and propelling their canoes along the river-banks, obstructed with snags and rapids, is truly surprising, and on many occasions called forth our hearty commendations. Ascending the rivers, all of which have constant downward currents, the canoe is kept within an arm's length of the shore, and fifteen miles is considered a good day's work, if the crew has a heavy load, but a light traveling-canoe often makes as much as thirty miles in a single day. Descending, paddles are used, and the craft is run in the center of the stream, to take advantage of the current, when fifty miles can be readily accomplished in one working-day. At night all hands abandon the canoes, to sleep on shore in the Indian huts or on the river-bank. The patrons invariably recommend this course on account of the danger of being attacked by alligators in the canoes at night.

High up the rivers, where there are a great many strong rapids, the Indians navigate the streams on the balsa, which consists of three unhewn logs, each about twelve feet long and eight inches in diameter, fastened together by wooden pins. An unusually light wood, the palo-mulato, is selected for the construction of balsas. They carry two or three persons, and draw only about six inches of water, and, being very light, the natives carry them on their shoulders around the rapids when it is not possible to ascend them.

The novelty of this mode of traveling, the dense overhanging tropical vegetation on either river-bank, the huge trees, covered with a thousand curious parasites and epiphytes, the beautiful hanging vines and creepers, the long lines of the feathery hymbal and green camolote, forming here and there trim borders to the river, and looking like well-kept hedges, the numerous flocks of screaming parrots, the monkeys chattering in the trees, and the water-fowls, in almost infinite number and variety, lining the beach and wading in the shallow streams, all combined to make the ascent of the rivers, as we went slowly along, day by day, exceedingly interesting and enjoyable. But we passed sleepless nights, tormented by myriads of insects and chilled by the cold winds and rain-storms.

CHAPTER IV.

INHABITANTS.

It is estimated that of the 8,000,000 inhabitants of the republic of Mexico, 5,000,000 are Indians, direct descendants of the Aztecs and other aboriginal tribes and races. On the Isthmus of Tehuantepec, as in all sparsely settled districts of the republic, the proportion of Indian population is much greater than this. The aborigines, although a conquered race, and reduced to the condition of laborers, possessing neither property nor education, have, nevertheless, identified themselves with the dominant European race, adopting their laws and their religion, and, to some extent, their civilization, differing in these respects greatly from the less fortunate Indians of the United States, or those that Columbus found inhabiting the islands of the West Indies. The latter race has become extinct, while the wretched condition of the former, our own Indian tribes, is well known to every one. This difference in favor of the Indians of Mexico is probably owing to their more civilized condition at the time of the conquest, and also to the fostering care of the Roman Catholic Church.

In the larger towns there are a few Americans, English, French, Germans, and Italians, who are generally engaged in mercantile pursuits, but the whole number of them on the Isthmus does not exceed two hundred. There is a larger class, composed of the direct descendants of the Spanish conquerors and European emigrants, mixed more or less with the aboriginal races. The officials and persons of wealth generally belong to this class. The Indians call them " gente de razon," people of reason. They are rather darker than Spaniards, and neither so large nor so handsome.

The Indians are found settled over the whole Isthmus, generally living in towns or villages, or large haciendas. They are of a mild and gentle disposition, little inclined to war or cruel practices. They seem to have but little natural fondness for hunting, although the country abounds in game. The men are rather smaller than the Indians of our own western plains, but, nevertheless, they are very muscular, and possess, many of them, wonderful endurance. In color they are lighter than our own Indians, and their features are much finer, and the expression of the face is more pleasing. The women are small and delicately made, and many of the young ones have beautiful figures, approaching nearer the classic models than any living female forms we have ever seen. Their hands and arms are particularly delicate and well-shaped, which characteristic, considering the great amount of manual labor they perform, is probably an inheritance from their Aztec forefathers, many of whom were accustomed to a life of ease and luxury. The hair is coarse, straight, and jet-black, and the men are without beards. The dress of the females consists of a skirt, usually of white linen, which is made by fastening a square piece of the material about the waist with a belt, so that the robe hangs gracefully about the hips and reaches below the knees; the chest and shoulders are often covered with a cape made of the same stuff, but it also often happens that no covering of any sort protects the upper part of the body. The men wear white cotton pantaloons, and have the singular habit of rolling up the legs as high as possible; the shirt is of the same material, and is worn outside the pantaloons. In the winter season the thermometer occasionally falls as low as 59°, but no additional clothing is ever put on. Both sexes wear sandals made of rawhide, which are tied to the feet with coarse thongs. One of the thongs always passes in the space between the great toe and the one next to it, and these toes are, in consequence, widely separated; and we often noticed this peculiarity in the feet of little Indian children who had never worn sandals. The male children go entirely naked until they attain the age of puberty; but the females, however young, are always clad as modestly as their mothers. The walls of the houses are usually made of bamboo, occasionally plastered with clay, and the roofs are of thatch, either palm-leaves or grass. Instead of nails, hinges, bolts, and so forth, the several parts are lashed together with "bijucos," or vines, which serve all the purposes of ropes, and last longer. These rude dwellings are destitute of floors, chimneys and windows. There are no tables nor chairs, and the people squat on the earth to take their food, the whole family eating from one dish in common. A hammock is found in nearly every house. These people are invariably hospitable to strangers, and often cheerfully give up their bed and hammock for their accommodation, for which they never make any charge; but if any food is taken, they expect to be paid for it. The dogs, pigs, and chickens occupy the house in common with the family. The women perform all the house-work, assist in cultivating the milpas, and prepare and cook the food. They rise before the men in the morning, often as early as three o'clock, and begin the preparation of the morning meal. We found the Indians remarkably honest and faithful attendants, and not one of our party had anything stolen during our residence on the Isthmus. The robberies in Mexico are rarely committed by this class.

Nearly all the men speak the Spanish language in addition to their own Indian tongue; the women, however, rarely know any other language than their own native dialects, which, for each tribe, is quite a distinct language, and is not generally understood except by the individuals of the same tribe. In conversation between Indians who understand and speak Spanish very well, we observed that they invariably employed their own guttural tongue, seeming to prefer it to the

Spanish language. Except in large Spanish towns, it is seldom that an Indian is found who is able to read and write. In large Indian villages of two thousand inhabitants, there are no schools of any sort. Formerly, when each village had its priest, a few of the children were taught to read and write. But it does occasionally happen that an Indian, in despite of the absence of an early education, and the feeling of caste, which is very strong against him, attains an eminent position in the state or in the army.

The Christian religion, introduced by the Spaniards more than three hundred years ago, is universally professed by the Indians, and not a trace of their ancient religion seems to remain among them. They appear to regard with horror and avoid with superstitious fear all those places reputed to contain remains or evidences of their former religion. Indeed, it is singular, but it is nevertheless quite true, that the Indians now-a-days pay more attention to the ceremonies belonging to the Christian religion than the white races who introduced it among them. We observed that, as the Indian villages were more remote from the centers of European civilization, the services of the church were more regularly performed, notwithstanding the absence of priests. In such remote Indian villages the "ave" and the "oracion" are constantly heard, while in the larger Spanish towns the churches and convents are used for barracks. The Indians have the right of suffrage, and very generally exercise it. In their own villages the president and alcalde are generally appointed from their own class, and exercise authority as Mexican officials and not as the chiefs of the tribe. There are, however, a few of the aboriginal laws and customs still in existence, as, for instance, the village or tribe possessing land as a common property. In their music, songs, and dances they have retained much that belonged to the original inhabitants of the country. The arts, for which this race was at one time quite celebrated, have nearly all been lost; perhaps the manufacture of pottery and certain sorts of dyed-fabrics are the only exceptions to this rule. In the marked preference for certain kinds of food and the manner of preparing it, much that belonged to the ancient Mexican is constantly noticed by the traveler. Corn or maize is the staple article of food, and takes the place of rice for the Asiatic, or wheat for the European. In preparing it for food the grains are soaked in lime-water for five hours, which loosens the husks or skins, when they are removed by rubbing with the hands. The corn is then placed on the metlatl, a flat stone, and ground to a fine pulpy mass, after which it is made into thin cakes, and baked on an earthen griddle. These cakes are very well known as the "tortillas," and, if well made and eaten when quite hot, are rather palatable. When they are baked brown, they are called "totoposti," and taste like parched corn, and foreigners generally prefer them in this form to the tortillas. They will keep for several weeks, and the Indians always take a supply of them when they go on a journey. Grinding corn according to the Indian plan is very laborious and tedious, and requires one woman to work about five hours daily to prepare enough corn for a family of four persons; but in spite of this, all attempts to introduce mills and hand-machines for grinding the corn have resulted in failure. Every male has a machete, a long knife resembling a sword, with which he builds his house, clears the land and plants the seeds, defends himself from wild beasts, and attacks his enemy in battle.

There are five distinct tribes found on the Isthmus, each of which occupies a different section of the country. The language of each tribe is quite distinct, and is neither understood nor spoken by the other tribes. The most friendly relations exist between all of them.

The Zapotecos inhabit the Pacific plains and the elevated table-lands from Tarifa to Petapa. They are the most intelligent as well as the most industrious Indians on the Isthmus, and, in personal appearance, are superior to any others. This race, at the present time, inhabits an extensive region along the Pacific coast, both east and west of Tehuantepec, and was once one of the most powerful of the aboriginal tribes. They were able to defy for a long time the Spanish soldiers, by their bravery and skill in war, qualities for which the race is quite celebrated to this day. Recent intestine wars have nearly desolated their section of the Isthmus. The cities of Juchitan and Tehuantepec have been repeatedly sacked and burned, and the country of the Zapotecos has greatly declined in wealth and prosperity in the last decade, and the population has materially fallen off. The women, many of them, are very handsome. They wear, instead of the ordinary plain white skirt, one composed of strips of various-colored material, with the strips so arranged as to encircle the body, which makes a very gay and pleasing costume. They are also extremely fond of the Tyrian purple skirt, the dye of which is obtained from a shell-fish (*Aplysia depilans*) found along the shores of the Pacific. The process of obtaining this dye is very tedious, for each shell only yields a drop or two of the liquid, which is emitted on gently squeezing the shell-fish. The fabric, when dyed, is very costly, a skirt (three or four square yards of material) not unfrequently being sold for twenty dollars. A stuff to imitate it is manufactured in England and sent here for sale, but the Indians instantly detect the difference, and always prefer the native article, although it is much more costly. The native fabric possesses a disagreeable fishy odor, which is said to be highly esteemed by the Zapoteco women. A head-dress, composed of a native white lace, is a striking feature in the costume of a Zapoteco female, and is, so far as our observation extends, confined to this tribe. A vocabulary of their language, which we took while residing among them, is appended to this report.

The Huaves, a small tribe, are confined to four towns near the Pacific Ocean, viz: San Mateo, Santa Maria, San Dionisio, and San Francisco. The men are tall, well-formed, and possess great strength and endurance, and the women are ugly and very repulsive in appearance. They have higher and broader foreheads than their neighbors, the Zapotecos, and they are greatly inferior to them in intelligence, and enterprise, and bravery. Fish is their principal article of food, the rivers and lagoons near their towns abounding in them, and fishing is their chief occupation. They supply the southern portion of the Isthmus with salt fish, which they carry on their backs in huge baskets for many miles from town to town seeking purchasers. They were but little inclined to sell us food or allow us shelter in their houses, and we only obtained what we required by making an official demand for the same on the alcalde. Their towns are rarely visited by strangers, and, at our approach, the women and children ran away and hid themselves, screaming as they ran, apparently overcome with fright.

It is believed by some persons that these Indians are the descendants of emigrants from Peru, before the discovery of America, and a tradition to this effect is said to exist among them. From the people themselves we were not able to get any information on this point. We asked one of the most intelligent of them what language he spoke as his native tongue, and he replied in Spanish, in a very lofty manner, "the language God gave my people." It is regretted that circumstances prevented us from collecting a vocabulary of the language spoken by this isolated and singular tribe, for it might have thrown some light on their origin and history.

The ignorance and simplicity of these people are very well shown in the following story which is related concerning them. At the time the French fleet which accompanied Maximilian was expected to land in Mexico, the president of the republic sent to each pueblo a request for a contribution of money, and at the same time directed that all the people should not fail to do their utmost to repel the invaders. The Huaves, in return, sent thirty dollars, and said that, should the expected fleet appear off their coast, they would immediately go out in their canoes and attack it.

The Soques, or Chimalapas, occupy the mountain towns of Santa Maria and San Miguel, and number altogether about two thousand souls. It is said they came quite recently from the neighboring state of Chiapas, and their distinct language and different personal appearance lend some credit to this report. In stature they are short, with large chests and powerful muscles. They are rather darker than the Indians of the plains, although the true color of their skin is often greatly obscured by the pinta or leprous skin-disease which is so common among them. Both men and women have very repulsive countenances, but they are quite harmless and docile. The men are extremely intemperate, and it is quite within the bounds of truth to say that half the males are constantly in a state of intoxication; but, strange enough, none of them are refractory or quarrelsome when in this condition. During our stay of fourteen days in the town of Santa Maria Chimalapa, where intemperance is so prevalent, we did not hear of nor see a single case of mania-a-potu, nor any other disease the result of drink, at which we were not a little surprised. The liquor most in common use is known as aguardiénte, or chinguirito, is colorless, and has the flavor of rum, for it is made from the juice of the sugar-cane. In nearly every Indian hut a primitive still is kept for this purpose. We did not see any females intoxicated, and at the fiestas we observed the women neither ate nor drank with the men, but served them; nor did they take any part in the singing and dancing. The men are very ignorant and superstitious, and exceedingly timid. They declined at first to accompany the party in the exploration of the headwaters of the Coatzacoalcos River from fear, so they said, of being destroyed by wild beasts, huge serpents, and violent tempests, all of which they assured us were to be met with in the region we proposed to visit.

The injurious and disgusting practice of eating earth is quite common in this tribe, and especially in the town of Santa Maria. The earth selected for this purpose is a very white clean sand, (kaolin,) which in appearance is not unlike the ordinary granulated sugar constantly seen on our tables. Little holes are seen about the streets and by the roadsides, a foot or more in depth, and large enough to admit the hand, from which the earth is obtained. In the house formerly occupied by the priest as a school there are great holes dug in the rude earthen plastering, which we were told were made by the pupils to get earth to eat during school-hours. The practice is most common among the children, and in a short time produces a dropsical condition of the whole body, with jaundiced skin and eyes, a dull, vacant stare, puffy cheeks, and a slow and unsteady gait. In answer to our questions, (made to a boy of fourteen years of age,) "Why do you eat this earth; do you like the taste of it?" He said, "It is one of my vices," and by his behavior seemed to be ashamed of it. The language is very harsh and gutteral, and a vocabulary of it, taken during our residence among them, is appended.

The Mijes, in personal appearance, habits, and language, resemble very much the Chimalapas, and are probably the same race, although they regard themselves as having a distinct origin, and are at present a separate tribe. They have but one village, San Juan Guichicovi, in the vicinity of which they cultivate a considerable quantity of corn and frijoles, and they also raise mules and cattle. They have expended a good deal of labor in making roads leading to their mountain village, and in this respect they are in advance of their Chimalapa neighbors, as they are, indeed, in many others. Intemperance is their besetting vice. The habit of drinking to excess is much more common among the mountain Indians than those inhabiting the plains, and this rule is quite universal on the Isthmus, the reason for which, however, is not very apparent.

On the Atlantic plains we find the Atzec or Mexican Indians, and they speak the Nahuatl, or ancient language of Mexico, used in turn both by the Toltecs and Atzecs. They are nearly equal to the Zapotecos in personal appearance and superior in physique, but they are more grave and not so intelligent. They are remarkably peaceful, and local rebellions are very rare among them. In cultivating the soil and cutting the valuable timber found on the Atlantic plains they find remunerative employment. Many of them are occupied as raftsmen and boatmen on the rivers, and, trained to these occupations from boyhood, become very expert and trustworthy.

There are a few Zambos or mulattoes, who chiefly inhabit the village of El Barrio, the most of whom are employed as muleteers. Their negro ancestors were introduced into the country as slaves, to cultivate the Marquesanas, when these estates belonged to the wealthy successors of Cortes. In many respects these mulattoes are superior to the aboriginal inhabitants surrounding them, abundant evidence of which is to be found in the recent increase in population and wealth of El Barrio, their town, which, less than fifty years ago, contained about a dozen houses; but it has now about fifteen hundred inhabitants, and is commercially the most important town in the central division of the Isthmus. The inhabitants we found on the banks of the Uspanapa River are all mulattoes, who settled there quite recently, emigrating from Tabasco. A French colony was started on the banks of this river in 1828, and their clearing, which is of considerable extent, is visible yet. Our guide informed us that most of the colonists died of the fever, and a number of others committed suicide. It is certain that not one of them is left. There are no inhabitants on the river higher up than thirty miles from its mouth, and it struck us as rather singular that the Indians have never occupied the fertile lands which border this fine river.

LANGUAGES OF THE ABORIGINAL TRIBES.

This vocabulary represents the language of the Zapotecos as it is spoken at Tehuantepec, and that of the Logues as it is spoken at San Miguel, Chimalapa:

English.	Zapoteco.	Logue.
Man.	Nge-é-hu.	Hát-ty.
Woman.	Gu-ná.	Yo-ma.
Boy.	Bah-du-nge-e-hu.	Chĭck-sháh.
Girl.	Bah-du-jap-áh.	Yo-ma-ú-nay.
Infant.	Bah-nu-é-ne.	Mas-sañ-ú-nay.
My father.	Be-sho-o-sé.	Há-tō
My mother.	Ne-áh-ah.	Mám-ma.
My husband.	Schē-lah.	Ha-a-yah.
My wife.	Schē-lah.	Meuh.
My son.	Schī-ne.	Téyn-man-na.
My daughter.	Schī-ne-jap-ah.	Téyn-man-na.
My elder brother.	Be-záh-nah-lu-go-lah.	At-sze.
My younger brother.	Be-zah-nah-we-ne.	Poh-at-tuk.
My elder sister.	Be-záh-nah-lu-go-lah.	Seut-zeh.
My younger sister.	Be-zah-nah-we-ne.	Poh-at-tuk.
An Indian.	Re-re.	Hàh-mo.
People.	Be-ny.	Penn.
Head.	E-káy.	Kén-păck.
Hair.	Gé-chah.	Wáh-ee.
Face.	Lu.	Wee-náh-kah.
Forehead.	Lu-kwah.	Kén-păck.
Ear.	De-á-gah.	Ta-a-tzénck.
Eye.	Be-zah-lú.	Wé-tam.
Nose.	Shé-lu.	Ké-nah.
Mouth.	Ru-wah.	Heup.
Tongue.	Lu-ché.	To-óty.
Language.		O-tó-e.
Teeth.	Lah-yah.	Tentz.
Beard.	Ge-chah-ru-wah.	Añ-wát-tzee.
Neck.	Yah-né.	Win-tú.
Arm.	Năh.	Shah.
Hand.	Nah-yah.	Dzán-kwe.
Fingers.	Be-kwé-ne.	Weé-kee.
Thumb.	Be-kwe-ne-ro.	Wán-te-wee-kee.
Nails.	Be-shú-gäh.	Ken-tshus.
Chest.	Lăh-je-dó-a	Tsóh-koy.
Belly.	En-dăh-ne.	Tzeck.
Female breasts.	She-je-gu-na.	Tzsú-tze.
Leg.	Ne-yáh.	Pú-ee.
Foot.	Ne-yáh.	Mán-ku-ee.
Toes.	Be-kwé-ne.	Man-ku-ee-wee-kee.

LANGUAGES OF THE ABORIGINAL TRIBES—Continued.

English.	Zapoteco.	Logue.
Bone.	Je-tah.	Päck.
Blood.	Ré-ne.	Nen-pin.
Town.	Ge-jé.	Kúm-ku-e.
Chief.	Sha-é-kah.	
Warrior.		Tuck-she-áp-pa.
House.	Yo.	Tenck.
Skin-lodge.	Yo-dah-ge-de.	Na-ác-ca-tenck.
Bow and arrow.		Say-hen-pét-ku-ee.
Sandals.	Gā-lah-gé-de.	Kén-ack.
Tobacco.	Gā-zah.	Tsa-we.
Sky.	Ge-bah.	
Cloud.		Úhp-sah.
Sun.	Gu-bé-jah.	Háh-mah.
Moon.	Bay-u.	Shay-pay.
Star.	Ba-lah-gé.	Mâá-tzah.
Day.	Je.	Háh-mah.
Night.	Wah-shé-ne.	Tsú-he.
Morning.	Ge-shé.	Hoh-he.
Early morning.		Ney-tsú-he-te.
Evening.	U-ah-gé.	Tzi-hé-an.
Dry season.	Gu-see-báh.	Hah-mah-ank-shun.
Wet season.	Gu-see-gé-ah.	Tu-ank-shun.
Wind.	Bee.	Shan-wah.
Thundering.	Ka-sge-jé.	Men-yen.
Lightning.	Kah yah po né-sa.	Tem-pah.
Rain.	Ne-sah-gé.	Tu.
Snow.		Tzú-ma.
Fire.	Ge.	Hu-ku-tah.
Water.	Ne-sah.	Nêah.
Earth.	Yu.	Năs.
Sea.	Ne-sah-dó.	Mé-ah.
River.	Ge-go.	Pah-hok.
Prairie.		Heuñ.
Hill.	Dă-ne.	Ko-tzch.
Mountain.	Ge-she-róh.	Tzá-ma-kue.
Stone.	Ge-ā.	Tza.
Salt.	Zé-de.	Ka-na.
Iron.	Ge-báh.	Téu-en-kue.
Forest.	Ge-she.	Win-tzám-a.
Tree.	Yah-gah.	Ku-ee.
Wood.	Yah-gah.	Ku-ee.
Leaf.	Ban-dáh-gah.	I-eé.
Bark.	Ge-de-láh-de.	Ku-ee-na-ka.
Grass.	Gé-she.	Mook.

S. Ex. 6——17

LANGUAGES OF THE ABORIGINAL TRIBES—Continued.

English.	Zapoteco.	Logue.
Pine.	Ge-re-bé-je.	Tchin.
Maize.	Shú-bah.	Mock.
Squash.	Ge-to.	Ú-koom.
Flesh.	Be-lah.	Shees.
Dog.	Be-ko.	Nŭ.
Wolf.	Gay-u.	Páh-ho.
Fox.	Bay-tay.	
Deer.	Be-jé-ñah.	Mén-āh.
Hare.	Be-au-ná.	Heuñ-kóh-e-ah.
Tortoise.	Be-go.	Tú-ke.
An animal, (indefinite.)	Máh-nĕ.	
Fly.	Be-ah-lá-ze.	Hén-hen.
Mosquito.	Be-u-sjé.	Ú-suh.
Snake.	Bāyn-dah.	Saáh-heen.
Rattlesnake.	Bāyn-dah-gu-be-sje.	Saah-káh-ka.
Bird, (thing that flies.)	Ma-né-re-pa-pa.	Hohn.
Egg.	Je-tah-bay-ray.	Bóh-hok.
Feathers.	Du-be.	Pench.
Wings.	Shé-ah.	Saah.
Turkey.	Tā-u.	We-ah-ku.
Pigeon.	Gú-gu.	Kú-ku.
Fish.	Băyn-dah.	Kóhe-kay.
Name.	La-ah.	Tim-neú-he.
White.	Nah-ke-ché.	Póh-ho.
Black.	Nah-yah-see.	Yenck.
Red.	Nah-zhé-ña.	Tza-patz.
Light-blue.		Tzu-tzhus.
Yellow.	Nah-gu-che.	Poots-poots.
Light-green.		Same as light-blue.
Great.	Nah-ró.	Ko-me.
Small.	Nah-wé-ne.	Waok-seng.
Strong.	Nah-ge-je.	Peu-me.
Old.	Nah-yu-sho.	Ah-pú-am.
Old man.	Re-go-lah.	
Young.	Nah-wé-ne.	Wack-seng.
Good.	Nah-sá-ka.	When-hén.
Bad.	Nah-jár-bă.	Ne-nah.
Dead.	Gă-to.	Ka-wum.
Alive.	Nah-bah-ne.	Hech-pah.
Cold.	Nah-nán-da.	Wa-é-ie.
Warm.	Nan-dá.	Nótz-pah.
I.	Näh.	Tus.
You.	Le.	Mish-ha.
He.	Lah-ve.	Taá-peu.

LANGUAGES OF THE ABORIGINAL TRIBES—Continued.

English.	Zapoteco.	Logue.
We.	Lah-ka-nó.	
Ye.	Lah-tú.	
They.	Lah-ka-bé.	
This.	Bu-re.	Yeu-pèuh.
That.	Be-re-ka.	Kaa-peuh.
All.	Ge ráh.	Wa-kus.
Many.	Stáh-le.	Schen-hen.
Who.	Tu.	Eé-weuh.
Far.	Ze-tu.	Yāh-heu.
Near.	Gah-sha.	Tó-meh.
Here.	Rah-ré.	Yeu-he.
There.	Rah-ré-ka.	Kā-hà.
To-day.	Ya-nah-jé.	Ga-e.
To-morrow.	Ge-shé.	Hó-he.
Yesterday.	Na-a-ge.	Téu-heuck.
Yes.	Yah.	Heu.
No.	Kah.	U-ee.
One.	Tu-be.	Tu-ma.
Two.	Tchú-pah.	May-stzan.
Three.	Tchā-nah.	Tu-wāng.
Four.	Tah-pah.	Māck-tá-shan.
Fve.	Gi-yu.	Mors-shan.
Six.	Tsho-pah.	Too-tán.
Seven.	Gáh-je.	Wens-too-tan.
Eight.	Shō-no.	Too-doo-tan.
Nine.	Gah.	Max-too-tan.
Ten.	Tche.	Mác-kan.
Eleven.	Tche-be-tu-be.	Mac-tu-ma.
Twelve.	Tche-be-tchu-pah.	Mac-ku-es-ta-kan.
Twenty.	Gàm-de.	Eps-shan.
Thirty.	Gan-de-be-tche.	Eps-ko-mac-kan.
Forty.	Tchú-pah-lah-te-gan-de.	Wes-tenk-eps-shan.
Fifty.	Tchu-pah-lah-te-gan-de-no-tche.	Wes-tenk-eps-co-mac-kan.
Sixty.	Tchā-nah-lah-te-gan-de.	Tenk-eps-shan.
Seventy.	Tcha-nah-lah-te-gan-de-no-tche.	Tenk-eps-co-mac-kan.
Eighty.	Tah-pah-lah-te-gan-de.	Mac-taps-shan.
Ninety	Tah-pah-lah-te-gan-de-no-tche.	Mac-taps-co-mac-kan.
One hundred.	Te-gah-yu-ah.	Moss-eps-shan.
One thousand.	Tche-gah-yu-ah.	Mac-eps-shan.

LANGUAGES OF THE ABORIGINAL TRIBES—Continued.

The verbs used here in the Zapoteco language are of the imperative mode. They have no infinitive. In the Logue language the action is expressed as going on in the passive sense.

English.	Zapoteco.	Logue.
To eat.	Gu-dó.	Kens-oi-pa.
To drink.	Go-a. (Eng. *a*.)	Uk-oi-pa.
To run.	Be-sho-ñe.	Yuk-poi-pa.
To dance.	Be-yáh.	Etz-pa.
To sing.	Béan-dah.	Wān-pa.
To sleep.	Gú-se.	Moung-pa.
To speak.	Gu-né.	O-tón-pa.
To see.	Bé-yah.	A-má-pa.
To love.	Gu-nash-ché.	
To kill.	Be-té.	Yah-kaá-pa.
To sit.	Gu-ré.	Tseún-pa.
To stand.	Gus-au-gáh.	Tén-pa.
To go.	Gus-záh.	Neúc-pa.
To come.	Gu-dáh.	Me-ún-pa
To walk.	Gus-záh.	Tung-á-pa.
To work.	Be-ne-jé-ña.	Yósh-pa.
To steal.	Gu-láh-nah.	Núm-pa.
To lie.	Bees-se-ghé.	U-naá-pa.
To give.	Be-dé.	
To laugh.	Be-shé-je.	Sheéck-pa.
To cry.	Be-kar-rhé-je.	Way-héy-pa.

TOWNS, VILLAGES, HACIENDAS, ETC.

Tehuantepec is situated on the left bank of the river of the same name, and is twelve miles from the sea. It is spread out over a valley, and on the sides of several hills, in such a manner as to make the situation a pleasing one. The river, a clear stream, fordable on horseback, and about a hundred yards wide, skirts along the town for a distance of half a mile, and affords a primitive but excellent water-supply. The inhabitants, about 12,000 in number, are principally Zapoteco Indians, but in this town there is a larger proportion of the European element—the descendants of the Spanish conquerors and other foreigners—than in any other locality on the Isthmus. Perhaps one-half of the houses are adobe with tiled roofs, and the remaining are built of bamboo, and all of them are of one story. Both inside and outside they are covered with whitewash, and this, combined with the white sand of the streets, and the entire absence of trees, or any green thing in them, produces a glare which is very unpleasant. There is a large plaza in the center of the town, where the people promenade in the cool of the evening, and listen to music, of which they are extremely fond. The streets are wide, and in a few places they are paved, but they are not regularly laid out. In the several old buildings in Tehuantepec, which was an important and populous city at the time of the Spanish conquest, we failed to discover any traces of the peculiar architecture of the Mexican aborigines. The old church and convent of Santo Domingo are said to have been built by one Cocijopi, the last cacique of the Zapotecos, but on examining these buildings they were found not to differ materially from many other similar structures in Mexico, and exhibit abundant evidence of having been constructed by the Spaniards, or at least under their direction. There is a small hotel here, and there are several shops where foreign goods of almost any sort can be purchased. In the summer this town is said to be very hot, and in the winter the streets are filled with dust and drifting sand. The public mail reaches Tehuantepec once a week, and this is the only town in the southern and central divisions of the Isthmus where this is the case. There is but very little commerce, and the people are becoming poorer every year. The manufactures were formerly of considerable importance, but of late years they have greatly declined.

Salina Cruz is the sea-port of Tehuantepec, with which it is connected by a good level road, the distance being about twelve miles. There are only six small houses here, and they are unoccupied, except during the occasional presence of a ship in the harbor. The harbor is completely protected from the northers by a semicircle of hills, and besides this it possesses several natural advantages, which render its improvement much less difficult than the harbor of La Ventosa. The construction of a custom-house has been commenced by the Mexican government. Fresh water for the ships in the harbor is at present very difficult to obtain, and the supply of it is limited.

La Ventosa is the name of a slight indentation of the coast-line at the mouth of the Tehuantepec River. There is no town at this point, and, indeed, there is not so much as a single hut here.

San Mateo is built in a clump of timber on the sandy shores of a small lagoon, which communicates with the sea, and is one of the principal towns of the Huave Indians. The dwellings, with one or two exceptions, are made of bamboo, and are located without any reference to regular streets. The population is now about 800, but, from the large size of the church, half in ruins, we concluded that at a former period it was much greater.

Santa Maria is located half a mile from the sea on the sandy beach, and is protected from the scorching rays of the sun by a few forest trees. The population does not exceed four hundred, all of whom are Indians. Their squalid dwellings are infested with fleas and vermin to so great a degree that to sleep or even to repose for an instant in them was impossible. We observed that the drinking-water, which is obtained from holes dug in the sand about the streets, is brackish and contains many impurities. It should be filtered before used.

Huilotepec is a small village of about fifty inhabitants, prettily located in the valley of the Tehuantepec River. Its inhabitants raise cattle and cultivate corn for the markets of Tehuantepec and Juchitan.

Juchitan was, until last winter, the most important town on the Pacific plains, except Tehuantepec, when, during a battle between its inhabitants and the troops of Oaxaca, it was set on fire, and fully one-half of the town was reduced to ashes. Before this calamity, it contained a population of ten thousand, and possessed considerable wealth. Although the inhabitants belong to the Zapoteco race, they are constantly spoken of on the Isthmus as "Los Juchitecos," and they are quite celebrated for their industrious habits, sobriety, and intelligence. They are the best cultivators of the soil found on the Isthmus; and in the various wars in which they have taken part, they have gained a reputation for bravery and endurance which is very creditable to their race. We visited Juchitan a few days after its destruction, and in the place of the former flourishing town we beheld a mass of smoking ruins; and all the people not killed in the battle had fled to the forest for safety, save a few old Indian women, who stood in sorrowful groups around the little heaps of ashes, the ruins of their former humble homes.

El Espinal is a village of four hundred inhabitants, on the left bank of the Rio de los Perros, four miles above Juchitan. This place is of quite recent origin, having sprung up about the residence of a bishop who lived here at a former period.

Iztaltepec is, since the destruction of Juchitan, the second town of importance on the Pacific slope, and has a population of six thousand souls. Of late years it has increased in size, owing to the fact that the repeated civil conflicts in Tehuantepec and Juchitan have caused many peaceably disposed persons to take up their residence in this town, which has been fortunate enough to escape the calamity of local rebellions. It is now the center of the indigo trade, and once a year a number of merchants assemble here for the purpose of buying the indigo grown by the natives.

San Geronimo is located on the right bank of the Rio de los Perros, five miles above Iztaltepec, and contains about two thousand inhabitants. The country surrounding it is slightly rolling, and is well adapted to growing indigo, corn, and garden vegetables, the latter being of a better quality than those of any other locality on the Pacific side.

Chihuitan, a small village of four hundred inhabitants, stands in the picturesque valley of Los

Perros, at the foot of the Sierra. This region is said to be particularly well suited to the cultivation of indigo, and sugar-cane also grows very well. Many of the residents are unfortunately afflicted with pinta.

Comitancillo is a little Indian village on the Estéro de Camotepec, at the point where the road leading from Tehuantepec to San Geronimo crosses it. The land is low, and is therefore readily irrigated, all the water of the estéro being turned to this use. The forest trees are considerably larger just here than those generally found on this side of the Cordillera.

Tlacotepec, a secluded little village of 250 inhabitants, is located on the same stream, at the very base of a large spur of the Cordillera. Half a mile west of the town, in a valley, there is a remarkable formation of coarse chalk, which is used by the natives as a purge. In a limestone mountain near the village there is a hollow cavity, which we were told was the entrance of a cave, but, on approaching it, it proved to be nothing more than a large indentation in the mountain side.

La Venta is the largest hacienda on the extensive estates known as the Marquesanas. The dwelling occupied by the owner of these famous estates is a large, well-built adobe, and surrounding it are about thirty inferior houses, which are occupied by the rancheros, the population altogether being about 150 souls.

Tarifa is also one of the haciendas of the Marquesanas, and is located on the broad, fertile plain of the same name, and contains twelve houses, all of an inferior sort.

Santiago is another hacienda of the same estate and on the same plain. It is smaller than that of Tarifa, and its herds are less numerous.

La Chivela is a large hacienda, beautifully situated on the plain of the same name. In addition to the ordinary dwellings of the rancheros, there is a well-built adobe house, one story high, with tiled roof and brick floors, which, through the kindness of Señor Maqueo, the owner, was occupied as the headquarters of the exploring party. This forms also a part of the Marquesanas. In the dry season the water-supply is deficient, and we were obliged to ride a distance of six miles to find a stream where a comfortable bath could be obtained.

El Barrio is a flourishing town of 1,500 inhabitants, most of whom are mulattoes. Many of the mules used in transporting cargoes across the Isthmus belong to this place, and many of the inhabitants follow the occupation of muleteers. There are several shops, where a variety of native and foreign articles are kept for sale, and there are also blacksmiths and shoemakers to be found in the town. The church, a substantial stone structure, is, like the town, of recent origin, having been finished in 1834. The town is located on a sandy ridge in the western end of the plain of Chivela, and the country in its immediate vicinity is barren.

Patapa is the oldest Spanish settlement in the mountainous section of the Isthmus, and is still the capital of the district, although El Barrio, distant from it only two miles, is a place of far more importance. The population does not exceed 1,000, and their number is said to be constantly on the decline. They are nearly all Zapoteco Indians.

Santo Domingo is a small village less than a mile from Patapa, of which it once formed a part. Its inhabitants are in all respects similar to those of Patapa.

San Miguel Chimalapa is located in the beautiful valley of the Chicapa, which, at this point, is more that 400 feet above the sea. High mountains, covered with tropical vegetation, surround this valley, converting it into a vast natural amphitheater, through which the river takes a tortuous course. This beautiful spot is the home of a portion of the wretched Chimalapas, who live in squalid huts, and pass half their existence in a state of intoxication. It is here that the best hammocks are manufactured, and it is, therefore, sometimes called the "hammock town." It was a novel sight to see the highways, as we rode into this village, obstructed with long threads of ixtle stretched across the road, which the natives were twisting into cords, for the manufacture of hammocks. The population is estimated at 500.

Santa Maria Chimalapa is an interesting Indian town, of 1,000 inhabitants. It is seldom visited by strangers, and on this account the characteristics of the aboriginal inhabitants are more marked than in any other locality on the Isthmus. The town is reached by only one very difficult road, barely passable for mules, which winds through the dense forests, often following the ridges in a very singular manner, thereby making the route a circuitous one. The town itself is located three miles from the Coatzacoalcos River, on a high, narrow ridge, the surface of which is composed of a remarkable white sand, or, more properly speaking, kaolin. There are three churches in this little place, and the foundation walls of a very large one, the construction of which was discontinued probably a hundred years ago; and there is also a "casa de ayuntamiento," where all the males of the village assemble several times a day to transact the public affairs of the community. The houses are small and squalid in appearance, and are constructed of bamboo and long grass, and they are not located with any reference to regular streets. The climate is damp, with a great deal of rain and cloudy weather, and, in consequence, malarial fever is quite prevalent among the natives, two of whom died of it during our stay in the village.

San Juan Guichicovi is a large Indian town, of 5,000 inhabitants, and is built on a high hill, at an elevation of several hundred feet above the surrounding country, and is spread over a considerable space. The houses are of an inferior sort, and the general appearance of the place is disagreeable, notwithstanding the fine location it enjoys. The people, like the Chimalapas, are very intemperate, and repulsive in appearance. They cultivate a considerable quantity of corn and frijoles, and raise mules and cattle. It is a common thing to find their patches of corn and frijoles, of an acre or two, in the midst of the dense forest, twenty miles or more from their village. There is an interesting old church, of enormous size, never completed, and which now serves to show how very great must have been the efforts made by the Spaniards at a former period to win the natives of this country over to the Christian religion.

Súchil is nothing more than a monterea of the mahogany-cutters, and contains ten small Indian houses. It is situated on the left bank of the Coatzacoalcos, at the head of canoe navigation; however, in the autumn and early winter the canoes proceed higher up than this. Canoes and boatmen can always be obtained here to descend the river. The rain-fall, just at this point, is very great, and, in consequence, the insects are unusually abundant and troublesome, so that the herds do not thrive at all. Considerable quantities of corn and tobacco are grown here.

Almagres is a flourishing Indian village, of 300 inhabitants, and is located on the right bank of the Coatzacoalcos, 22 miles above Minatitlan. At this point there is a high, sandy bluff, on which the present town was commenced as a French colony, in the year 1821, but there is now only one of the original families left, and the place has become, in all respects, like the usual Indian villages met with all over the Isthmus. So far, all attempts to settle this region with European colonies have been unsuccessful.

Minatitlan is the principal sea-port on the Isthmus, and possesses more wealth than any other town, and its population is estimated at 1,000, a considerable number of whom are foreigners. Owing to the construction of the houses with boards and shingles, the town is very unlike any other on the Isthmus, and might easily be taken for a village in one of the Southern States. In the winter, the town is enlivened by the presence of a number of ships, loading with the precious woods of the country. About ten thousand tons of mahogany and cedar are exported from this port every season; and, besides, there are considerable quantities or fustic, indigo, hides, and tobacco, which go to make up the not unimportant foreign commerce of the place.

Coatzacoalcos is a little village of 17 houses, and is situated at the mouth of the river of the same name. The inhabitants are fishermen and pilots; and the captain of the port of Minatitlan has also his official residence here.

There are several other important towns on the Isthmus, which, however, we had not an opportunity to visit.

LABORERS.

The last census of the Isthmus of Tehuantepec gives the number of inhabitants as 82,395, but since this enumeration was made the population, from civil wars and other causes, has greatly fallen off, and probably does not now exceed 50,000, of whom 30,000, at least, are females; for here the females outnumber the males to an extent which is very unusual. Of these 20,000 males, about 15,000, young and old, generally Indians, belong to that class from which laborers may be obtained; and of these, perhaps one in ten, or fifteen hundred persons, will be about as many of the present, inhabitants of the Isthmus as will be likely to seek employment as permanent laborers in constructing an interoceanic ship-canal. There is little doubt the Indians of other parts of Mexico, contiguous to the Isthmus, would gladly accept employment on this work, and many of them, judging from the accounts we received of their habits and powerful physiques, possess excellent natural qualifications for the sort of laborers needed. About three reals, or thirty-seven and a half cents, is the average price of a day's labor, the workman for this amount furnishing his own subsistence. The full pay of a Mexican soldier is only twenty-five cents a day, with which he is expected to supply his own food and support his wife, who, owing to the absence of a commissary department in the army, invariably accompanies her husband in the campaigns for the purpose of collecting and transporting his food. These people are already well accustomed to clearing land, cutting timber, driving mules and horses, and some of them are excellent watermen. They are not unruly nor quarrelsome in disposition; nor are they, judging from their tolerance of, and subordination to, all foreigners, likely to be jealous of laborers of the European or Asiatic races. They are looking forward with delight to the time when they shall have employment of this sort on the Isthmus. The first question they generally asked us was, when is "La Compañia Americana" coming? referring to the company which has a grant for constructing a railroad across the Isthmus of Tehauntepec. Once while we were there a report spread over the Isthmus that this company had already arrived at Minatitlan, and so great was the joy that the towns and houses were illuminated, and innumerable bómbas were fired off. We were informed by Americans and others residing on the Isthmus that, when they cultivated large indigo plantations, their field-laborers, who were the native Indians, were generally industrious, and could be relied on, in time of peace, as permanent workmen.

PEARL FISHERIES.

Along the Pacific coast, a few miles west of Salina Cruz, there are extensive beds of pearl-oysters, from which the natives have taken, from time to time, many valuable pearls. Within a few years past an attempt was made by a foreign company to fish these beds with the modern apparatus used in this sort of work, but the undertaking was singularly unfortunate. The first diver was accidentally drowned a day or two after commencing work, and his successor failed to meet the expectations of the company, and the whole thing was abandoned. Some seasons the Indians inhabiting the coast collect a considerable number of pearls by diving into the sea unaided by any apparatus, and this work is said to be more remunerative than any other employment within the reach of these people; but, notwithstanding this, there are other seasons when, for some unknown reason, they cannot be induced to engage in this work. An intelligent American citizen, who was at one time interested in these fisheries, informed us that the mother-of-pearl they collected was sold for enough to pay all the expenses of working the fisheries, and the value of the pearls was all clear profit.

CHAPTER V.
NATURAL HISTORY.

Our collections in natural history are small, on account of the limited facilities we had for collecting. Most of the specimens came from the vicinity of La Chivela, our headquarters, and Minatitlan. The collection, though small, is interesting, both from the new species contained in it, and by it widening the range of other determined species.

WARM-BLOODED VERTEBRATA.

CHEIROPTERA.—Aribeus perspiccilatum, Allen. Schizostoma elongatum, Tomes; two species. Saccopterynx lepturus. (?)

EDENTATA.—Dasypus novacinctus. Cyclothurus dorsolis, Gray.

AVES.—Falco cachinnans, Ceryle carbonisii, Tshudi, in alcohol. Xanthoruus mesomelas, Licht. Muscicapa melancholica, 2 spec., in alcohol. Garrulus gubernatrix, Temm. Psittacus ara canga, Linn. Ramphastos carinatus, Swain. Celeopicus castaneus, Licht. Iringa hypoleucos. Parra cordifera, 2 spec., 1 skin, in alcohol.

COLD-BLOODED VERTEBRATA, DETERMINED BY EDW. D. COPE.

REPTILIA.—Elaps ornatissimus, Jaw., (with distinct armuli.) Masticophis margaritiferus, Schl. Oxybelis acuminatus, Wier. Coniophanes fissidens, Gthr. Oxyrrhopus plumbens. Hydrops lubricus, Cope, sp. nov.

LACERTILIA.—Sphaerodactylus glaucus, Cope. (Adult of two inches; labials $\frac{5}{4} \frac{6}{4}$; tail, orange-red. See Proc. Ac. Nat. Sci., 1865, 192. Scales smooth, flat.) Cyclura acanthura, Wier. Cyclura pectinata, Wier. Sceloponis, Amioa, Cnemidaphorus, Plistodon.

BATRACHIA.—Systoma ustum, Cope, (Engystoma Mexicanum, Peters.) Bufo agua, Bufo stemosignatus, Gthr. Hylodes, rhodopis, Cope.

FISHES.—Philypnus dormitator, C. V. Tetragonopterus streetsii, Cope, sp. nov. Xiphophorus hellerii, Heck. Fundulus, sp. 1. Fundulus, sp. 2.

Hydrops Lubricus, Cope, sp. nov.—Head short, broad, little distinct from neck; scales entirely smooth, poreless; posterior grooved; tooth not much larger than those in front of it; parietals still longer, somewhat contracted behind; rostral broad, low; loreal small, higher than long; temporals 1—2, first in contact with two labials. Superior labials eight, fourth, and fifth bounding rather small orbit; seventh wider above than below. Inferior labials 10 or 11, 4.5 in contact with anterior, 1.5 with posterior or longer geneials scales in 21 rows; anal divided; tail, $4\frac{1}{6}$ times in total length; ground-color above, a stone-brown. A blackish lateral band extends from the end of the muzzle to the end of the tail, including all between the approximated edges of the second and sixth rows of scales. A dark brown shade extends throughout the length on the vertebral, and the serial of scales on each side of it. Below the second row of scales, white, (in life, yellow;) a large black spot marking the third from each end of each gastrostege and urostege, thus forming two series. Labial plates above and below pale, with a black spot; gulars and geneials similar. Total length, two feet; gastrosteges, 162; urosteges, 71.

This species was found on the bank of the Coatzacoalcos River, in the department of Vera Cruz, Mexico. It is excessively smooth, so much so as to produce the sensation of an oiled surface when the finger is passed over the scales.

Tetragonopterus streetsii.—Cope, sp. nov. radii D 11, A 25; scales 7-41-6. Maxillary bone elongate, the extremity extending to below the anterior part of the pupil, its margin toothless. Profile nearly plane, rising into the convex dorsum at the supra-occipital crest; muzzle obtuse; jaws nearly equal. Interorbital region transversely convex, as wide as the diameter of the orbit. Dorsal fin originating a little behind that of the ventral. General form elongate rhombic. Depth 2.5 times in length, less caudal fin; length of head 4 times in same. Eye, 3.2 times in head. Total length, 5 inches. Color of superior half of head and body blackish, a vertical clavicular dark band; a leaden band from its upper margin to basis of caudal fin, terminating in a pyriform black blotch of considerable size, which is prolonged on the caudal radii. Below, yellowish white. Fins, unicolor. From the Coyolapa River, a branch of the Coatzacoalcos, among the Cordilleras.

This species may be allied to those mentioned by Bocourt from the rivers of Belize and Peten, (American Sci. Nat., XI,) but it will be impossible ever to recognize them from the notes attached to the names.

The *Insecta* undetermined, consisting of Coleoptera and Lepidoptera.

ARACHNIDA.—Mygale avicularia. Buthus biaculeatus. Phrynus. (?)

CRUSTACEA.—Boscia dentata, Milne Edwards. Remipes strigillatus, Stimpson. Pachycheles mexicanus, Streets, sp. nov. Panulirus gracilis, Streets, sp. nov. Cambarus astecus, Saussure. Palaemon dasydactylus, Streets, sp. nov. Palaemon ruber, Streets, sp. nov. Palaemon fluvialis, Streets, sp. nov.

Pachycheles mexicanus, Streets, sp. nov.—Carapax broadly oval, about as broad as long, slightly convex antero-posteriorly, surface shining, but minutely granular through the lens; anterior portion of the carapax deflexed, triangular, and furrowed, a small white spot at the tip; neither spines nor teeth anywhere on the body; eyes small, supra-arbital, border concave and inflated. Carpus as broad as long; three teeth on the anterior border; two slightly elevated ridges of granules on the superior surface; hand broad and large, the right larger than the left; fingers hooked at their extremities, denticulated; surface of the carpus and hand more coarsely granulated than the carapax; the granules extend to the ends of the fingers. Color red, with patches of a lighter shade; three posterior pairs of legs striped; the last article furnished with a few stiff hairs. Length of the carapax 0.018 inch; the hand, 0.025 inch. Habitat—Gulf of Tehuantepec, Mexico.

Panulirus gracilis, Streets, sp. nov.—Antennary ring armed with two spines, situated near together on the anterior border; behind these, and separated more widely from each other, are two rudimentary spines, seen through the lens; two stout horns projecting forward over the base of the ophthalmic peduncles; surface of the carapax covered with spines, larger anteriorly than posteriorly; also furnished with a few stiff hairs, attached mostly to the spines; epistoma armed with three spines; abdomen smooth; the transverse sulci, except the last, interrupted in the middle; a pit between the last nearly connects them, separated by two very narrow bands on either side of the pit. Color, reddish brown; external antennæ striped with bands of white. Length, 0.09 inch. Habitat—Gulf of Tehuantepec.

Palaemon dasydactylus, Streets, sp. nov.—Rostrum long and slender, reflexed, extends beyond the lamellar appendices of the external antennæ; armed on the superior margin with nine or ten teeth, and six or seven on the inferior margin; the first tooth on the upper margin small, situated more directly on the carapax than, and separated from, the following six, which are situated together; the seventh and eighth separated by a wider space; last tooth quite small; apex of the rostrum pointed; the fifth tooth on the upper margin (counting from the carapax) nearly over the first on the lower margin; eighth over the last on the lower margin; those, with but six teeth on the inferior margin, have the last under the seventh of the superior margin; the first is constant in its situation. Two external flagella of the internal antennæ united for a very short distance; smaller flagellum very short; all the others very long. First pair of legs short and slender; carpus more than twice the length of the hand; fingers half the length of the hand, slightly pubescent; second pair of legs very long; carpus not quite as long as the hand; fingers cylindrical and straight along their approximated surfaces, not as long as the palmer portion of the hand, densely downy; under surface of this pair of legs covered with spinules to the base of the fingers; the spinules on the carpus arranged in four parallel rows, of which the anterior and posterior contain the largest spinules; posterior legs rough to the feet, pubescent.

This species can very readily be distinguished from *P. mexicanus*, (Saussure,) which it more closely resembles, by having six or seven teeth on the inferior margin of the rostrum. The carpus in *P. mexicanus* is longer than the hand, and the terminal segment of the abdomen is armed with three spines. In *P. dasydactylus*, the terminal segment of the abdomen is armed with five spines, one in the middle and one at either extremity, and a larger articulated one on either side of the middle. Length, from the tip of the rostrum to the end of the terminal segment, 4.037 inches. Habitat, Tide-water of the Coatzacoalcos River, Isthmus of Tehuantepec.

Palaemon ruber, Streets, sp. nov.—Rostrum long and slender, more reflexed than in the preceding species; longer than the lamellar appendices of the external antennæ; armed on the superior margin with nine or ten teeth, and six on the inferior margin; sixth tooth on the upper margin over the first on the lower; the last on the lower margin half way between the eighth and ninth on the upper margin; those with but nine teeth on the superior margin have the first below, under the space between the fourth and fifth; the last midway, under the space between the seventh and eighth of the superior margin. Inner free flagella of a deep red color. Anterior pair of legs slender and delicate; carpus more than twice the length of the hand; hand slightly pubescent; second pair of legs slender, smooth on the upper surface; under surface beset with very minute spiniform granules, seen only through the lens; carpus longer than the hand, twice the length of the palmer portions of the hand; fingers cylindrical, straight, less than half the length of the hand; posterior legs smooth.

This species is very closely allied to *P. mexicanus*, (Saussure,) and may prove to be nothing but a variety of that species. The measurements of the second pair of legs of *P. ruber* agree with De Saussure's description as far as they extend, but it differs widely from the measurements of his figure. *P. mexicanus* has but four or five teeth on the inferior margin of the rostrum. The terminal segment of the abdomen in *P. ruber* is armed with three small teeth, and two longer movable spines, situated one on either side of the middle tooth. The hand is very largely beset with hairs. Length, ——. Habitat, same as the preceding.

Palæmon fluvialis, Streets, sp. nov.—Rostrum short, lanceolate, somewhat arched above, not as long as the lamellar appendices of the external antennæ, reaching to the end of the second joint of the antennæ; superior margin armed with seven teeth, the inferior margin with two, situated near the point of the rostrum. One specimen of this species has but four teeth above and one below. Two flagella of the internal antennæ united for a very short distance; spines on the lateral portion of the carapax very small; first pair of legs slender; hand more than half the length of the carpus; hand of the second pair, stout; carpus shorter than the palmar portion of the hand, gradually enlarged toward the hand; fingers cylindrical and straight, shorter than half of the hand, the same length as the carpus, beset with a few stiff hairs; legs smooth; length, 1.03 inches. This is a fresh-water palæmon, taken from a tributary of the Coatzacoalcos River, among the Cordilleras.

MOLLUSCA.—Ampularia cumingii, bulimus powisianus, petit, pachycheilus laevissimus, sowerby glandina?

JOHN C. SPEAR,
Surgeon, United States Navy.
THOMAS H. STREETS.

JULY 14, 1871.

E.

REPORT

UPON THE

SANITARY CONDITION AND CLIMATIC INFLUENCES

OF

THE COATZACOALCOS RIVER, MEXICO.

BY

HORATIO N. BEAUMONT, PASSED ASSISTANT SURGEON, U. S. N.

ON BOARD UNITED STATES STEAMER KANSAS, OFF MINATITLAN, MEXICO,
April 19, 1871.

SIR: In obedience to your order, I have the honor to submit the following report upon the sanitary condition of the Coatzacoalcos River, based upon personal experience since our arrival at Minatitlan, in November, 1870.

The division of the Isthmus to which this report will be confined is known as the "Atlantic plains," comprising a breadth of country of about fifty miles, and extending from the Gulf of Mexico to the base of the Cordilleras.

This portion of the Isthmus consists of several rich and extensive alluvial basins, which are traversed by as many rivers, of which the Coatzacoalcos, which drains the waters of the northern slope of the Cordilleras, is the principal, and occupies the central portion of the Isthmus.

This river flows through a non-mountainous district of alluvial soil, and drains miles of flat, low, marshy country for a distance of nearly seventy miles before it reaches the Gulf.

The country along the Coatzacoalcos, from its mouth to Minatitlan, (the highest point reached by the United States steamer Kansas,) is an extensive plain, covered with thick forests and dense wild grasses, intersected by numerous tributaries of the river, and for the greater part of the year is nothing more than a vast marsh.

The Coatzacoalcos, as well as all the rivers draining the waters of the northern slope of the Cordilleras, is subject to annual overflow, by which these extensive alluvial fields and woodlands are completely inundated, and remain, after the subsidence of the waters, a month or more, covered with the vegetable and animal matters, whose decomposition is productive of the malarial gases which produce the intermittent and remittent fevers to which this whole country is so subject.

The northerly winds prevail from December to the end of March, and frequently last for several days, blowing with great violence, and changing the temperature (which averages, during November, December, and January,) from 81° to 68 or 70° within a few hours.

During the prevalence of the northers, the atmosphere is heavy, and the damp mists are very productive of rheumatism and ague, and necessitate a thorough change of clothing, especially at night.

The rainy season begins in July and ends in November, although there is more or less rain throughout the greater portion of the year. It is during this season that the annual inundation takes place, and for a month or more the country is flooded so that it is possible to pass in boats from one river to another. At this season of the year, the temperature is said to be 82° or 83° at noon, when it rains; but never below 78°. When the sky is clear and the sun shines brightly, the thermometer ranges between 89° and 91° from 10 o'clock a. m. to 4 p. m., while at night it falls to 78° or 76°.

The principal cause of disease, throughout the year, is the decomposition of vegetable and animal matter.

The country is thickly wooded, and covered with tall, dense grasses and shrubs, which prevent the sun's rays from reaching the ground, and give rise, by their decomposition, to the miasmatic and gaseous matters which produce fever. During the winter, the sudden changes of weather are productive of disease; and, in consequence of a sudden check of perspiration, with a tendency to internal congestion, the northers are always accompanied by an addition to the sick-list.

During the summer the changes are equally as great, when the frequent rains, which are not sufficient in quantity to inundate the country, only aid by their sudden evaporation to produce vegetable effluvia.

During the period of complete inundation, I am informed that the greatest health prevails, and from the fact that vegetable decomposition cannot go on during such period, we would naturally coincide in the opinion.

The most unhealthy periods are at the beginning and close of the rainy season, or, in other words, when there is just sufficient heat and rain to favor the generation of malaria.

Judging from the nature of the country, i. e., the low, marshy wastes on either side of the Coatzacoalcos, and other rivers draining the northern slope of the Cordilleras, intersected by the numerous small streams, which are alternately large and small, and from the circumstances of the inundation depositing accumulated animal and vegetable matter to decompose upon the subsidence of the waters, I consider the least healthy portion of the Isthmus to be the Coatzacoalcos basin.

From my own experience, both on board ship and at Minatitlan, I am prepared to say that I do not think the country unhealthy, nor does the climate predispose to other endemic diseases than intermittent fever in its various forms. During our stay here and at Coatzacoalcos Bar, for the last six months, the sick-list has averaged over sixteen daily, while about as many cases have occurred daily in the town of Minatitlan, a town consisting of about one thousand inhabitants.

The necessary exposure of the crew to the sun, in the performance of surveying duty, &c., the confinement on board ship, (there being allowed only sixty-four cubic feet of air to each man,) with a very imperfectly ventilated berth-deck, not to mention the cheapness of liquor, ("aguadiente,") and the frequent indulgence of the sailors while on shore, have, no doubt, been the immediate causes of a so much larger average on board ship than on shore. By an examination of the accompanying statistical report, it will be seen that there have been very few admissions to the sick-list, with the exception of cases of intermittent and remittent fevers, and I may mention that of the latter there has not been one patient who had not already had several attacks of the former, and whose debilitated condition did not more conduce to the fever than the original poison.

The fact that, out of 270 persons admitted to the sick-list with fever alone, only two have died, and sixteen remain under treatment, speaks favorably of the non-malignancy of the disease, and I have no hesitation in stating that, with the exception of diseases of spleen, liver, and bowels which so frequently accompany fever in the tropics, I could not have expected the same good results in many malarious districts of our own country. The diseases of diarrhœa, hepatitis, splenitis, icterus, and melancholia, mentioned in the accompanying report, are more the consequences of the fever than original diseases, and, if intermittent fever be excepted, the average number of sick since our arrival here will be much smaller than could have been reasonably expected upon any expedition where the vicissitudes of climate and exposure would be so unavoidable. It is stated by authority of the oldest inhabitants that yellow fever has never been known here. The cholera prevailed once (in 1850) with great mortality, but did not extend beyond the Atlantic plains. With the exception of malarial diseases, and the various diseases of the portal system which prevail in all tropical countries, I have no hesitation in pronouncing that the Coatzacoalcos River and its vicinity is a healthy locality, and if the forest were cut off, and a system of drainage established, I know of no reason why its sanitary condition should not be as good as can be expected in any new country within the tropics.

I have the honor to remain, very respectfully, your obedient servant,

HORATIO N. BEAUMONT,
Passed Assistant Surgeon, U. S. Navy.

Captain R. W. SHUFELDT,
Commanding Tehuantepec and Nicaragua
Exploring Expedition, Minatitlan, Mexico.

F.

OFFICIAL CORRESPONDENCE

CONNECTED WITH

THE U. S. EXPEDITION FOR EXPLORATIONS AND SURVEYS

FOR A

SHIP-CANAL ACROSS THE ISTHMUS OF TEHUANTEPEC, MEXICO.

No. 98.]
DEPARTMENT OF STATE,
Washington, September 12, 1870.

SIR: Captain R. W. Shufeldt, a distinguished officer of the Navy of the United States, has been appointed chief of a surveying party to ascertain the practicability of a ship-canal between the two oceans by way of the Isthmus of Tehuantepec. He will be accompanied by a few other officers. It is probable that the party will start for that quarter about the first of next month. No objections to the survey on the part of the Mexican government are anticipated; you will, however, inform the minister for foreign affairs of the captain's purpose, and will request such orders to the local authorities as may serve to check any hostility on their part, or on that of the people of the region to be traversed. The captain would be happy if the Mexican government would, on its part, detail an engineer officer to accompany the Expedition, to take part in its labors, and to verify their results. He would also be glad to be apprised of the views of the Mexican government upon the subject, at as early a period as may be practicable, by a communication addressed to him at Vera Cruz, to the care of our consul there.

Though Mexico herself is largely interested in the practicability and success of so great an enterprise, other countries, especially those concerned in commerce, and, perhaps above all, the United States, have deep stake in its realization.

I am, sir, your obedient servant,

HAMILTON FISH.

THOMAS H. NELSON, Esq.,
&c., &c., &c., *Mexico.*

LEGATION OF THE UNITED STATES,
Mexico, October 18, 1870.

SIR: I herewith transmit a copy of the correspondence between this legation and the Mexican secretary for foreign affairs, in regard to the proposed survey of the Isthmus of Tehuantepec, with the view to ascertain the feasibility of a ship-canal across the same. You will perceive that the Mexican government will cheerfully co-operate with the Expedition, and furnish such assistance and protection as may be required. Trusting that the expectations of the friends of the great enterprise may be fully realized,

I have the honor to be, with great respect, your obedient servant,

THOMAS H. NELSON.

Captain R. W. SHUFELDT,
Commanding United States Surveying Expedition, Vera Cruz.

Inclosures.

A. Mr. Nelson to Mr. Lerdo.
B. Mr. Nelson to Mr. Lerdo.
C. Mr. Lerdo to Mr. Nelson.
D. Mr. Lerdo to governors of Vera Cruz and Oaxaca.
E. Mr. Lerdo to minister of war.
F. Mr. Lerdo to Mr. Nelson.
G. Mr. Nelson to Mr. Lerdo.

A.

LEGATION OF THE UNITED STATES,
Mexico, October 6, 1870.

SIR: Captain R. W. Shufeldt, a distinguished officer of the Navy of the United States, has been appointed chief of a surveying party to ascertain the practicability of a ship-canal between the two oceans by the way of the Isthmus of Tehuantepec. He will be accompanied by a few other officers. I have been instructed to ask the permission of the Mexican government to make the said survey, and to request such orders to the local authorities in the region to be traversed as may serve to facilitate the object of the Expedition and protect the surveying party.

Captain Shufeldt would be happy if the Mexican government would, on its part, detail an engineer officer to accompany the Expedition, to take part in its labors, and to verify their results.

As it is the purpose of Captain Shufeldt to start for the Isthmus in a very short time, I respectfully request from your excellency an early answer to this communication.

I have the honor to remain, with great respect, your excellency's obedient servant,

THOMAS H. NELSON.

His Excellency S. LERDO DE TEJADA,
Secretary for Foreign Affairs, Mexico.

B.

[Unofficial.]

LEGATION OF THE UNITED STATES,
Mexico, October 14, 1870.

MY DEAR SIR: I beg leave to call the attention of your excellency to the contents of my note of the 6th instant, asking permission of the Mexican government for a surveying party from the United States to examine the Isthmus of Tehuantepec, to ascertain whether it is practicable to construct a ship-canal across the same; and also requesting your excellency to cause the proper orders to be issued directing the local authorities in that region to facilitate the purposes of the Expedition, and protect the surveying party.

Desiring to transmit to my Government the response of your excellency, by the extraordinary mail which will leave this city to-morrow, for the reason assigned in the said note, I trust it will be convenient for your excellency to favor me with an answer to-day.

I remain, with great respect, your excellency's obedient servant,

THOMAS H. NELSON.

His Excellency S. LERDO DE TEJADA,
Secretary for Foreign Affairs, Mexico.

C.

[Translation.]

DEPARTMENT OF FOREIGN AFFAIRS,
Mexico, October 13, 1870.

SIR: I have the honor to reply to your excellency's note of the 6th instant, to the effect that Captain R. W. Shufeldt, a distinguished officer of the American Navy, has been appointed chief of an Exploring Expedition to determine upon the practicability of a ship-canal between the two oceans, across the Isthmus of Tehuantepec.

Your excellency informs me that you have received instructions to ask the permission of the Mexican government to carry the said explorations into effect, which permission the President gladly grants, recognizing all the advantages which that work will produce if it shall prove practicable.

I send your excellency herewith two copies of the communications which I have addressed to the governors of the States of Vera Cruz and Oaxaca, requesting them to notify the respective local authorities of each of those two states, to aid as far as possible the objects of the Expedition, and protect the exploring party.

I also send your excellency, herewith, a copy of a communication which I have addressed to the minister of war, in order that he may notify in a similar manner the commanders of the federal forces in Minatitlan, and at other points of the territory which the Expedition is to pass over.

The President has considered the proposal which your excellency was pleased to make, and has determined that the department of public works appoint a commission, which, on the part of the Mexican government, may accompany the said Expedition, and take part in its labors.

I will have the honor to communicate to your excellency, at the proper time, whatever the department of public works may inform me concerning the time of the departure of this commission, and if your excellency will have the goodness to let me know the time of Captain Shufeldt's arrival, I will inform the said department.

I take this opportunity to renew to your excellency the assurances of the very distinguished consideration with which I am, respectfully, your excellency's obedient servant,

S. LERDO DE TEJADA.

His Excellency THOMAS H. NELSON,
    Minister Plenipotentiary of the United States, in Mexico.

D.

[Translation.]

DEPARTMENT OF STATE,
    OFFICE OF FOREIGN AFFAIRS,
        American Section.

His excellency the minister plenipotentiary of the United States of America in Mexico has informed this department, by a note of the 6th instant, that Captain R. W. Shufeldt has been appointed chief of an Exploring Expedition to determine upon the practicability of a ship-canal between the two oceans across the Isthmus of Tehuantepec; that he will be accompanied by a few other officers, and that he proposes to proceed to the Isthmus very soon.

He has also informed me in the said note that he has been instructed to request the permission of the Mexican government to carry the exploration into effect, and that proper orders be issued to the local authorities of the territory to be traversed to aid the objects of the Expedition and protect the exploring party.

The President of the republic, having taken the subject into consideration, has been pleased to grant the said permission, and has directed that you be requested to instruct the local authorities of that portion of your state which will be traversed by the Expedition, to aid and protect, as far as possible, the exploring party.

I beg you will immediately issue such orders in advance, and if I shall receive a previous notification of the precise time of Captain Shufeldt's arrival, I will let you know at once.

Independence and liberty. Mexico, October 13, 1870.

LERDO DE TEJADA,
    Citizen Governor of the State of Vera Cruz, Vera Cruz.

CITIZEN GOVERNOR *of the State of Oaxaca, Oaxaca.*

E.

[Translation.]

DEPARTMENT OF STATE,
    OFFICE OF FOREIGN AFFAIRS,
        American Section.

By a note of the 6th instant, his excellency the minister plenipotentiary of the United States of America in Mexico has informed me that Captain R. W. Shufeldt has been appointed chief of an Exploring Expedition to determine upon the practicability of a ship-canal between the two oceans across the Isthmus of Tehuantepec; that he will be accompanied by a few other officers, and that he proposes to proceed to the Isthmus very soon.

He has also informed me in the said note that he has been instructed to request the permission of the Mexican government to carry the explorations into effect, and that proper orders be issued to the local authorities of the territory to be traversed to aid the objects of the Expedition and protect the exploring party.

The President of the republic, having taken the subject into consideration, has been pleased to grant the said permission, and has directed that you be informed of the fact, in order that you may issue the necessary orders to the commanders of the federal forces at Minatitlan, and at other points of the territory to be traversed, in order that, as far as possible or necessary, they may aid and protect the exploring party.

I beg that you will immediately issue such orders in advance, and if I shall receive a previous notification of the precise time of Captain Shufeldt's arrival, I will let you know at once.

Independence and liberty. Mexico, October 13, 1870.

LERDO DE TEJADA.

CITIZEN MINISTER OF WAR.

F.

[Translation.]

DEPARTMENT OF FOREIGN AFFAIRS, (*Unofficial,*)
Mexico, October 14, 1870.

ESTEEMED SIR: I have received your excellency's unofficial note of to-day, in which you express a desire to send by the extraordinary mail which is to be sent from this city for the American packet, my reply to your excellency's note of the 6th instant, relative to the Exploring Expedition appointed by the United States of America to determine upon the practicability of constructing a ship-canal between the two oceans across the Isthmus of Tehuantepec.

My reply was already drawn up yesterday, but has not been sent until to-day, owing to a delay occasioned by the preparation of the copies of the accompanying documents.

I improve this opportunity to inform your excellency, in case you have not yet been notified, and for your convenience in sending your correspondence, that the postmaster general has to-day sent me word that the extraordinary mail for the American packet will start from this city the day after to-morrow, the 16th instant, at 9 o'clock a. m.

I am, very respectfully, your excellency's obedient servant,

S. LERDO DE TEJADA.

His Excellency THOMAS H. NELSON,
Minister Plenipotentiary of the United States of America in Mexico.

G.

LEGATION OF THE UNITED STATES,
Mexico, October 15, 1870.

SIR: I have the honor to acknowledge the receipt of your excellency's note of the 13th instant, concerning the proposed survey of the Isthmus of Tehuantepec, in which I am informed that his excellency the President gladly grants permission to the surveying party to make the exploration of the Isthmus, recognizing all the advantages which the construction of a ship-canal would produce, if it shall prove practicable. Your excellency was kind enough to inclose copies of the communications which had been addressed to the governors of the States of Vera Cruz and Oaxaca, requesting them to notify the local authorities of those States to aid, as far as possible, the objects of the Expedition, and protect the exploring party; also, a copy of a communication which was addressed to the minister of war, in order that he should notify in a similar manner the commanders of the federal forces in Minatitlan and at other points of the territory which will be traversed by the Expedition. I am also advised that his excellency the President has determined that the department of public works shall appoint a commission to accompany the Expedition, and take part in its labors.

I will have the honor to transmit copies of your excellency's note and the accompanying papers to the Secretary of State of the United States, who, as well as my Government, will be gratified at the judicious and considerate measures which have been adopted by your excellency's government to facilitate the objects of the Expedition.

I will take pleasure in announcing to your excellency the time of the arrival at Vera Cruz of Captain Shufeldt and the surveying party from the United States, so that the proper arrangements may be made for the commission to be appointed by the department of public works to join them.

Renewing the assurances of my highest consideration, I have the honor to remain your excellency's obedient servant,

THOMAS H. NELSON.

His Excellency S. LERDO DE TEJADA,
    Secretary of Foreign Affairs, Mexico.

Printed in Dunstable, United Kingdom